Women, Armies, and Warfare in Early Modern Europe

Women, Armies, and Warfare in Early Modern Europe examines the important roles of women who campaigned with armies from 1500 to 1815. This included those notable female individuals who assumed male identities to serve in the ranks, but far more numerous and essential were the formidable women who, as women, marched in the train of armies. While some worked as full-time or part-time prostitutes, they more generally performed a variety of necessary gendered tasks, including laundering, sewing, cooking, and nursing. Early modern armies were always accompanied by women and regarded them as essential to the well-being of the troops. John A. Lynn II argues that, before 1650, women were also fundamental to armies because they were integral to the pillage economy that maintained troops in the field.

John A. Lynn II earned his Ph.D. from the University of California at Los Angeles. He is the author of *Bayonets of the Republic: Tactics and Motivation in the Army of Revolutionary France, 1791–94* (1984); *Giant of the Grand Siècle: The French Army, 1610–1715* (1997); *The Wars of Louis XIV, 1667–1714* (1999); *The French Wars 1667–1714: The Sun King at War* (2002); and *Battle: A History of Combat and Culture* (2003 and 2004). He has edited *Tools of War: Ideas, Instruments, and Institutions of Warfare, 1445–1871* (1990), and *Feeding Mars: Logistics in Western Warfare from the Middle Ages to the Present* (1993). He has also published eighty chapters, articles, and papers. He has served as president of the United States Commission on Military History and as vice-president of the Society for Military History. In addition, he has been awarded the Palmes Academiques at the rank of chevalier from the French government and the Wissam al Alaoui at the rank of commander from his Majesty, King Mohammed VI of Morocco.

Women, Armies, and Warfare in Early Modern Europe

JOHN A. LYNN II

CAMBRIDGE UNIVERSITY PRESS

CAMBRIDGE
UNIVERSITY PRESS

32 Avenue of the Americas, New York NY 10013-2473, USA

Cambridge University Press is part of the University of Cambridge.

It furthers the University's mission by disseminating knowledge in the pursuit of education, learning and research at the highest international levels of excellence.

www.cambridge.org
Information on this title: www.cambridge.org/9780521722377

First published 2008

A catalogue record for this publication is available from the British Library

Library of Congress Cataloguing in Publication data
Lynn, John A. (John Albert), 1943–
Women, armies, and warfare in early modern Europe / John A. Lynn II.
p.   cm.
Includes bibliographical references and index.
ISBN 978-0-521-89765-5 (hbk. : alk. paper)
1. Women and war–Europe–History.   2. Camp followers–Europe–History.
3. Women soldiers–Europe–History.   4. Military art and science–Europe–History.
I. Title.
U 21.75.L 96 2008
355.0082′094–dc22
2008028107

ISBN 978-0-521-89765-5 Hardback
ISBN 978-0-521-72237-7 Paperback

This book about women of strength, endurance, and courage is dedicated to my granddaughter
Helena Grace Lynn

Contents

List of illustrations

Acknowledgments

Writing *Women, Armies, and Warfare in Early Modern Europe* has been a great ride. Begun simply as a chapter in another manuscript, it grew to such proportions that it clearly demanded to be a book of its own. The subject matter took charge, and I followed where it led me. At first I wanted to stay in my comfort zone, restricting the tale to a military history focused on women with early modern armies, but well into the project it became clear that it also needed to be a work of women's history *per se*, or at least as much as I could make it.

During this journey I accumulated many debts, and I would like to acknowledge those who contributed so much. The early Europe reading group at the University of Illinois would not let me settle for less and encouraged me to strive for more. Many thanks to Clare Crowston, Jennifer Edwards, Amanda Eisemann, Caroline Hibbard, Craig Koslosky, David O'Brien, Dana Rabin, and Carol Symes. Beyond these colleagues, I benefited from those who braved reading the entire manuscript at various stages: Fred Jaher, Barton Hacker, Lynn Hunt, Frank Tallett, and the second reader for Cambridge University Press. Drawing on his own considerable expertise, Brian Sandberg provided me with a particularly knowledgeable and helpful reading.

I also gained from the translation help of Kelly De Vries, Mary Beth Ailes, Alex d'Erizans, and, Jacob Baum. Above all, Jacob Baum gave me access to important material that I otherwise could not have employed.

This is the kind of book that relies upon the work of many scholars who, through their books and articles, have taught me much and provided me with a great many of the sources used here. I have followed many a footnote and found gold. Thank you for all you have given and all I have gained.

Illustrations play a substantial role in this volume; they are not simply amusing pictures. Assembling them required help from a number of libraries, museums, and collections. These include: Library of the University of Illinois at Urbana-Champaign; Lilly Library, Indiana University;

Huntington Library; Bibliothèque de Genève; Library of the University of Amsterdam; Hertzog August Bibliothek, Wolfenbuettel; British Museum; Bibliothèque National; Musée de l'image, Epinal; Germanisches National-museum, Nürnberg; Albertina Museum, Vienna; National Army Museum, London; Staatliche Graphishe Sammlung, Munich; Art Resource; Bridgeman Art Library; Lukas, Art in Flanders; and the very helpful people at Abaris Books.

And thanks to my wife, Andrea Lynn, not only for her talents as an editor but also for enduring as I became so obsessed with the formidable women who populate the pages. Being a writer herself, she understands how the book kidnaps the author.

Introduction: Identifying Issues and Questions

In the early seventeenth century, a military commentary by Jacob von Wallhausen cautioned: "When you recruit a regiment of German soldiers today, you do not only acquire 3,000 soldiers; along with these you will certainly find 4,000 women and children."[1] Two hundred years later, British regulations stipulated: "The number of women allowed by Government to embark on service are six for every hundred men, inclusive of all Non-Commissioned Officers' wives, [an ample number which] should never be exceeded on any pretext whatsoever, because the doing so is humanity of the falsest kind."[2] These quotations begin our story, because the continuities and contrasts between them set the twin directions of this inquiry.

Each quotation confirms the presence of camp women with early modern armies in the field. Such women endured the rigors of the march and the hard life of the camp; and, even if they did not fight in the line of battle, they were exposed to risks of injury, illness, and death, plus a danger almost exclusively reserved for them, rape. Ultimately, camp women belonged to the army and were integral to its military functions. It is the first goal of this book to explore their lives on campaign in as much detail and with as much humanity as possible.

Yet these two excerpts also reveal an important change in campaign life for these women. During the sixteenth century and the first half of the

---

[1] Jacob von Wallenstein, *Kriegskunst zu Fuss* (Graz: 1971), p. 7. Originally published in 1615.

[2] British regulations for the Corps of Riflemen, 1801, in Noel T. St. John Williams, *Judy O'Grady and the Colonel's Lady: The Army Wife and Camp Follower Since 1660* (London: 1988), p. 19. These reflect the 29 October 1800 order issued by the duke of York, pp. 17–18.

seventeenth century, mercenary bands arrived with great crowds of women in their trains, but from the second half of the seventeenth century and through the eighteenth century, the number of women that accompanied troops radically declined. The plebian women who are the subjects of this study were always present with early modern armies, because they performed tasks essential to the health and well-being of the common soldiers who were their partners. However, if a British unit could march with only six women per one hundred men, why did earlier forces include so many more? The second goal of this book is to come to grips with this question.

THE HISTORY OF WOMEN ON CAMPAIGN

The history of noncombatant camp women who accompanied early modern armies across Europe remains woefully under explored. This is not meant to imply that contemporaries and historians have failed to comment on women with armies, but they have almost always reserved the discussion to those rare but fascinating women who bore arms in battle or siege. The more mundane women who scrubbed clothing and tended fires have not seemed worth much commentary.

Surprisingly, interest in the subject of women associated with European armies came centuries before the rise of women's history as an academic field. Popular culture regaled seventeenth- and eighteenth-century audiences with books, pamphlets, articles, and songs about women who dressed as men, adopted male identities, and bore arms. Their stories appealed to audiences as amusing, unusual, and, sometimes, titillating adventures. These cultural products will be discussed at length in Chapter IV: Warrior Women: Cultural Phenomena, Intrepid Soldiers, and Stalwart Defenders.

Tales of women warriors continued to attract a wide readership during the nineteenth century. Authors presented such stories as engaging curiosities, patriotic models, and examples of extraordinary womanhood. They appeared throughout the 1800s, but are more prevalent from the mid-century and later. British examples include T. J. Llewelyn Prichard's *The Heroines of Welsh History* (1854) and Ellen Clayton's *Female Warriors* (1879).[3] British accounts were not always full of

---

[3] T. J. Llewelyn Prichard, *The Heroines of Welsh History: Comprising Memoirs and Biographical Notices of the Celebrated Women of Wales* (London: 1854); Thomas Carter, *Curiosities of War and Military Studies: Anecdotal, Descriptive and Statistical* (London: 1860); Ellen C. Clayton, *Female Warriors: Memorials of Female Valour and Heroism, from the Mythological Ages to the Present Era*, 2 vols. (London:

praise; Julie Wheelwright demonstrates that Victorian works sometimes criticized military women for violating the boundaries of their gender.[4] The French read of their military women in such works as Alfred Tranchant and Jules Ladimir's *Les femmes militaires de la France* (1866) and J. Pichon's *Les femmes soldats* (1898).[5]

Several modern works also concentrate on female soldiers and sailors, cashing in on the interests of the reading public, attempting to make scholarly sense of the phenomenon or even mining the past for political messages. Those meant for a popular market vary in quality, with one of the best being David Cordingly's *Heroines & Harlots* (2002).[6] Other works carry more practical subtexts, advocating fuller participation of women in the military, particularly in the combat branches—the female warrior as woman empowered. Linda Grant De Pauw's *Battle Cries and Lullabies* straddles the line between history and modern agenda.[7]

Much of the serious scholarship written by academics during the past two decades continues the tradition of history-by-vignette, sketching the lives of those exceptional women who dressed as men to stand in the

---

1879); and Menie Muriel Dowie, *Women Adventurers: The Adventure Series*, vol. 15 (London: 1893).

[4] Julie Wheelwright, "Amazons and Military Maids: An Examination of Female Military Heroines in British Literature and the Changing Construction of Gender," *Women's Studies International Forum* 10, no. 5 (1987): 489–502.

[5] French works include Alfred Tranchant and Jules Ladimir, *Les femmes militaires de la France* (Paris: 1866); Nicolas Edouard Delabarre-Duparcq, *Histoire militaire des femmes* (Brest: 1873); Edouard de Beaumont, *L'Epée et les femmes* (Paris: 1881); and J. Pichon, *Les femmes soldats* (Limoges: 1898).

[6] Earlier twentieth-century works include Reginald Hargreaves, *Women-at-Arms: Their Famous Exploits Throughout the Ages* (London: 1930); and C. Romain, *Les guerrières* (Paris: Berger-Levrault, 1931). More recent examples of such works include John Laffin, *Women in Battle* (London: 1967); J. David Truby, *Women at War: A Deadly Species* (Boulder, Colorado: 1976); Suzanne J. Stark, *Female Tars: Women Aboard Ship in the Age of Sail* (London: 1996); David E. Jones, *Woman Warriors: A History* (Washington, DC: 1997); and David Cordingly, *Heroines & Harlots: Women at Sea in the Great Age of Sail* (London: 2002). A book dealing with women at war, although not in uniform, is Alison Plowden, *Women All on Fire: The Women of the English Civil War* (Stroud, Gloucestershire: 1998). A recent scholarly compendium on individual military women is Reina Pennington, ed., *Amazons to Fighter Pilots: A Biographical Dictionary of Military Women*, 2 vols. (Westport, CT: Greenwood Press, 2003).

[7] Linda Grant De Pauw, *Battle Cries and Lullabies: Women in War from Prehistory to the Present* (Norman, OK: 1998). She discusses women and war on several levels, stressing the examples of particular individuals, although she also deals with camp women a bit. Her mix of scholarly skill and enthusiastic credulity can be frustrating, and the book must be used with care. Also see works of more explicit modern advocacy, as Erin Solaro, *Women in the Line of Fire* (Emeryville, CA: 2006).

ranks. The most thought-provoking modern scholarly survey of cross-dressing women soldiers is Julie Wheelwright's *Amazons and Military Maidens* (1989).[8] Alfred Young provides an exhaustive treatment of one early modern woman soldier; however, his subject is not European, but a heroine of the American Revolutionary War, Deborah Sampson.[9] Some of the most sophisticated modern studies in this vein explore women soldiers as female transvestites, individuals who overthrew the signs and confines of gender.[10] Other historians are asking interesting questions about the loyalties and motivations of women who stood in the line of battle, either openly as women or masquerading as men, during the Wars of the French Revolution. They follow new approaches, but their focus remains women warriors, not camp women.[11] A number of intriguing works have examined the cultural representation of women at war, for example, Dianne Dugaw's *Warrior Women and Popular Balladry* (1996).[12] A few additional works address those civilian women who

---

[8] Wheelwright, *Amazons and Military Maids* (London: 1989).

[9] Alfred Young, *Masquerade: The Life and Times of Deborah Sampson, Continental Soldier* (New York: 2005).

[10] See Rudolf M. Dekker and Lotte C. van de Pol, *The Tradition of Female Transvestism in Early Modern Europe*, trans. Judy Marcure and Lotte Van de Pol (Basingstoke, Hampshire: 1989) ; Sylvie Steinberg, *La confusion des sexes: Le tranvestissement de la Renaissance à la Révoltution* (Paris: 2001) ; and Joseph Harris, *Hidden Agendas: Cross Dressing in 17th-Century France* (Tubingen: 2005).

[11] See Rudolf M. Dekker and Lotte C. van de Pol, "Republican Heroines: Cross-Dressing Women in the French Revolutionary Armies," trans. Judy Marcure, *History of European Ideas* 10, no. 3 (1989) : pp. 353–63; Dominique Godineau, "De la guerrière à la citoyenne. Porter les armes pendant la Révolution française et la Révolution française", *Clio* 20 (2004): p. 43–69; Jean-Clément Martin, "Travetissements, impostures la communauté historienne: À propos des femmes soldats de la Révolution et de l'Empire," *Politix: Revue des sciences sociales du politique*, 74 (impostures), 19, no. 74 (2006) : pp. 31–48; and Barbara Ann Day-Hickman, "The Heroic Imaginary: Women Soldiers in the Republican and Imperial Wars," paper presented at the 2006 meeting of the Society for French Historical Studies, University of Illinois at Urbana-Champaign.

[12] Wheelwright, "Amazons and Military Maids"; Keith Moxey, *Peasants, Warriors, and Wives: Popular Imagery in the Reformation* (Chicago: 1989, 2004); Dianne Dugaw, *Warrior Women and Popular Balladry* (Chicago: 1996); Ulinka Rublack, "Wench and Maiden: Women, War and the Pictorial Function of the Feminine in German Cities in the Early Modern Period," trans. Pamela Selwyn, *History Workshop Journal*, 44 (January 1997), pp. 1–21; Simon Barker, "Allarme to England!: Gender and Militarism in Early Modern England," in *Gender, Power, and Privilege in Early Modern Europe*, Jessica Munns and Penny Richards, eds. (Harlow: 2003), pp. 140–58; Scarlet Bowen, "'The Real Soul of a Man in her Breast': Popular Oppression and British Nationalism in Memoirs of Female Soldiers, 1740–1750," *Eighteenth-Century Life* 28, no. 3 (Fall 2004): pp. 20–45.

took part in the defense of their towns when they were threatened by besieging armies. Here the work of Brian Sandberg stands out.[13]

Two unique volumes deal with women with the troops. Beate Engelen, *Soldatenfrauen in Preußen*, concentrates on soldier wives in Prussian garrisons during the eighteenth century.[14] Engelen provides important insights in this study, particularly about marriage, but her focus and questions are quite different from those that concern me here. She explores the relationships between the numerous soldiers' wives and the municipal civil communities where they were garrisoned during peacetime to tell us more about society. My study, however, surveys the contributions of those women on campaign with the troops in the early modern combat zone to learn more about the conduct of war. Holly A. Mayer's *Belonging to the Army* discusses male and female camp followers in the train of the Continental Army, giving us a good sense of the military community during the American Revolution. However, she does not concentrate on women in particular, does not have a European focus, and treats only a few years, 1775–83.[15] Not only is my study centered on women and on European armies, but much of its value derives from broadly considering military evolution over three centuries.

---

[13] Brian Sandberg, " 'Generous Amazons Came to the Breach': Besieged Women, Agency and Subjectivity during the French Wars of Religion," *Gender & History*, vol. 16, no. 3 (November 2004): pp. 654–88. Rublack, "Wench and Maiden," also deals with townswomen who contributed to the defense of their homes. For a popular account of female defenders in the English Civil War, see Plowden, *Women All on Fire.*,

[14] Beate Engelen, *Soldatenfrauen in Preußen. Eine Strukturanalyse der Garnisonsgesellschaft im späten 17. und 18. Jahrhundert* (Münster: 2004).

[15] Holly A. Mayer, *Belonging to the Army: Camp Followers and Community during the American Revolution* (Columbia, SC: 1996). See as well the brief and sketchy work, Walter Hart Blumenthal, *Women Camp Followers of the American Revolution* (Philadelphia: 1952).

Just as military history enjoys a large popular readership, it also benefits from the contributions of earnest and enthusiastic students of the past from outside universities and other institutions of higher learning. The historical reenactment community supplies some of these. Consider the work of Don N. Hagist published in *The Brigade Dispatch*, a reenactors' newsletter, particularly his four part, "The Women of the British Army, A General Overview. Part 1 – Who & How Many," The Brigade Dispatch, vol. XXIV, no. 3 (Summer 1993): 2–10; "Part 2 – Sober, Industrious Women," vol. XXIV, no. 4 (Autumn 1993): 9–17; "Part 3 – Living Conditions," vol. XXV, no. 1 (Spring 1995): 11–16; "Part 4 – Lives of Women and Children," vol. XXV, no. 2 (Summer 1995): 8–14. This is republished conveniently on the web at http://www.revwar75.com/library/hagist/britwomen.htm#110. See also the work of John U. Rees, 'The Multitude of Women': An Examination of the Numbers of Female Camp Followers with the Continental Army," *The Brigade Dispatch*, three parts: vol. XXIII, no. 4 (Autumn 1992): 5–17; vol. XXIV, no. 1 (Winter 1993): 6–16; vol. XXIV, no. 2 (Spring 1993): 2–6.

Thus, no book takes on directly the lives and roles of European camp women, from the sixteenth through the eighteenth centuries. Instead, the subject is dealt with exclusively in a scattering of articles and chapters, among which only two require attention here, and both of these pieces have been around for some time.[16] In 1981, Barton Hacker published the most important article on women with early modern forces, "Women and Military Institutions in Early Modern Europe: A Reconnaissance." In his classic piece, Hacker establishes that many women performed work integral to the well-being of military forces in the field, including the gender-defined tasks of laundering, sewing, and nursing. He also notes other ways in which such women aided their male companions, thus presenting women as something other than "camp followers," a term often used as a synonym for prostitutes. Yet Hacker does not really address the decline in the number of camp women after 1650. He makes passing reference to military reforms in the late seventeenth and eighteenth centuries, but does not go into much depth.

Unlike Hacker, Peter H. Wilson's 1996 article, "German Women and War, 1500–1800," offers an explanation for the decreasing presence of women, but it does not stand up well. Wilson questions that women were essential to the functioning of armies on campaign, particularly after

[16] The useful and enjoyable, St. John Williams, *Judy O'Grady and the Colonel's Lady*, includes interesting materials about army wives on campaign, but deals only briefly with plebian camp women, 1660–1815. See as well, Dianne Graves, *In the Midst of Alarms: Women in the War of 1812* (Montreal: 2007). The regrettably small number of scholarly articles and chapters includes: Barton Hacker, "Women and Military Institutions in Early Modern Europe: A Reconnaissance," *Signs: Journal of Women in Culture and Society* 6, no. 4 (1981): pp. 643–71; Peter H. Wilson, "German Women and War, 1500–1800," *War in History*, vol. 3, no. 2 (1996): pp. 127–60; Brian Crim, "Silent Partners: Women and Warfare in Early Modern Europe," and Scott Hendrix, "In the Army: Women, Camp Followers and Gender Roles in the British Army in the French and Indian Wars, 1755–1765," in *A Soldier and A Woman: Sexual Integration in the Military*, ed. Gerard J. DeGroot and Corinna Peniston-Bird (New York: Longman, 2000), pp. 18–48; Barton Hacker and Margaret Vining, "From Camp Follower to Lady in Uniform: Women, Social Class and Military Institutions before 1920," *Contemporary European History* 10 (2001): pp. 353–73; Barton Hacker and Margaret Vining, "The World of Camp and Train: The Changing Role of Women in Early Modern Armies," *Sovereign Arms: Armies and Fleets in the World between Lepanto and the French Revolution, 1571–1789* (Rome: 2002); and Mary Elizabeth Ailes, "Camp Followers, Sutlers, and Soldiers' Wives: Women in Early Modern Armies (c. 1450–c. 1650)," *A Companion to Women's Military History*, Barton C. Hacker and Margaret Vining, eds. (Leiden: 2010). To these should be added Wilhelm Haberling, "Army Prostitution and Its Control: An Historical Study," in Victor Robinson, ed., *Morals in Wartime* (New York: 1943), pp. 3–90; this chapter includes a fruitful discussion of 1500–1800 with excellent sources.

1650. He then argues that military authorities expelled women from military camps because Reformation and Counter-Reformation concepts of morality lowered the status of women and confined them in more restricted roles. His argument may convince historians who privilege cultural explanations, but as this volume will demonstrate, Wilson fails to appreciate women's critical contribution to the troops and the camp economy.

Only by transforming the discussion can we give camp women their due. This requires positioning the lives and labors of camp women in the contexts of military, community, and women's history. In particular, bringing together military and women's history invites interpretive tensions. To be blunt, the two fields tend to be wary of one another. Military historians are likely to regard the history of women and gender as an agenda-driven field fortified by a nearly impenetrable barrier of arcane theory, a sort of intellectual barbed-wire entanglement. Historians of women often disdain military history as a hide-bound traditional field, unable to see beyond war and the state, dominated by men, dismissive of women, and usually blind to modern theoretical approaches. This does not make for a happy marriage.

And yet I propose a union. Let me reassure military historians that this is the work of one of their own who fully intends to give the study of warfare and military institutions its proper significance. Women described here are not transformed into anything other than what they were; their portraits are meant to come as close as possible to historical accuracy. The arguments will be direct and language as jargon-free as possible. Also, this volume is guided by the assumption that understanding women's presence and roles with early modern armies entails, above all, knowledge of the history of armed conflict. At the same time, *Women, Armies, and Warfare* hopes to demonstrate that any attempt to describe early modern warfare without reference to the women who accompanied its armies is doomed to be at best incomplete and, most probably, distorted.

To those who come at this work from gender history, let me promise to do my best by your specialty and beg a bit of indulgence if I do not bring out what you would regard as the full variety and richness of the gender issues raised in these pages. I am admittedly new to your town, but I will try to be respectful and leave no rubbish in my wake. I believe the same historical facts that are required for an understanding of women's contributions to early modern warfare should also give these female noncombatants considerable significance for the history of women and gender. Complexities of femininity and masculinity within the very masculine environment of the military camp may add new insights to the discussion of early modern gender boundaries. Women who engaged in petty commerce within the camps experimented with an economic leeway similar to but greater than that accorded their sisters in civil society. The presence of women with armies and the daily life issues fundamental to them emerge as matters of significance to the traditional "big" historical subjects: war, military institutions, and state formation.

I propose that the women who accompanied early modern armies were always important to the well-being of the troops, and before 1650 they were actually vital to the maintenance of military forces on campaign. During the sixteenth and early seventeenth centuries, when legions of women accompanied soldiers into the field, logistical realities determined strategy and operations, such as movements of armies on campaign and pillage of civilian communities in their paths. Women were significant factors and actors in this plunder-driven campaign economy. On the demand side, they and their children were extra mouths to feed, while on the supply side, women were active in pillaging and, more subtly, apparently played a key part in managing the take from plunder.

In the second half of the seventeenth century the framework of warfare changed; definitive military and governmental reforms fundamental to state formation increased state support of armies and allowed a decline in the numbers of women traveling with the troops. Women were no longer necessary to fill the gap between what armies required and what states could provide. Only when armies could make do with fewer women, did their numbers decrease.

Admittedly, this study remains preliminary because detailed monographs that allow for a more definitive evaluation are still lacking. Hacker called his article a "reconnaissance," and to borrow his metaphor, we are still reconnoitering. A large part of my purpose here is to scout directions for further advance.

EVIDENCE AND THE LACK OF EVIDENCE

Despite the ubiquity of plebian women with troops on campaign, official records are disappointingly sparse on this subject. Those who employed soldiers usually did not accept responsibility to feed and maintain the women who accompanied them; therefore, these women remained "off the books" and had to take care of themselves in one way or another. Maurizio Arfaioli concludes in his study of the sixteenth-century

Florentine Black Bands that although these mercenaries were known to bring many women, "Their presence is more easily inferred than proven."[17] To establish their numbers and examine their roles with the troops, we must cobble together diverse sources that vary in their subject, form, and reliability.

Several forms of popular culture speak of women with military forces. I employ songs, literature, plays, and other public performances, but bear in mind that such works of popular culture expressed their authors' points of view and the tastes of their intended audiences. Often these works were formulaic, because authors felt comfortable with a set pattern, and the public liked to hear the story told a certain way. Thus, songs about women soldiers portrayed them as driven by a desire to stay with or seek lovers and husbands, although, in fact, most such women adopted male identities to escape misery from crushing economic poverty or intolerable personal situations. Contemporary books also had their own conventions. A literary conceit among seventeenth- and eighteenth-century works disguised entirely fictional accounts as legitimate memoirs or collections of correspondence, in a mode similar to Daniel Defoe's *Robinson Crusoe*. At the same time, however, openly fictional accounts by certain authors can serve as valuable sources: The German author of picaresque novels, Johann Jacob Christoffel von Grimmelshausen, was carried off as a boy by raiding troops and became a soldier during the Thirty Years War, and the Irish playwright George Farquhar was an officer recruiting for his regiment when he wrote his comedy, *The Recruiting Officer*.

Popular prints, drawings, and paintings also provide windows into military life, including that of women with the troops.[18] For some periods and regions, graphic sources are particularly numerous; for example, a rich harvest of woodcuts depicts sixteenth-century German mercenaries, known as Landsknechts, and Swiss mercenaries, known as Reisläufers.[19] While visual media can be compelling, it is important to recognize that contemporary engravings and paintings are not

---

[17] Maurizio Arfaioli in his *The Black Bands of Giovanni* (Pisa: 2005), p. 68.

[18] In preparation for this study I collected some six hundred contemporary images. Here I am exploring a wealth of graphic material earlier exploited by Barton Hacker. David M. Hopkin provides a sophisticated discussion of popular prints in his *Soldier and Peasant in French Popular Culture 1766–1870* (Woodbridge, Suffolk: 2003).

[19] On these German and Swiss military woodcuts, see J. R. Hale, "The Soldier in Germanic Graphic Art of the Renaissance," *Journal of Interdisciplinary History* 17, no. 1 (Summer, 1986).

snapshots; they are creations of talented and imaginative artists. Of course, it is important to recognize that some of these artists were unfamiliar with military life, while others knew it well. Urs Graf (circa 1485–1529) carried arms as a Reisläufer, and the English artist, Marcellus Laroon (1679–1772), spent many years in military service; thus, the works of these men have an eye-witness character. Jacques Callot (circa 1592–1635) seems to have been acquainted with his subjects, and the prolific artists of the Watteau family lived in the French garrison towns of Valenciennes and Lille during the eighteenth century.

Sometimes common motifs tell us something, as in the German fashion of showing Landsknechts paired with their women, indicating that these soldiers typically formed such partnerships, whether sanctioned by the church or not. It is also important to realize that artists plagiarized one other, so later engravers duplicated works by the talented and original Jacques Callot, simply updating the clothing and detail but retaining the theme and layout.[20] Owing to the lack of formal records, graphic sources are important mainstays of this study, but they are used with care and some skepticism. Often the most reliable aspects of such artistic sources are the details that set the scene behind and around the main characters.

Contemporary treatises and memoirs provide some accounts of women's activity, although these are usually terse. As historian Simon Barker observes: "Non-fictional military narratives rarely dwell on the involvement of women in the extensive camp infrastructure that, for centuries, determined the success or failure of armies as they engaged ... at a little distance away on the field of battle itself."[21] Contemporaries usually described women who followed the camps as moral dangers and logistical embarrassments. Such women populate the works of moral crusaders who disparaged casual sexual liaisons and advocated Christian marriage.

---

[20] For example, Callot's depiction of recruitment and pay in his large format "Les misères et malheurs de la guerre" was updated into early eighteenth century garb and reproduced as the payment of troops in at least two different prints. See Jean Delmas, ed., *Histoire militaire de la France*, vol. 2, De 1715 à 1871 (Paris: 1992), pl. 2, between 12 and 13 and Jean-René Bory, *La Suisse à la rencontre de l'Europe : l'épopée du service étranger : du Concile de Bale (1444) à la Paix de Westphalie (1648)* (Lausanne: D. Perret, ca. 1978), p. 183, pl. 317. Callot's works are also reflected in the series by Romeyn de Hooghe on the brutal conduct of French troops in the Dutch Netherlands, 1672–74. See the series reproduced in Georg Hirth, *Picture Book of the Graphic Arts, 1500–1800 (Kulturgeschichtliches Bilderbuch aus drei Jahrhunderten)* (New York: 1972), vol. 5, pls. 2680–90.

[21] Barker, "*Allarme to England!*," p. 141.

Military reformers wanted to strip armies of all impediments, including women, in order to make them more nimble in the field. Still, such contemporary descriptions can be of greater value than sources drawn from popular culture, when evaluated in light of the authority of the writer and the purpose of the account.

I am aware that in turning to popular art and literature, as well as professional military commentaries, I am not hearing the actual voices of the women I wish to study. Rather I am hearing the men who offered their own observations or, in a paradoxical reversal of the cross-dressing woman soldier, pretended to speak as women with the army. There really is very little chance to escape this limitation at present. Only occasionally were the plebian and usually illiterate camp women able to speak for themselves in testimony, appeals, and petitions. Much the same can be said for common soldiers. My attempt to identify diaries or memoirs of French common soldiers from the seventeenth century when I was writing *Giant of the Grand Siècle* turned up not a single example. The only existent journal of a private soldier from the Thirty Years' War seems to be that of Peter Hagendorf.[22] Quite probably industrious historians will uncover more examples of women's voices in the future, but the larder is pretty bare at present. I have used what is available in as fair a manner as possible, and I expect the reader to understand that woodcuts are not photographs and popular tales are not depositions, and that the artists and authors are all men.

It might be expected that contemporary military regulations and edicts were definitive sources for army practice, as they are in a modern military; however, that was not necessarily the case. Military commanders and the states they served often lacked the effective authority to impose compliance with official edicts and directives. Therefore, a military article of war, ordinance, or regulation stipulating a certain practice could have simply indicated the desires of those in charge without reflecting the actual conduct of armies. At times, military directives were issued by administrators or officers who realized that the troops either would not or could not obey because circumstances did not allow. In fact, official directives could be seen as proof of a problem, rather than as evidence of its solution. Thus, repeated declarations about enforcing discipline might indicate that defiant troops needed to be brought to heel, not that their commanders were asserting their authority.

---

[22] Peter Hagendorf, *Ein Soeldnerleben im Dreissigjaehrigen Krie*, Jan Peters, ed. (Berlin: 1993).

Administrative records and the accounts of legal proceedings provide the most reliable and useful information. These were not meant for public consumption but for official eyes. Such documents include formal complaints to government officials, requests for military pensions, interrogations of those guilty of military infractions, and records of court cases. Unfortunately, such valuable records, while quite plentiful for the late seventeenth and eighteenth centuries, are disturbingly meager for earlier years.

MEASURING WOMEN'S PARTICIPATION ON CAMPAIGN

Because the numbers of women who took part in early modern military campaigns are a critical matter in this study, let us begin by presenting some data. Early modern armies traveled with large retinues of non-combatants. During the sixteenth and early seventeenth centuries the total number of such camp followers was extremely high in relation to the number of troops. During his invasion of Italy in 1494–95, Charles VIII (1483–98) of France calculated that he had to feed 48,000–50,000 people – termed "mouths" – each day to maintain an army of 20,000 combatants.[23] The Franciscan monk, Johannes Pauli, commented on armies in the 1520s: "If there were 10,000 travelers, there were also 20,000 concubines."[24] When the duke of Alba marched troops north to the Spanish Netherlands in 1573, communities were required to prepare food stores for 16,000 mouths, although the number of infantry and cavalry totaled only 9,600.[25] When Bergen-op-Zoom was besieged by Spinola's army in 1622, Dutch observers condemned it as "a small army with so many carts, baggage horses, nags, sutlers, lackeys, women, children, and rabble which numbered far more than the Army itself."[26]

---

[23] Philippe Contamine, *Histoire militaire de la France, vol. 1, Des origines à 1715* (Paris: Presses Universitaires de France, 1992),:232.

[24] Pauli in Haberling, "Army Prostitution and Its Control," p. 32.

[25] Geoffrey Parker, *The Army of Flanders. and the Spanish Road* (Cambridge: 1972), p. 87.

[26] C. A. Campen (ed.), *Bergues sur le Soom assiégée* (1622, edn. Brussels, 1867), p. 247, in Parker, *Army of Flanders*, p. 176. It is fair to note that Parker also lists municipal figures that suggest few women with the troops. However, these were tallies by local administrators responsible for recording how many women accompanying troops were to be given food and quarters at municipal expense. The problem is that it is unclear what standard the administrators applied in recognizing the claims of such women. In one instance, only eighty-five women are noted for 6,975 troops. This figure is preposterously low, being only a one woman for every eighty-two men. Could this tally represent only some officers' wives? Parker, *The Army of Flanders*, Appendix I, p. 288.

Sebastien Bürster reported that when General Aldringer marched to relieve Constance in 1633, his fighting force numbered "some 30,000 soldiers, but including the baggage train around 100,000 people."[27]

Documents of the same period argued that a high percentage of such "camp followers" were women. We have already seen Wallenhausen's estimate that 3,000 German troops would be accompanied by 4,000 women and children during the early seventeenth century. At the camp of Langenau in 1630, 368 cavalrymen had with them a total of 475 camp followers, 168 of which were women and children.[28] Many articles of war and other regulations tried to set the number of women, notably prostitutes, at a much lower figure, but such regulations usually seem to have been honored primarily in the breach.

By the late seventeenth century, the number of camp followers, and the number of women in particular, had decreased sharply. Reports from Dijon, dating 1692–1710, show an average of fifteen women per French infantry battalion, among those battalions that explicitly reported women.[29] For example, on 21 April 1709, the second battalion of the Regiment of Ponthieu arrived with 32 officers, 26 sergeants, 472 men in the ranks, and 22 women, or about five women per one hundred men. These numbers probably accurately reflect the average for the army as refashioned by Louis XIV. A letter dated 1772, a half-century after that great monarch's death, commented on the "fifteen or twenty women who are in the train of each unit."[30]

In 1758, the British also allowed ten women per company for an expedition to the West Indies, but British troops fighting in North America at this time were allowed but six women per hundred.[31] The 1801 regulation quoted earlier also held the number at six women per

---

[27] Sebastien Bürster, *Sebastien Bürster's Beschreibung des schwedischen Krieges 1630–47*, ed. F. von Weech (Leipzig: 1875), p. 17, in Geoff Mortimer, *Eyewitness Accounts of the Thirty Years War 1618–48* (Basingstoke, Hampshire: 2002), p. 33. In 1648, the last year of the Thirty Years War, the Bavarian army had 40,000 fighting men with another 100,000 camp followers. Herbert Langer, *The Thirty Years' War*, trans. C. S. V. Salt (New York: 1980), p. 97.

[28] Langer, *The Thirty Years' War*, p. 97.

[29] Dijon Municipal Archives, H228 (1692), 232 (1698), 235 (1707), 241 (1707), 243 (1709), 244 (1710), 256.

[30] Letter of 30 January 1772 in Albert Babeau, *La vie militaire sous l'ancien régime*, vol. 1 *Les soldats*, and vol. 2 *Les officiers* (Paris: 1890), 1:204.

[31] Mayer, *Belonging to the Army*, p. 10. This figure does not include hired nurses.

hundred men, which in a full strength battalion of 1,000 men would provide sixty women.[32] It would appear that the allotment was often more generous, in fact, because the Judge Advocate General reported that in December 1813, Wellington's 60,000 British troops were accompanied by 4,500 British "wives on the strength" along with "700 Portuguese and 400 Spanish women as sutlers, vivanderas, washerwomen," making for a total of 5,600 women, or a bit over nine women per one hundred men.[33] These figures are still significant, but are much, much lower than those during the Thirty Years' War.

British figures match up well with eighteenth-century German numbers. A Prussian circular of 23 August 1733 commanded that the number of women with troops in the field could not exceed ten per hundred men.[34] The troops which served Frederick the Great brought with them five to twelve women per company, typically all wives.[35] At mid-century, the army of Maria Theresa sent three to five wives, usually strong peasant women, with each company.[36] Later Hapsburg regulations further restricted the number of women that could go into the field.

The number of six women per hundred men also seems to have typified at least some units of the Continental Army in the fledgling United States. In the early 1780s, regiments were allowed to draw sixteen rations for every fifteen men to take care of accompanying women.[37] This would mean that American regulars were expected to have six or seven women for every hundred men.

LITTLE URSULA

Though essential, numerical data are cold and impersonal, but the women I have studied were warm and full of personality. Before going further, we should meet one of these women, or at least one as

---

[32] Hacker, "Women and Military Institutions," p. 660–61. See also regulations in Cordingly, *Heroines & Harlots*, pp. 104–05, and Richard Holmes, *Redcoat: The British Soldier in the Age of Horse and Musket* (London: 2002), p. 294.

[33] Quoted in Michael Glover, *Wellington's Army in the Peninsula, 1808–1814* (New York: 1977), pp. 159–60, in Hacker, "Women and Military Institutions," p. 655.

[34] Haberling, "Army Prostitution and Its Control," p. 53.

[35] Christopher Duffy, *The Army of Frederick the Great* (Newton Abbot, Devonshire: 1974), p. 59.

[36] Christopher Duffy, *The Army of Maria Theresa: The Armed Forces of Imperial Austria, 1740–1780* (New York: 1979), p. 57.

[37] Mayer, *Belonging to the Army*, pp. 103 and 129.

interpreted in a sixteenth-century woodcut by Erhard Schön.[38] (see Plate 1). Here Hans is accompanied by Urschelein, Little Ursula.[39] They are young and strong. He carries only his weapons, but she carries a pack; in fact, the metaphor of the woman being her partner's "mule" appears in military commentaries. Hans has decided to leave his unrewarding job as a cobbler to march off to the Italian province of Friuli, controlled by Venice.[40] He is off to the wars, where in the past he has "won great wealth and manifold honors." This must be braggadocio or a lure to Little Ursula, because a man who has won "great wealth" need not work at a cobbler's bench. Little Ursula states that she is abandoning the unprofitable craft of spinning in hope that "so much may be my winning" through plunder.[41] These two have left behind low-paying jobs to go with the army, not for cause and country but for booty, which is about the only way such a plebian couple could accumulate wealth during the period of fighting.

Little Ursula has possibly struck the kind of bargain known as a May Marriage, contracted between parties in the spring for the duration of a campaign (see Chapter II). She is "pretty" and her bargain with Hans unquestionably involves sex; she will be "a cobbler's whore" but this does not mean she intends to prostitute herself. She belongs to the cobbler as his woman, but since they are not married, she describes herself as a "whore." She will lay with Hans, but that will not be the end of her duties. She must take care of his clothing, nurse him if need be, and perform whatever camp duties military authorities require. Perhaps Hans has taken her with him out of affection, but it is more likely that he brought her out of need. She is as important to his survival in the field as

---

[38] Walter L. Strauss, *The German Single-Leaf Woodcut, 1550–1600*, 3 vols. (New York: 1975), vol. 3, p. 1072. The plate is dated as 1568, and bears the name of Wolfgang Strauch, who was active in Nuremberg during 1554–72. However Heinrich Röttinger, *Erhard Schön und Niklas Stör* (Berlin: 1925) identifies the original as by Erhard Schön (1491–1542). Moxey, *Peasants, Warriors, and Wives*, p. 91, pl. 4.19 and p. 153, n. 51, makes the same conclusion. We know that the woodcut plates used to produce prints were saved, sometimes modified, and reused; this seems to have been the case here. This is available in both Strauss and Moxey; Moxey cites it as photo, Geisberg, Woodcut, vol. 3, cat. no. 1213.

[39] "Little Ursula," the soldier's sweetheart seemed to have been a stock character. Hale, "The Soldier in Germanic Graphic Art of the Renaissance," p. 92.

[40] I thank Jacob Baum for translating the poem that accompanies the woodcut. The poem states the destination as "Frigaul," which Baum translated as Freigau, but which Moxey, *Peasants, Warriors, and Wives*, pp. 90–91 and p. 153, n. 51, states is Friuli.

[41] Olwen Hufton, *The Prospect Before Her: A History of Women in Western Europe, vol., 1500–1800* (New York: Vintage Books, 1998), p. 98, labels spinning a pauper's craft.

PLATE I. *The Cobbler and His Girl*, a woodcut attributed to Erhard Schön, 1568.

The texts of the poems are as follows:

Little Ursula
My Hans I want to run with thee
To the Bright Band in Friuli.
Perhaps so much may be my
    winning
Much more than ever I could
    whilst spinning.
With yarn and twine I'll spin no
    more

Cobbler
In good health, pretty Little Ursula
Shall we go hence into Friuli.
The making of shoes I shall abandon.

When in many wars I have won

Great wealth and manifold honors,

| To become thereafter a Cobbler's whore. | Who then knows whom fortune favors? |

The Illustrated Bartsch, vol. 13, commentary, ed. Walter L. Strauss (New York: Abaris Books, 1984), pl. 222 , p. 401. Used with permission from Abaris Books.

are his weapons. She will pillage with Hans to supply herself and him with the necessities of life. Seeking, protecting, and managing plunder will be essential roles for her.

And she must face the fatigues and dangers of life on campaign. Should Little Ursula lack strength, endurance, and courage, she will not last, but she probably knows that. What she probably does not fully realize is the slim chance that she and Hans will return from the wars with full purses. Little Ursula may dream of riches, but she will be lucky simply to get by. She has chosen a hard life in a deadly arena.

* * *

We will learn a great deal about Little Ursula, and thousands of women like her, in the pages to come. Before we encounter her again, however, we must master some of the context that will allow us to appreciate her character and contributions. Chapter I: Situating the Story: Armies, Communities, and Women will discuss the contexts of this study, outlining some relevant aspects of military, community, and women's history. Such background is essential, particularly because this volume hopes to appeal to a mixed audience, some who know little about military history and some who are new to the history of women and gender. In Chapter II: Camp Women: Prostitutes, "Whores," and Wives, we return to Ursula and her sisters, first examining the identities of camp women and the relationships between women and men and between women and women. Chapter III: Women's Work: Gendered Tasks, Commerce, and the Pillage Economy, surveys the kinds of work women performed and their roles in the campaign economy. Chapter IV: Warrior Women: Cultural Phenomena, Intrepid Soldiers, and Stalwart Defenders discusses warrior women, including those unusual women who assumed male dress and identity to fight as soldiers in battle and the more common phenomenon of women who helped to defend their towns and homes from attacking armies. Based on the findings in the preceding chapters, the Conclusion will bring us full circle and offer answers to the fundamental questions about the participation of women posed at the start of this introduction.

Situating the Story: Armies, Communities, and Women

During the decades following the Peace of the Pyrenees (1659), Louis XIV and his ministers addressed the deficiencies of the French army and of the state apparatus that supported it. As was typical of the military forces of the early seventeenth century, his troops had committed destructive and brutal excesses on campaign, and all too often the victims were his own subjects. In his memoirs of 1666, Louis confided, "I was resolved to spare nothing to reestablish, at every point, discipline in the troops that served under my authority."[1] He used the word "reestablish," but, in fact, he could not restore something that had never been; rather, the king and his agents would create something new. The administrative and military reforms instituted by the French monarchy inspired and typified a powerful wave of change that transformed European armies, primarily during the second half of the seventeenth century. Military excess and reform constitute the first of the three contexts in which we must consider the presence and roles of those women who accompanied troops into the field.

What we will call the *campaign community* provides the second context. Soldiers in the field did not march alone, but as part of communities in which they lived symbiotically with male and female noncombatants. Armies on the march resembled cities in complexity and size, exceeded in population only by the largest European urban centers. While campaign communities understandably imported some standards and practices from civilian life, they established many of their own, some consciously antithetical to civilian values. Moreover, in order to survive, campaign communities preyed upon those unfortunate populations that lay in the path of the armies, creating a vicious dynamic between civilians and campaign communities.

---

[1] Louis XIV, *Oeuvres de Louis XIV*, Philippe Grimoard and Grouvelle, eds., 6 vols. (Paris: 1806), 2:91–92 in André, *Le Tellier*, 605.

The women who made up an important part of the campaign community remained women of their time. Therefore, the third context that we must consider is the history of women and gender in early modern Europe. Contemporary definitions of masculinity and femininity and the range of opportunity, independence, and power open to women helped to shape the campaign community. Thus, when Louis XIV banished prostitutes from military encampments in a series of reform edicts promulgated in 1684–87, he was not simply seeking to improve the discipline and health of his troops; his actions reflected Counter-Reformation condemnation of sexual sin and elevation of marriage.

These three contexts link the lives of women on campaign with major historical themes, most importantly the conduct of war, the rise of the state, the boundaries of gender identity, and the independence, status, and power of women in early modern Europe. Facing danger as they struggled to carry heavy burdens over primitive roads while baking in the sun or shivering in the rain, these women demand our attention, and our respect.

MILITARY EVOLUTION AND THE NECESSITY TO PILLAGE

Crowds of women did not accompany armies without good reason, and the marked decrease in their participation after 1650 had its causes. To explain this rise and ebb requires that we understand two aspects of early modern military history: army evolution and pillage. Driven by necessity and aspiration, military forces evolved in style and capacity. The three centuries discussed in this volume witnessed the dominance and decline of two styles of forces, the *aggregate contract army* and the *state commission army*, followed by the emergence of a third, the *popular conscript army*.[2] Each of these styles corresponded to the changing realities of contemporary government and society, as well as to advances in weaponry, logistics, and command. Early modern armies had no choice but to commandeer goods and services as they marched. This varied from the relatively benign necessity of foraging fodder, to the resented imposition of quartering troops and the destructive brutality of pillaging towns. The weak states that fielded aggregate contract armies could only maintain them by tolerating pillage, even though pillage undermined discipline, hampered operations, and discredited rulers. Plundering also poisoned the relations between the campaign and civilian communities, which became predator and prey.

---

[2] For a discussion of army evolution, see John A. Lynn, "The Evolution of Army Style in the Modern West, 800–2000," *International History Review* 18, no. 3 (August 1996): 505–45.

The Evolution of Army Style in Early Modern Europe

Field forces of the ~~aggregate~~ contract army (1450–1650) relied on diverse hired, often foreign, units combined into an army, usually for brief periods of time. Even though rulers might summon feudal arrays in emergencies, they were in sharp decline throughout this era. Rulers generally signed on entire bands of soldiers by means of a kind of business contract with their captains. The most notable sixteenth-century mercenary units, the Swiss Reisläufers, who rose to prominence during the late Middle Ages, and their subsequent rivals, the German Landsknechts, provided a ready supply when needed.

Sometimes hired at the last moment, these units arrived quickly and ready to fight; they were armed, trained, and organized. When François I faced invasion from Henry VIII to the north and Charles V to the east in 1544, he contracted in July for 16,000 Swiss, who reached France in time to form the heart of his main army at the camp de Jalons in late August, stalling the forces of Charles V in September.[3] Such mercenary bands could be purchased "off the shelf" for a particular campaign and then dismissed as soon as they were no longer needed. Thus, there was little reason to maintain armies from year to year, or even over the winter, when weather prohibited campaigning.[4]

Mercenary troops of the aggregate contract army exercised considerable leverage. Their captains created the units and struck deals with employers, whether they be governments, princes, or simply ambitious contenders for power. The critical point here is that, while men might join a mercenary company as individuals, they then became part of a unit that was contracted as a whole. It is illuminating to consider them as a special form of labor, organized and empowered to bargain with prospective employers. They had to be courted and cared for, and a generous offer might steal them away from their paymasters. For example, in 1515, shortly before the battle of Marignano, François I offered a handsome bribe to the council of the Swiss mercenaries fighting for his opponent,

---

[3] See Ferdinand Lot, *Recherches sur les effectifs des armées françaises des Guerres d'Italie aux Guerres de Religion, 1494–1562* (Paris, 1962), pp. 87–114.

[4] James B. Wood's excellent examination of the French royal army during the Religious Wars underscores how major military forces might exist for only a matter of months, or even weeks, in the late sixteenth century. James B. Wood, *The King's Army: Warfare, Soldiers, and Society during the French Wars of Religion, 1562–1576* (Cambridge: 1996). Peter H. Wilson characterizes this phenomenon in Germany, "Prior to the retention of permanent cadres in peacetime after 1648, most German soldiers served on temporary contracts which often expired when either winter or lack of funds halted operations." "German Women and War, 1500–1800," *War in History*, vol. 3, no. 2 (1996), p. 134.

Maximilian Sforza. Some of the Reisläufers accepted the French gold and marched away.[5] These same Swiss would also haggle for back pay, further leveraging their bargaining power with the imminence of battle.[6]

Aggregate contract armies might also include forces raised privately by great nobles in the names of their rulers or in rebellion against them. This period provided a magnificent theater for the private army, both in the service of and in opposition to the monarch. As Brian Sandberg observes, "Nobles were the principal organizers of warfare during the French Wars of Religion of the sixteenth and seventeenth centuries, employing their military offices, clientage networks and wealth to mobilize armies and wage warfare."[7] As did military entrepreneurs, nobles with their own forces pursued their own interests; they were players to be reckoned with.

While situations varied, those who assembled aggregate contract armies usually failed to pay them regularly or even at all. These shortages in pay were particularly disastrous because soldiers were usually expected to purchase their own food; thus, empty pockets meant empty stomachs. In 1594, troops from the Spanish Army of Flanders charged that they had not been paid for 100 months. A body of 15,000 Swiss soldiers serving the French kings received nothing from 1639 to 1648.[8] Lack of pay often caused troops to mutiny against their masters. The Spanish Army of Flanders suffered over forty-five mutinies from 1572 though 1607, including the horrendous sack of Antwerp in 1574.[9] Mutinies often resembled labor strikes; soldiers chose their own leaders, made demands for pay and better working conditions, and bargained with their employers until a settlement was reached.[10]

---

[5] Charles Oman, *A History of the Art of War in the Sixteenth Century* (London: 1937), p. 163

[6] See the comments by J. R. Hale, "The Soldier in Germanic Graphic Art of the Renaissance," *Journal of Interdisciplinary History* 17, no. 1 (Summer, 1986), p. 93. Swiss serving the French precipitated the battle of Bicocca in 1522 by complaining that they had yet to be paid and insisting that Lautrec, the French commander, fight the enemy the next morning or they would return home for lack of compensation. The result was a bloody defeat of Lautrec's army.

[7] Brian Sandberg, "'The Magazine of All Their Pillaging': Armies as Sites of Second-Hand Exchanges during the French Wars of Religion," in Lawrence Fontaine, ed., *Alternative Exchanges: Second-Hand Circulations from the Sixteenth Century to Today* (New York: 2007), pp. 76–96.

[8] Julius R. Ruff, *Violence in Early Modern Europe, 1500–1800* (Cambridge: Cambridge University Press, 2001), p. 54.

[9] Parker, *The Army of Flanders*, p. 185.

[10] Spanish troops, for example, were able to force the authorities to change their basic wage structure by mutinying in 1590. Parker, *The Army of Flanders*, p. 159.

Voyla les beaux exploits de ces cœurs inhumans   L'un pour avoir de lor iouente des Supplices,   Et tour d'vn mesme accord commettent meschamment
Ils rauagent par tout rien neschappe à leur mains   La autre a mil forfaicts anime les complices ;   Le vol, le rapt, le meurtre, et le violement. 5

Ifrael. ex. Cum Priuil. Reg.

PLATE 2. Jacques Callot, *Pillage of a Large Farmhouse* from *Les misères et malheurs de la guerre*, Paris, 1633.[11] Snark/Art Resource, NY. Bibliothèque Nationale, Paris, France.[1]

[11] This series in large-format includes other scenes of pillage as does the similar series Callot did in small format. For Dutch paintings and engravings of pillage scenes, see Jane Susannah Fishman, *Boerenverdriet: Violence between Peasants and Soldiers in Early Modern Netherlands Art* (Ann Arbor, MI: 1982), Pls. 6, 8, 25, 26, 37, 38, and 40.

Unfortunately, poorly paid and ill-fed troops commonly resorted to another form of collective disobedience; they pillaged villages and towns, which will be discussed at length later in this chapter. The pillaging soldier became the archetypical symbol of the aggregate contract army, and demonic troops served as the subject of contemporary artists, such as Jacques Callot (see Plate 2.)

By the mid-seventeenth century, the shortcomings of the aggregate contract army as an instrument of state power fostered evolution toward the state commission army (1650–1790), a military force that was better supported and more tightly controlled by princes. Regulation and uniformity became the rule in everything from organization to clothing. Princes relied on standardized regiments, preferably composed of their own subjects whenever possible. France led the way in national recruitment, but even under Louis XIV, as much as one-quarter of the army might still be composed of foreign regiments during wartime.[12] States without the manpower resources of France could be much more dependent on recruitment from beyond their own borders. Individual, foreign-born recruits could sign on with regiments already a permanent part of another state's forces. The majority of Prussian army recruits were foreigners during peacetime; in 1768, for example, about fifty-six percent of the soldiery was foreign born.[13] Another alternative was to hire the troops of lesser, usually German, states to supply additional complete regiments for a limited time. This created a new kind of military labor market exploited by such principalities as Hessen-Kassel and Württemberg.[14] Even foreign troops were organized and commanded in accord with new standards of hierarchy and obedience Officers received commissions from state authorities to maintain or create units that they recruited, equipped, and trained according to rules set by a more effective and intrusive military administration. Most of the rank and file enlisted

---

[12] In 1690, for example, foreign regiments composed about 24 percent of French infantry. John A. Lynn, *Giant of the Grand Siècle* (Cambridge: 1997), p. 332.

[13] According to Duffy, *Army of Frederick the Great*, p. 55, in 1751 only 50,000 of Prussia's 133,000 troops were native born. In 1768 the figure stood at 70,000 of 160,000, and in 1786, 80,000 of 190,000. On the number of foreign troops in Piedmontese service in 1734, see Sabina Loriga, *Soldats – Un laboratoire disciplinaire: l'armée piémontaise au XVIIIe siècle* (Paris: 2007) pp. 36–37, and Tables 1/1 and 1/3, pp. 237–39. In 1734, this Italian state fielded 26,000 native troops and 14,000 foreigners.

[14] On such armies for hire, see Rodney Atwood, *The Hessians: Mercenaries from Hessen-Kassel in the American Revolution* (Cambridge: 1980) and Wilson, *War, State and Society in Württemberg, 1677–1793*.

voluntarily as individuals. Such individual recruits who signed on to serve their prince or government lacked the leverage enjoyed by the members of the mercenary bands of earlier days. As armies grew larger, most European states also turned to selective forms of conscription to add needed manpower. Only Russia relied exclusively on conscripted troops.

Reorganized and reformed government administrations proved themselves more reliable pay masters.[15] Also supply and support services improved significantly, although they were hardly perfect. Permanent magazines, regular supply of food, provision of uniforms, and other important administrative innovations typified the state commission army. Soldiers in distress also received more compassionate treatment. Most states created better health services, which included military hospitals, and disabled veterans were accepted as wards of the state, symbolized by the creation of old soldiers' homes, such as the Hôtel des Invalides in Paris (1674) and the Royal Hospital at Chelsea (1682).[16] The growth of military administration, the need for states to mobilize and disperse resources to their forces, and the existence of standing armies influenced the development of more powerful, centralized, and bureaucratic governments.

Troops who were better supplied and more regularly paid, and who lacked the fierce independence of the mercenary bands and private armies who preceded them, were more dependable and obedient. Louis XIV was justly proud of the better behavior and discipline of his troops, and, of course, Prussian discipline became legendary under Frederick William I and Frederick II, the Great. The state commission army still witnessed excesses and abuses, but they were less frequent and rarely as extreme as those that typified aggregate contract armies. Governments eventually curtailed plunder by armies, particularly attacks on loyal populations, which had been as vulnerable to abuse as were enemy civilians.[17] The

---

[15] On pay in the French army of the seventeenth century, see Lynn, *Giant of the Grand Siècle*, pp. 148–58. J. Cognazzo, serving with Austrian forces during the Seven Years War reported: "I never knew of an instance when an officer went short of his monthly salary, or the soldier did not have his pay dispensed meticulously on the appointed day." Christopher Duffy, *The Army of Maria Theresa*, p. 55. A century before such regularity of pay would have been nothing short of miraculous. Also see Duffy's comments on the regularity of pay, p. 124.

[16] See as well similar reforms in a smaller army, such as hospitals provided by Savoy/Piedmont, Loriga, *Soldats*, pp. 38–39.

[17] See my "How War Fed War: The Tax of Violence and Contributions during the *Grand Siècle*," *Journal of Modern History* 65, no. 2 (June 1993) pp. 286–310, for the way in which Louis XIV worked to prohibit the plunder and abuse of his subjects by his own army.

LES QUATRES VERITEZ
Du fiecle D'aprefent: Sur *le Chant* Ceſt le Prince d'Orange:

Je prie Dieu pour vous tous: ❦ Pour vous mes tres chers Freres Je prie inceſſament Dieu qui de vos miſeres Prendra le foin dans toutes vos affaires Vous tirans des tourments

Le prêtre. Je prie Dieu pour tous Trois.

Le foldat Je vous garde tous trois

Je vous gar-de tous trois Je me tiens en poſture Pour main tenir vos droits, Pour les maux que j'endure foir et matin ainſi je vous aſſure : Et vous garde tous trois

Je vous nourris tous trois jour et nuit je travaille, Ou j'exerce mes bra Je n'ay denier ni maille et bien fouvent je couche fur la paille Pour vous nourrir tous trois.

Le payſant je vous nourris tous

Le procureur Je vous mange tous

Je vous man ge tous trois Moy qui fuis De Juſtice j'aime s bien les Proces Et par mon artifice : je trouveaſſe de force et de malice pour vous manger tous trois. FIN

A ORLEANS CHEZ   LETOURMI

PLATE 3. *Les Quatres Veritez* (*The Four Truths*), a popular print by Jean-Baptiste Letourmy, ca. 1780. *Les Quatre Veritez*, a theme of popular art during the eighteenth century, shows a priest, a peasant, a soldier, and a *procureur*, a government legal official. The priest says he prays for the other three; the peasant feeds them; and the soldier protects, *garde*, them. Interestingly, it is the *procurer* who admits he will *mange*, i.e., eat, them. *Manger* is a verb associated with armies consuming all the resources of an area in the seventeenth century.[18] But here the soldier protects, and it is the *procureur* who "eats" the others.

Musée de l'image, Epinal, France.

[18] See, for example, the comment by Louvois about enemy forces who would destroy, *manger*, Alsace. Letter from Louvois to Vauban, 25 August 1687, in Rochas d'Aiglun, *Vauban, sa famille et ses écrits*, 2 vols. (Paris: 1910), 2:280.

better-behaved troops of the state commission army who guarded a prince's lands and subjects were now seen as protectors rather than as predators (see Plate 3). The eighteenth century is often described as the era of limited war, in part because troops were less rapacious.

With a more secure government and administrative base, this form of army grew to unprecedented size; the sheer figures for army growth provide incontrovertible evidence of effective reforms. French forces grew impressively during the second half of the seventeenth century. Wartime levels of 60,000–80,000, which typified French armies since the late Middle Ages, increased to wartime highs that reached 450,000 on paper in 1693, a figure that can be discounted to about 360,000 actual troops.[19] Significantly, French peacetime forces grew at a much greater rate, expanding from a level of 10,000 men early in the seventeenth century to about 150,000 men by the 1680s, becoming a true standing army.[20] The growth of other armies paralleled that of the French; consider the expansion of the forces that served Brandenberg-Prussia, Russia, and even smaller states, such as Savoy/Piedmont.[21]

The popular conscript army (1790–1870), pioneered during the French Revolution, began its dominance at the end of the period covered in this volume. This form again witnessed army expansion, but not quite as dramatic as had occurred with the state commission army. In mid-1794 revolutionary France fielded about 1,000,000 troops on paper, well over twice the size of Louis XIV's forces. Under Napoleon, French numbers decreased to roughly 650,000. The greatest changes came with an expectation that patriotic sentiment would provide fundamental motivation and with reliance upon universal conscription as the primary method of raising troops. As a consequence, armies ideally became

---

[19] My most recent calculations of army size are explained in "Revisiting the Great Fact of War and Bourbon Absolutism: The Growth of the French Army during the *Grand siècle*" in *Guerra y sociedad en la monarchia hispanica: Política, estrategia y cultura en la Europa moderna (1500–1700)*, Enrique Garcia Hernán and Davide Maffi, eds. (Madrid: 2006), pp. 49–74. An earlier work on the subject is my "Recalculating French Army Growth During the *Grand siècle*, 1610–1715," *French Historical Studies*, 18 (Fall 1994), pp. 881–906.

[20] There is some reason to date the standing army back to the early aggregate-contract army, but French forces maintained in peacetime then rarely exceeded 10,000 men.

[21] With a population of only about five million subjects, the Prussian peacetime army of 133,000 in 1751 or 190,000 in 1786 was the largest army per capita in Europe. Duffy, *Army of Frederick the Great*, p. 55. Given its small population (2.5 million inhabitants), the fact that Savoy/Piedmont supported 26,652 troops in 1733 or 31,196 in 1760 gave it a large force in proportion to population, one with a military participation percentage approaching that of France. Loriga, *Soldats*, p. 237, table 1.

exclusively national in character, and the revolutionary government disbanded foreign regiments in the name of creating an army of the French people. While the extreme and rapidly changing situation of the Revolution caused a good deal of flux, military forces eventually became even more subject to direct government control.

Military historians have long considered the French Revolution as a great watershed in the nature of war and military institutions. Wars between peoples replaced wars between kings, and nationalism united entire populations in great struggles. During the Wars of the French Revolution, the common French soldier was exalted as a patriotic hero, an example of civic virtue.[22]

Taking What They Needed: Foraging, Quartering, and Pillaging

Early modern European military practice expected troops to get much of what they needed from local populations. On the march, armies had no alternative but to feed their many horses on fodder foraged from fields close at hand. Lacking barracks, which were relatively rare even in garrison towns until well into the eighteenth century, troops quartered in civilian homes. Foraging and quartering could be carried out in a more or less regular fashion with control and compensation, but they also could degenerate into theft and bullying. The most extreme form of commandeering, pillage, was by nature a brutal outrage, but troops of aggregate contract armies often had few alternative means of sustaining themselves. By requisitioning with proper sanction or simply stealing at the point of a sword, early modern soldiers took what they needed, or wanted, fueling hostility between the campaign community and civilian populations.

Foraging for animal fodder was the most basic and least destructive form of requisition; it also illustrated the absolute necessity for troops to live off the land. The tens of thousands of horses needed by even a moderate-sized army consumed far more fodder than could be effectively hauled by wagon.[23] This meant that foraging parties, sometimes

---

[22] For discussions of the common soldier as hero, see Jean-Paul Bertaud, *La Révolution armée* (Paris: 1979) and John A. Lynn, *The Bayonets of the Republic: Motivation and Tactics in the Army of Revolutionary France, 1791–94*, corrected edition (Boulder, CO: 1996; first edition published by the University of Illinois Press in 1984).

[23] A horse consumed about fifty-five pounds of fresh, or green, fodder each day, or twenty pounds of dried fodder and grain. An army of 60,000 men with 40,000 horses would thus consume 1,100 tons of green fodder, or 400 tons of dried fodder, each day, and it simply

numbering in the thousands, had to harvest forage from the surrounding
fields. Peasants sometimes received compensation for this requisition;
sometimes it simply amounted to outright theft, which might involve
force of arms.

Quartering put troops and their women on a collision course with
rural and town populations. Forced to house soldiers and their partners,
civilians saw the sanctity of their homes compromised. Regulations
might state that those quartered by the local population only had the
right to a bed to sleep, a place by the fire, and certain bare essentials;
however, they often demanded more, threatening householders with
violence.[24] Jules Mazarin, the first minister of France 1642–61, compared quartering troops to paying the primary land tax, the *taille*: "Three
days of quartering soldiers is more of a problem for an individual
than is paying the *taille*."[25] In a seventeenth-century poem, a soldier
announces to his woman, "his dearest little treasure," that war will soon
begin again:

> So now let's go to it,
> Drink and stuff ourselves
> But let the peasants pay.[26]

could not transport this quantity with it. See the classic article on logistics, G. Perjés,
"Army Provisioning, Logistics and Strategy in the Second Half of the 17th Century," *Acta
Historica Academiae Scientiarum Hungaricae* 16, nr. 1–2 (1970) pp. 1–52. See as well my
discussions in John A. Lynn, *Feeding Mars* (Boulder, CO: 2003), chaps. 1 and 7; Lynn,
Giant of the Grand Siècle, chap. 4.

[24] On French quartering during the seventeenth-century see Lynn, *Giant of the Grand
Siècle*, chap. 5. For visual images of seventeenth-century abuses during quartering and
peasant revenge in response to such abuses, see David Vinckboons, *Boerenverdriet*
(Peasant Sorrow) and *Boerenvreugd* (Peasant Joy), ca. 1615, in Fishman, *Boerenverdriet*, Pls. 14 and 15. These two plates are particularly interesting, and they should be
interpreted on several levels. First, they display the antagonism between abusive
soldiers, who demand food and service from peasants, and the peasants, who have
seized the soldiers' weapons and drive the soldiers and their women away with deadly
force. Second, Jane Fishman also points out that this illustration ridicules bullying, but
cowardly, soldiers. Third, she sees this pair of works by Vinckboons as an inversion of
roles, with "the rout of the soldiers by the peasantry" (p. 39). See as well the plates by
Bolswert after Vinckboons, Fishman, *Boerenverdriet*, Pls. 16–19. For another view of
peasants driving off a soldier, see the playing card design by Peter Floetner (ca. 1520)
showing a man with a pitchfork and a woman with a broom driving out a Landsknecht
with drawn sword. Max Geisberg, *The German Single-Leaf Woodcut, 1500–1550*
(New York: 1974), III, p. 817.

[25] Mazarin in André Corvisier, *La France de Louis XIV, 1643–1715: Ordre intérieur et
place en Europe* (Paris: 1979), p. 108.

[26] Een nieu liedekin vant beghin des Kriegs, 1621," in P. Leendertz, ed., *Het
Geuzenliedboek* (Zutphen: 1924), v. 1, #206, in Fishman, *Boerenverdriet*, p. 36.

In addition, living in close quarters with soldiers put civilian wives, daughters, and serving maids at risk of rape.[27] There was also the threat of less violent but still disastrous seductions in which serving maids seem to have been common targets.[28] All in all, quartering troops was so onerous that it could be used as a form of punishment; notably when Louis XIV wanted to compel his Protestants to convert to Catholicism, he quartered troops with them in the infamous *dragonnades*.[29] Abuses by quartered troops were at their worst with the aggregate contract army, and research on the French army indicates that quartering became much more benign in the eighteenth century.[30] However, troops still abused the practice; the tsar's soldiers ransacked Russian peasant homes at the end of the eighteenth century, leaving them as if plundered by Tartar raids.[31]

Pillage was the most extreme form of requisition committed by the early modern campaign community, and because plundering occupies such a critical role in this volume, we will need to explore it at some length.

Political masters were notoriously irregular in paying their troops during a time when troops were supposed to rely on their wages to buy essential supplies. Referring to the Thirty Years War, Sir James Turner (1615–86) commented that although men were supposed to be mercenaries fighting for pay, "if you will consider how their wages are paid, I suppose, you will rather think them Voluntaries, at least very generous, for doing the greatest part of their service for nothing."[32] Cash-strapped governments could not

---

[27] For example, Mac-Myer, a Scot in Danish service during the Thirty Years' War, raped the daughter of the Danish peasant family at whose house he was quartered. R. Monro, *Monro, His Expedition with the Worthy Scots Regiment Called Mac-Keys*, ed. William S. Brockington (Westport, CT: 1999), pp. 53–54.

[28] See the discussion in Rublack, "Wench and Maiden," pp. 12–18.

[29] For the best recent discussion of the *dragonnades*, see Roy L. McCullough, *Coercion, Conversion and Counterinsurgency in Louis XIV's France* (Leiden: 2007). So hated was the practice, that even the founding fathers of the United States wrote the third amendment to the Constitution as a safeguard against quartering troops.

[30] Claude C. Sturgill, "Changing Garrisons: The French System of Etapes," *Canadian Journal of History*, 20, #2 (August 1985): 193–201.

[31] Christopher Duffy, *Russia's Military Way to the West: Origins and Nature of Russian Military Power, 1700–1800* (London: 1981), p. 130.

[32] Sir J. Turner, *Pallas Armata: Military Essayes of the Ancient Grecian, Roman and Modern Art of War* (London: 1683), pp. 198–99. Some commanders even saw an advantage to paying troops irregularly. The great Spanish general Ambrosio Spinola stated, "To keep the troops together it is a good thing to owe them something." Parker, *The Army of Flanders*, p. 173. Sinola's harsh logic held that troops would be less likely to desert if they expected to receive back pay in the future. However, if underpaying troops might keep an army together, it practically guaranteed a breakdown in discipline as troops turned to plunder as a form of compensation and to supply necessities.

nd eliminate pillage without destroying their armies. Commenting on the Spanish in Naples in 1504, Guicciardini bemoaned that "the Spaniards in Italy were the first that presumed to maintain themselves wholly on the substance of the people."[33] Pierre de Brantôme (1539–1614), writing from his experience of late sixteenth-century warfare, shared this distaste, "It is deplorable that our soldiers dedicate themselves to pillage rather than to honourable feats, but it is all due to their not being paid."[34] Allowing troops to take what they wanted was accepted as a distasteful but practical necessity. As the *Mercure françois* put it in 1622, "One finds enough soldiers when one gives them the freedom to live off the land, and allowing them to pillage supports them without pay."[35]

Troops victimized whatever population was close at hand, even if it was loyal to the government served by the army. One contemporary observer described the conduct of the Florentine Black Bands in 1527, as they marched through Florentine territory, claiming that they were "worse than Turks. In the Valdarno they have sacked three Florentine villages, raped women and perpetrated other very cruel things."[36] French troops regularly ravaged the French countryside during the first half of the seventeenth century.[37]

Besieging armies also inflicted an especially unfettered form of pillage upon towns and fortresses that resisted them too resolutely. The customs

[33] Guicciardini in John R. Hale, *War and Society in Renaissance Europe, 1450–1620* (Baltimore: 1985), p. 189.
[34] Brantôme in Hale, *War and Society in Renaissance Europe*, p. 189.
[35] *Mercure françois* in Charles Tilly, *The Contentious French* (Cambridge, MA: 1986), p. 123. Louis XIV expressed almost exactly the same sentiment in his memoirs for the year 1666: "Of late, some commanders are found who have made great armies subsist for a long time without giving them any pay other than the license of pillaging everywhere." Louis, memoirs for 1666, Louis XIV, *Mémoires de Louis XIV*, Charles Dreyss, ed., 2 vols. (Paris: 1860), 1:249.
[36] Arfaioli, *The Black Bands of Giovanni*, p. 58.
[37] See my "How War Fed War," and *Giant of the Grand Siècle*, chap. 6. The Army of Flanders, sent by Philip II to secure control of his ancestral lands in the Low Countries was noted for his brutality in the late sixteenth and early seventeenth centuries. The Dutch issued orders condemning the conduct of their own troops in the 1580s, charging that: "both cavalry and foot soldiers in his Excellency's, ours, and the country's service, forgetting all military discipline, rove here and there, exploiting and plundering without restraint, even robbing and stealing ... and as we daily understand ... governors, colonels and captains, forgetting all proper discipline, on their own initiative threaten the villages and country folk with extortion, damage their goods, and torment their persons," a 1580s Plakkat issued repeatedly by the States General in Fishman, *Boerenverdriet*, p. 4. The Army of Flanders, sent by Philip II to secure control of his ancestral lands in the Low Countries, was noted for its brutality in the late sixteenth and early seventeenth centuries.

of siege warfare varied, but if a garrison held out so stubbornly that the town had to be taken by storm, a costly business for the attackers, no quarter would be offered. This freed the victorious attackers to do as they wished for several days, plundering, torturing, and raping. The sack of towns also terrorized other fortresses into accepting terms quickly to avoid such a horrendous fate.[38] In the pillage of Magdeburg that followed its fall on 20 May 1631, troops broke in, fires broke out, and the final death toll reached 25,000, or eighty-five percent of the city's population.[39] Similar fates awaited Drogheda and Wexford at the hands of Cromwell's troops as they "pacified" Ireland in 1649. The next year when the town of Kilkenny rejected Cromwell's call to surrender, he threatened to sack the city if he took it by storm, and the good citizens, mindful of the fate of Drogheda and Wexford yielded, even paying his troops to compensate them for foregoing the plunder of the town.

Pillage was all-too-often a necessity, but it also became a motivation for soldiers who hoped for booty. Erasmus captured much of the truth in his colloquy, "Of a Soldier's Life." In it, Hanno confronts the soldier, "It was not the Love of your Country, but the Love of Booty that made you a Soldier," to which, the soldier replies, "I confess so, and I believe very few go into the Army with any better Design." He also admits, "The Hope of Booty made me valiant."[40] Hans and Little Ursula certainly intended to come home with considerable loot.

Pillage could be a free for all, in which individual members of the campaign community could simply take whatever they laid their hands on; plundering, however, could be the more coordinated work of an entire unit: The troops collected the booty and piled up all they had found. It was then be appraised and all were given their share according to agreements between officers and men.[41] As Sandberg points out, Callot seems to portray the latter in his engraving detailing the pillage of a convent by troops who gathered their booty at a central location.

[38] See the analysis that Francisco de Vitoria offered in the 1540s. Francisco de Vitoria, *Relectio de iure belli* in Francisco de Vitoria, *Political Writings*, ed. Anthony Pagden and J. Lawrance (Cambridge: 1991), pp. 293–327, in Geoffrey Parker, "Early Modern Europe," in *The Laws of War: Constraints on Warfare in the Western World*, Michael Howard, George J. Andreopoulos, and Mark R. Shulman, eds. (New Haven: 1994), p. 49.

[39] Ruff, *Violence in Early Modern Europe*, p. 56.

[40] Erasmus, "Of a Soldier's Life," in *The Colloquies of Erasmus*, trans. N. Bailey, ed. E. Johnson (London: 1878), p. 62. Available on the internet.

[41] Sandberg, "The Magazine of All Their Pillaging," p. 86.

One wonders how many soldiers actually made their fortunes during these campaigns. Anecdotal evidence argues that most soldiers ended their service as poor as they had begun. When Erasmus's Hanno probes, "Well, have you brought home a good Deal of Plunder then?" the soldier shrugs, "Empty Pockets."[42] The mercenary soldier Sydnam Poyntz complained that he and his men received "nothing from our Generall but what we got by pillage which as the Proverb is lightly come as lightly goes."[43] Still, enough soldiers returned with hefty purses so that their good fortune fed a lottery-type psychology; individuals were attracted by the prospect of big rewards even if the chances were small. In studying the Spanish Army of Flanders, Geoffrey Parker concludes, "Many ordinary volunteers, poor men when they enlisted, left the Army with 1,000 ducats in their purse and, in rural Castille at least, a man with 1,000 ducats to his name was rich, one of the *villanos ricos* (rich peasants) who ruled the village."[44]

If the aggregate contract army was plunder-driven, the state commission army was not. Soldiers still welcomed booty, but private pillage was no longer essential to an army's existence. Although brutal pillage and destruction by soldiers did not totally disappear after 1650, it markedly declined. Abuse of civilian communities and the devastation of the countryside were then used as strategic gambits, as was the case for the French in the Dutch Netherlands (1672–74) and the Palatinate (1688–89), or for Marlborough's army in Bavaria (1704). But pillage as a necessary compensation for ill-paid or ill-supported troops ceased to be the rule for western European armies.

State commission armies continued to help support themselves in the field by extorting payments from hostile and even neutral populations, but they did so in a far more regular and reasonable manner by imposing contributions. These were war taxes, often assessed in relation to the taxes paid in peacetime by an area to its prince. Ideally, contributions were imposed under the supervision of civilian administrators attached to the army. The French even used printed forms with blank spaces to be completed with the name of the village or town, the amount to be paid, and the date(s) payment was due. Should a town or village refuse to agree, or should it renege on its commitment, it would be threatened with

---

[42] Erasmus, "Of a Soldier's Life," p. 62.

[43] Sydnam Poyntz, *The Relation of Sydnam Poyntz 1624–1636*, ed. A. T. S. Goodrick (London: 1908), p. 51, in Mortimer, *Eyewitness Accounts*, p. 30.

[44] Parker, *The Army of Flanders*, p. 183. The loot from a fallen town could be impressive; after they took Dundee in 1651, Oliver Cromwell's army sent home sixty shiploads of booty. Ruff, *Violence in Early Modern Europe*, p. 57.

burning – "execution" in the language of the day. But if it paid up, it gained a degree of protection.

THE CAMPAIGN COMMUNITY

Because the violent excesses discussed above were not simply the work of soldiers but of campaign communities, the latter should be regarded as important agents of history, helping to shape the conduct of warfare and to drive military and administrative reforms meant to bring military forces to heel.[45] The men and women who populated the camps constituted a special and influential European community, one that rivaled in size the major towns of the day.

At the start, it is important to realize that the troops and those attached to them interacted in two distinct kinds of the communities: garrison and campaign communities. The former involved military units living for long periods in towns and/or fortresses, while the latter typified armies in the field. Garrison communities formed when troops assumed a sedentary existence either during peacetime or when they occupied towns for extended periods during wartime, as in the case of garrison battalions.[46] Particularly with the rise of large standing armies after 1650, battalions and regiments took up peacetime residence in towns where they could live a more regular existence, raising families and pursuing a trade in off-duty hours.[47] During the late seventeenth and eighteenth centuries, garrison life was regular enough so that armies with a large proportion of married soldiers even established garrison schools for the education of the soldiers and their children.[48] Troops within garrison communities interacted on a

---

[45] This volume is not the first to reconceptualize an early modern army as a campaign community. Holly A. Mayer did so with her very valuable work, *Belonging to the Army: Camp Followers and Community during the American Revolution* (Columbia, SC: 1996), in which she speaks of a "Continental Community." I actually adopted this conceptual key before I read Mayer's work, but she clearly got there first.

[46] For references to French Garrison battalions during the seventeenth century, see John A. Lynn, *Giant of the Grand Siècle*, pp. 182, 469, and 522.

[47] For a treatment specifically of women in the Prussian garrison community of the eighteenth century, see Beate Engelen, *Soldatenfrauen in Preußen. Eine Strukturanalyse der Garnisonsgesellschaft im späten 17 und 18. Jahrhundert* (Münster: Lit, 2004). She defines the garrison community as "the social community of people with a legal or only familiar, conditional relationship to the army in the time of the standing army of the eighteenth century," p. 203. In fact her concern is overwhelmingly the peacetime community, when the relationship between soldiers' wives and the civil community was rich.

[48] In 1692, Frederick I founded a school for all soldiers' children in Berlin, and the first garrison school in Potsdam was established in 1721 (Engelen, *Soldatenfrauen*

constant and regular basis with the civilians who inhabited the towns where the units were stationed. In this volume, we will occasionally discuss these garrison communities, often to contrast them with campaign communities. But campaign communities will be the main focus, because the emphasis here is on women as participants in the actual conduct of war. It is worth noting, however, that the difference between garrison and campaign communities became less distinct when field armies went into winter quarters during wartime. Then, soldiers could temporarily live the life of the towns.

It is essential to define an early modern force in the field as a campaign community, because it hardly fit the modern definition of an army. Although soldiers constituted its teeth and claws, a considerable number of noncombatants accompanied the troops into the field as we have seen. These civilians were often referred to as "belonging to" or "serving with" the army, although they were not formally enrolled in a fighting unit.[49] Noncombatants who marched with the troops fell into three categories: soldiers' women, servants or "boys," and service personnel. Although soldiers' women are the major focus of this volume, we must briefly mention the other noncombatant members of the campaign community.

Troops brought servants with them. Those who attended common soldiers were referred to as "boys," an appropriate description as they were usually youths.[50] Servants comprised a significant proportion of a troop's number. A count of servants with the Black Bands in the late 1520s identified 806 servants for 2,954 troops, while a Spanish cavalry

---

in Preußen, p. 211). Peter the Great established the first Russian garrison school for Russian troops in 1721. On the various garrison schools established in Russia, see Duffy, p. 130. Although some overseas garrisons formed regimental schools during the late seventeenth century, the first such school, which taught both children and adults, was founded in England in 1762 for the First Regiment of Guards in London. E. A. Smith, "Educating the Soldier in the Nineteenth Century," *Journal of the Society for Army Historical Research* 65, no. 264 (Winter 1987): 201–02.

[49] For example, see the use of language in Matthew Bishop, *The Life and Adventures of Matthew Bishop of Deddington in Oxfordshire* (London: 1744), pp. 222–24, and American terminology in Mayer, *Belonging to the Army*, p. 5.

[50] Many illustrations show boys in the baggage train with women. For example, see the woodcut by Hans Sebald Beham, ca. 1530, in Andrew Cunningham and Ole Peter Grell, *The Four Horsemen of the Apocalypse: Religion, War, Famine and Death in Reformation Europe* (Cambridge: 2000), pp. 105–6, Pls. 3.4 and 3.5. Their small stature and lack of facial hair clearly show them as boys; several carry weapons, which they may be carrying for their masters.

company of 110 men claimed 117 servants in 1577.[51] The experienced soldier, Sir James Turner, complained that during the Thirty Years' War, "a Gudget or Boy was allowed to serve two Souldiers, *inde* for 10,000 Souldiers, 5,000 Gudgets, the very Vermine of an Army."[52] As Turner indicates, boys were of low status in the camp and had limited resources. With the formation of a state commission army, the number of soldiers' servants declined sharply, but they did not disappear entirely.[53]

Armies were also attended by civilian service personnel. Civilian entrepreneurs contracted with the state to provide troops with bread and other food stuffs, and sent thousands of bakers, teamsters, and other staff to the field.[54] Civilians drove the teams that pulled baggage wagons and artillery pieces. Turner estimated that a Swedish army of 15,000 troops during the Thirty Years' War required 1,796 wagons, each with its teamster, to which would be added a requisite number of stable boys to help care for the animals.[55] The French army did not replace civilian teamsters with uniformed drivers in the artillery until the Revolution.[56] Additionally, a variety of civilian craftsmen, including carpenters, blacksmiths, and wheelwrights, accompanied armies.[57] Beyond this, merchants and peddlers, known as sutlers in English and *vivandiers* or *vivandières* in French, accompanied the troops to sell them liquor, food, and other goods. Turner estimated that his hypothetical Swedish force

---

[51] Arfaioli, *The Black Bands*, p. 65. Maurizio Arfaioli writes that the Florentine government "recognized the Bands' high percentage of servants as a necessary evil and as another concession they made to their seemingly insatiable mercenary troops," p. 67. See this and other accounts of servants with troops in Parker, *The Army of Flanders*, appendix I, pp. 288–99.

[52] Sir J. Turner, *Pallas Armata*, p. 275. Coquault supports this, complaining that during the rebellion of the Fronde (1648–53), an army of 20,000 men still had 10,000 "valets" alone. Oudard Colquart, *Mémoires*, p. 132 in Babeau, *La vie militaire*, 1:198–99.

[53] A touching illustration shows men of the army late in the reign of Louis XIV including a *goujat* dutifully trudging along carrying two muskets. *Costumes militaires: infanterie*, in Philippe Contamine, *Histoire militaire de la France*, vol. 1, *Des origines à 1715* (Paris: Presses Universitaires de France, 1992), between pp. 402–03, Pl. 84. For a discussion of servants in the Continental army see Mayer, *Belonging to the Army*, particularly pp. 58 and 162–63.

[54] See Lynn, *Giant of the Grand Siècle*, chap. 4, concerning the supply of food by private contractors, *munitionnaires*.

[55] Turner, *Pallas Armata*, pp. 274–75.

[56] See Lynn, *Giant of the Grand Siècle*, chap. 14, concerning the organization of artillery during the seventeenth century, and Lynn, *Bayonets of the Republic*, p. 209, on the militarization of artillery teamsters by 1800.

[57] For a discussion of the civilian tradesmen who accompanied an army see Mayer, *Belonging to the Army*, chapter 6.

would include 220 such sutlers.[58] Service personnel included women as well as men, particularly among the sutlers. The term "camp women" is used here to reference both soldiers' women and female service personnel.

We know that a campaign community could contain a host of noncombatants equal to or even greater than its number of combatants in the days of the aggregate contract army.[59] So, when Gustavus Adophus led 26,000 Swedish and 16,000 Saxon troops to the battlefield of Breitenfeld in 1631, these forces and their entourages formed a campaign community with a larger population than Bordeaux, Strasbourg, or Turin.[60] It is no exaggeration to describe military camps as marching cities. Even after the number of women was culled with the formation of the state commission army, the number of noncombatants with a force in the field was still substantial.[61]

Aspects of life in the campaign community reflected civilian practices and values, but the campaign community also had unique parameters.[62] Towns tended to be closed communities that retained the right to banish citizens, particularly women, for acting against local standards. The campaign community, however, was essentially open, with its population in constant flux, stabilized primarily by oft-transgressed prohibitions against desertion. Craft and commerce in European civilian communities were regulated to some extent by local law and tradition, but above all they were controlled by guilds. Although military authorities regulated camp life to a degree, no institutions analogous to guilds limited economic life and opportunity within the campaign community. In addition, the campaign community usually overturned the standards of propriety and morality that governed conduct in civilian life.

---

[58] Turner, *Pallas Armata*, pp. 274–75.

[59] And these numbers do not count the thousands of peasants conscripted for manual labor by armies besieging towns and fortresses. Vauban argued that digging the entrenchments surrounding a fortress could require 15,000 to 18,000 peasants and 2,000 to 3,000 wagons. Sébastien le Prestre de Vauban, *De l'attaque et de la défense des places* (The Hague: 1737), p. 5. Their labor was requisitioned for only a short time, and they did not enter the campaign community in any real sense.

[60] Pierre Guillaume and Jean-Pierre Poussou, *Démographie historique* (Paris: 1970), p. 207.

[61] Don N. Hagist, "The Women of the British Army in America," http://www.revwar75.com/library/hagist/britwomen.htm#110, references a planning document presented in J. Alomon, *The Remembrancer or Impartial Repository of Public Events*, vol. 3, p. 310, that estimates that a British army of 30,000 would be accompanied by an equal number of attendants, women, and children, but this may well be for the garrison army, not for campaign forces, which cut down for mobility.

[62] See Sheilagh Ogilvie, "How Does Social Capital Affect Women? Guilds and Communities in Early Modern Germany," *American Historical Review* (April 2004): 325–59.

Entering the Community

Common people may have willingly joined the campaign community, but those who chose this path probably followed it because they had few if any other alternatives. Noble officers had complex rationales that drew them to military service – power, honor, and, at times, financial gain – but the plebian folk who are the focus of this volume usually joined the military community simply in order to survive.

The overwhelming reason that men chose early modern military life was because their opportunities in the civil world were unacceptable or had completely disappeared. A German woodcut dating from the 1530s makes this point with a poem attached to an illustration of a Landsknecht. A tailor complains that "I must sit long hours for little pay with which I can hardly survive," so he decides to try his luck in "the open field to the sound of pipes and drums."[63] Sydnam Poyntz confessed his reason for enlisting during the Thirty Years' War: "My necessitie forced mee, my Money being growne short, to take the manes of a private soldier."[64] By correlating British recruitment with economic cycles in the early 1800s, Edward Coss demonstrates that recruits were scarce when they had other economic alternatives, and plentiful when times were hard because of cyclical or seasonal unemployment.[65] The fact that prisoners of war often signed on to serve with the army that had captured them underscores both the recourse to military service to escape misery and the lack of dedication to any cause other than personal survival.[66]

---

[63] Woodcut by Nicolas Stör, *The Tailor*, in Keith Moxey, *Peasants, Warriors, and Wives: Popular Imagery in the Reformation* (Chicago: 1989, 2004), p. 90, Pl. 4.18. See as well Pl. 4.17, *The Shoemaker*.

[64] Sydnam Poyntz, *The Relation of Sydnam Poyntz 1624–1636*, ed. A.T.S. Goodrick (London: 1908), p. 45, in Mortimer, *Eyewitness Accounts*, p. 29. Troops raised in North Holland to fight against Spain adopted such illustrative *noms de guerre* as Without Money, Seldom Rich, Gambled-Away. Ruff, *Violence in Early Modern Europe*, p. 53. Also consider the rationale for enlistment in the army of Louis XIV in André Corvisier, *L'armée française de la fin du XVIIe siècle au ministère du Choiseul: Le soldat*, 2 vols. (Paris: 1964), 1:317. See eighteenth-century French testimony of misery in Archives départmentales, Illeet-Vilaine, 8B 561, 14 July 1771 and 21 November 1787 in Naoko Seriu, "Faire un soldat: Une histoire des hommes à l' épreuve de l'institution militaire," Ph.D. diss., Ecole des Hautes Etudes en Sciences Sociales, 2005, p. 133.

[65] Edward James Coss, "All for the King's Schilling: An Analysis of the Campaign and Combat Experiences of the British Soldier of the Peninsular War, 1808–1814," Ph.D. dissertation, The Ohio State University, 2005, ch. 2. Loriga shows that the poorer areas supplied the most recruits to the eighteenth-century Piedmontese army. Loriga, *Soldats*, p. 121–23.

[66] On enrollment of prisoners of war, see Peter Hagendorf's tale in *Ein Soeldnerleben im Dreissigjaehrigen Krieg*, in Mortimer, *Eyew itness Accounts*, ed. Jan Peters (Berlin: 1993). See the convenient practice of prisoners switching sides during the English Civil

Other factors lead men to choose life as a soldier. A taste for adventure or personal circumstances such as an unwanted marriage could bring a man to bear arms. Mercenaries might also serve foreign masters because they had been forced to depart their own countries, as was the case for many Irishmen and Scots.[67] Much has been written claiming that towns conveniently expelled their problem citizens by forcing them into military service, but such claims may well be overstated.[68] And, of course, there was the lure of plunder.

We have little explicit evidence to explain why women opted to join the campaign community. Logic and what little information we have suggest that women entered the campaign community for much the same kinds of economic reasons as did men. Such women might also have been attracted by the fool's gold of plunder, as was Little Ursula (see Plate 1). Full-time or part-time prostitutes marched with the troops, and what we know of prostitutes in civilian life shows that they were most often driven into the trade by poverty. [69] As Daniel Defoe's heroine

Wars and the Wars of Louis XIV in Tallett, *War and Society in Early Modern Europe*, p. 130, and J. W. Wright, "Sieges and customs of war at the opening of the eighteenth century," *American Historical Review*, xxxix (1934), p. 643, in Tallett, *War and Society in Early Modern Europe*, p. 274, no. 88.

[67] Gráinne Henry, *The Irish Military Community in Spanish Flanders, 1586–1621* (Dublin: 1992), pp. 23–27 and 74–75, in Mary Elizabeth Ailes, "Camp Followers, Sutlers, and Soldiers' Wives: Women in Early Modern Armies (c. 1450–c. 1650)," *A Companion to Women's Military History*, Barton C. Hacker and Margaret Vining, eds. (Leiden: 2010), and Mary Elizabeth Ailes, *Military Migration and State Formation: The British Military Community in Seventeenth-Century Sweden* (Lincoln, NE: 2002), pp. 10–11.

[68] See the testimony of Barnabe Rich (ca. 1540–1617), an Englishman, who claimed "When they set forth soldiers, either they scoure their prisons of thives, or their streets of rogues and vagabonds" in Simon Barker, *"Allarme to England!*: Gender and militarism in early modern England," in *Gender, Power, and Privilege in Early Modern Europe*, Jessica Munns and Penny Richards, eds. (Harlow: 2003), p. 149. This echoes the common English claim that their soldiers were the "scum of the earth," a turn of phrase used from Queen Elizabeth to the duke of Wellington. Elizabeth I in Barker, *"Allarme to England!,"* p. 149, and Wellington in conversation with Stanhope, November 4, 1831, on Wikipedia, http:// en.wikiquote.org/wiki/Arthur_Wellesley. And yet recent careful research by Edward Coss effectively challenges the notion that the English simply emptied the jails and the poorhouses, Coss, "All for the King's Schilling."

[69] See the treatments of prostitution in Olwen Hufton, *The Prospect Before Her: A History of Women in Western Europe, vol. 1, 1500–1800* (New York: 1998); Ruth Mazo Karras, *Common Women: Prostitution and Sexuality in Medieval England* (Oxford: Oxford University Press, 1996); Emlyn Eisenach, *Husbands, Wives, and Concubines: Marriage, Family, and Social Order in Sixteenth-Century Verona* (Kirksville, MO: 2004); Mary Elizabeth Perry, *Gender and Disorder in Early Modern Seville* (Princeton, NJ: Princeton University Press, 1990); and in the broader and more popular account Hilary Evans, *Harlots, Whores & Hookers: A History of Prostitution* (New York:

Moll Flanders explained, "Vice came in always at the door of necessity, not at the door of inclination."[70] The special case of women of common birth who dressed as men in order to serve as private soldiers indicates the same desperation; they usually adopted this extreme course as an alternative to poor economic prospects or unacceptable family circumstances.[71] These women might also have been drawn by a sense of adventure.

The circumstances that brought men and women into the campaign community might have been generated by the war itself. Refugees from destroyed villages and pillaged towns could find themselves serving in the ranks or following the camp because they had no other option. Troops seized individual men and women. The author, Johann Jakob Christolffle von Grimmelshausen, was himself captured by soldiers as a boy during the Thirty Years' War and then served in the ranks; he put his Simplicissimus character in a similar situation. Peter Hagendorf, who wrote the only surviving diary composed by a common soldier during the Thirty Years' War, reported taking women as booty and bringing them to camp.[72] For many, once they entered the campaign community, other options disappeared. A female camp follower bemoaned at the close of the Thirty Years' War: "I was born in war, I have no home, no country and no friends; war is all my wealth and now whither shall I go?"[73]

Taplinger Publishing Company, 1979). For a graphic example, see Wolfgang Strauch, *Tailor and Seamstress* in Walter L. Strauss, *The German Single-Leaf Woodcut, 1550–1600*, 3 vols. (New York: 1975), vol. 3, p. 1075. In the accompanying poem the tailor is convincing the poor seamstress that she can make more as a prostitute with him as her helpful pimp.

[70] Daniel Defoe, *The Fortunes and Misfortunes of the Famous Moll Flanders, &c. Who was born in Newgate, … Written from her own memorandums* (London: 1722), p. 155.

[71] See the discussion of why women assumed male dress and identities to serves as soldiers in Rudolf M. Dekker and Lotte C. van de Pol, *The Tradition of Female Transvestism in Early Modern Europe*, trans. Judy Marcure and Lotte Van de Pol (Basingstoke, Hampshire: 1989) and in Fraser Easton, "Gender's Two Bodies: Women Warriors, Female Husbands and Plebeian Life," *Past and Present*, no. 180 (2003): 131–74.

[72] Hagendorf, *Ein Soeldnerleben im Dreissigjaehrigen Krieg*, in Mortimer, *Eyewitness Accounts*, p. 35. Hagendorf released the women he took, but there must have been women who were taken and stayed with the camp, either because they had no home to return to or because they felt themselves too shamed to return.

[73] Quoted in Charles Blitzer and the Editors of Time-Life Books, *Age of Kings* (New York: 1967), p. 52, in Hacker, "Women and Military Institutions," p. 654.

The above excerpt identifies another minority born into the campaign community itself. Some of the children of soldiers and camp women grew up with the army and intermarried. The number of children in the train of regiments during the sixteenth and seventeenth centuries must have been great, but we have no firm statistics on the number of girls who stayed in the campaign community as adults.

Libertine Lifestyle

The alienated and the desperate must also have been enticed by the lurid side of the campaign community. Camps have always been filled with the young owing to the physical demands of war and, to a lesser degree, because of the difficulty of soldiering once one has established a family and secured a place in society. Studies of contemporary records reveal that the great majority of common soldiers were in their late teens and their twenties.[74] Certainly there were always old-hands around, but most were young men with young men's ideas of pleasure and pride. Such individuals cut adrift from their pasts probably saw an adventurous and sexualized libertine lifestyle as an attractive compensation to an otherwise hard and dangerous existence. J. R. Hale concludes that soldiers did not sign up enticed by the meager pay but, "for the chance of booty and for a life which, although subject to savage punishments for breaches of military law, was free from many of the moral and behavioral constraints within civilian society."[75]

In the European imagination, and to a large extent in reality, the campaign community was noted for its libertine ways, typified by drinking, gambling, and wenching.[76] A sixteenth-century woodcut by the

[74] The average age of French troops from the Thirty Years' War seem to have been about twenty-four Robert Chaboche, "Les soldats français de la Guerre de Trente Ans, une tentative d'approche," *Revue d'histoire moderne et contemporaine* 20 (1973), p. 23. During the mid and late eighteenth century, about half French troops were age twenty-five or younger. See the discussion of age and other characteristics of French troops, 1716–94, in Lynn, *Bayonets of the Republic*, pp. 44–61. Muster records for the army that served Empress Maria Theresa show that in peacetime recruits were in their early or mid-twenties, but that during wartime they were often in their late teens. Duffy, *The Army of Maria Theresa*, p. 51. See Coss, "All for the King's Schilling," ch. 2, p. 10, for similar results for the British army ca. 1800.

[75] Hale, "The Soldier in Germanic Graphic Art of the Renaissance," p. 96.

[76] David M. Hopkin, *Soldier and peasant in French popular culture 1766–1870* (Woodbridge, Suffolk: 2003), p. 17, comments that in the woodcuts of Landsknechts and Reisläufers, "more common were those images which treated mercenary bands as alternative societies, exciting, threatening and repulsive in turns."

sometimes Swiss mercenary, Urs Graf, advertised this image by embla-
zoning a standard bearer's flag with a wine bottle, dice, and a pack of
cards.[77] This perception of military life was strongest in the period before
1650; greater regimentation and discipline, as well as the decline in the
numbers of camp women, tempered the perception and the reality under the
state commission army. At the height of its excess, the libertine lifestyle of
the campaign community represented a kind of anti-morality that set
proper civilian virtue on its head.[78] In his *Espeio y deceplina militar* (1589),
Francisco de Valdés observed grimly, "The day a man picks up his pike to
become a soldier is the day he ceases to be a Christian."[79]

Gambling was a particularly attractive pastime for soldiers, even though
it often emptied their purses and led to violent and sometimes deadly disputes. In Plate 4, Landsknechts drink, gamble, and draw swords against one
another. One of them vomits on a crucifix, defiling religion. In the midst of
the deadly brawl, another startled soldier sees a devil at the table. The
details of this engraving mirror an account written by Peter Hagendorf,
who repeated a story about a player who saw another devil at the table.[80]

Prints of camp life commonly display gambling as men wager away
their meager earnings or their booty at cards or dice games. Often the
playing table is a drum laid on the ground.[81] Drawn knives or swords
seem an all-too-frequent climax to the game.[82] Grimmelshausen

---

[77] Hale, "The Soldier in Germanic Graphic Art of the Renaissance," pp. 92–93.

[78] It may also be that the wilder aspects of life in the campaign community simply elevated
the disreputable conduct of civil society's ruffians and ne'er-do-wells to a perverted
community standard. The great Counter-Reformation cardinal, Gian Matteo Giberti
(1495–1543), complained that poor men "consume all they have earned during the
week for their children and their wife, gambling, carousing, and whoring on Sundays."
Giberti in Eisenach, *Husbands, Wives, and Concubines*, p. 17.

[79] Francisco de Valdés, *Espeio y deceplina militar* (Brussels: 1589), fo. 40v, in Geoffrey
Parker, "Early Modern Europe," in *The Laws of War: Constraints on Warfare in the
Western World*, Michael Howard, George J. Andreopoulos, and Mark R. Shulman, eds.
(New Haven, CT: 1994), p. 44.

[80] "On one occasion there was such a cursing and swearing at the gaming area. Then when
one of the players bent down after a dice, for they were playing on a table and it had fallen
off, he saw someone with a cloven hoof standing by the board. This figure began: 'Oh Lord
Jesus, what kind of gamblers have we got at this table!' Then he suddenly disappeared,
leaving a foul stench behind him." Hagendorf, *Ein Soeldnerleben im Dreissigjaehrigen
Krieg*, p. 95, in Mortimer, *Eyewitness Accounts*, p. 75.

[81] For gambling on a drum head see Gaëtane Maës, *Les Watteau de Lille* (Paris: Arthena,
1998), p. 317, and Langer, *The Thirty Years' War*, trans. C. S. V. Salt (New York:
1980), p. 80, Pl. 75.

[82] For other drawings of fights over gambling see: Langer, *The Thirty Years' War*, p. 80, Pl.
75, and Georg Hirth, *Picture Book of the Graphic Arts, 1500–1800 (Kulturgeschichtliches*

PLATE 4. Petrarch Master, *Landsknechts in Tavern Brawl*, a woodcut in Franchesco Petrarca, *Von der Artzney bayder Glück, des guten vnd widerwertigen*, published by Heinrich Steyner in 1532. Note the gambling in the background and the money on the main table. Gambling quarrels often precipitated violence. The Landsknechts in the left background continue playing as if nothing unusual is happening even as the fight rages and a devil appears at the table.

Lilly Library, Indiana University.

accounts for the creation of camp gambling grounds via an old soldier explaining, "It was in order to prevent these killings, and because some men gambled away their muskets and horses, even their rations, that [the authorities] not only allowed gambling in public again, but provided this yard for it so that the guard would be on hand if any trouble breaks out."[83]

Stories of heavy drinking abound, and drunkenness made bad situations worse when fights erupted. Drinking also interfered with duty. One example is that cannons being transferred from Freiburg to Breisach traveled without an ecort, because the cavalry picked for the escort was too drunk to ride.[84]

Bilderbuch aus drei Jahrhunderten, hrsg. Georg Hirth), 6 vols. (New York: Benjamin Blom, 1972), vol. 5, Pl. 2453.

[83] Grimmelshausen, *Simplicissimus*, p. 156.

[84] Mortimer, *Eyewitness Accounts*, p. 37.

In contrast to the restricted life of a peasant village, the camp offered brief trysts with prostitutes as well as longer term, but still temporary, liaisons with other camp women.[85] In Erasmus's "The Soldier and the Carthusian," the soldier explains that he has no money because "whatsoever I got of Pay, Plunder, sacrilege, Rapine and Theft, was spent in Wine, Whores and Gaming."[86] The escapades of Courage, the female anti-hero in Grimmelshausen's *The Life of Courage, the Notorious Thief, Whore, and Vagabond* provide more literary evidence of a community with very different sexual mores than the civil world.

In the libertine lifestyle of the campaign community, violence was common currency.[87] Soldiers routinely brawled and dueled. A sixteenth-century woodcut of a Landsknecht, Valentine Scarface, includes accompanying text which boasts: "And whoever annoyed me, Promptly had to fight me."[88] In *Simplicissimus*, one soldier who had merely been slapped by another, dashed the brains of the offender, explaining to Simplicissimus, "I would be a coward and rather die if I did not have my revenge. Only a knave would let himself be bullied like that."[89] It came down to manliness and one's standing in the military community. Fighting could be a kind of initiation; French soldiers reported clandestine duels of this kind in the mid-eighteenth century, where the weapon used was sometimes a bayonet.[90]

---

[85] Colin Jones observes that in addition to pillage, "women and drink" were the "unofficial wages of war." Colin Jones, "The Military Revolution and the Professionalisation of the French Army under the Ancien Régime," in Clifford J. Rogers, ed., *The Military Revolution Debate* (Boulder, CO: 1995), p. 153.

[86] Erasmus, "The Soldier and the Carthusian," p. 266. In "Of a Soldier's Life," p. 64, the soldier explains that he spent all his money on "Whores, Sutlers [who sold alcohol], and Gamesters."

[87] To a degree, soldier violence mirrored plebian violence in the civilian world. See, for example, peasant sword fights in Walter L. Strauss, *The German Single-Leaf Woodcut, 1550–1600*, 3 vols. (New York: 1975), vol. 1, p. 56, Moxey, *Peasants, Warriors, and Wives*, pp. 36–7, Pl. 3.1; pp. 40–1, pl 3.2; p. 44, Pl. 3.4; and p. 55, Pl. 3.11. On Amsterdam knife fighting see Ruff, *Violence in Early Modern Europe, 1500–1800*, p. 123–24.

[88] Erhard Schon, Scarface, Moxey, *Peasants, Warriors, and Wives*, p. 92, Pl. 4.21.

[89] Grimmelshausen, *Simplicissimus*, p. 78–9. Simplicissimus also fought a duel himself, pp. 226–27.

[90] See accounts of soldier dueling from Victor Barrucand, ed. La vie veritable du citoyen Rossignol, vainqueur de la Bastille (1759–1896) (Paris: 1896), pp. 30–31, and 33 in duels in Seriu, "Faire un soldat," pp. 270–74. Noted historian Jean Chagniot concludes, "Combat with edged weapons was in effect a kind of rite of initiation for the recruit, and he dare not hide from it under penalty of being discredited." Jean Chagniot, *Paris et l'armée au XVIIIe siècle* (Paris: 1985), p. 589.

Summary

Grimmelshausen, a veteran himself, summed up the ardor and excess of the libertine lifestyle during the Thirty Years' War: "Their whole existence consisted of eating and drinking, going hungry and thirsty, whoring and sodomizing, gaming and dicing, guzzling and gorging, murdering and being murdered, killing and being killed, torturing and being tortured, terrifying and being terrified ... pillaging and being pillaged."[91]

The Meaning of Dress within the Campaign Community

Many men and women of the campaign community displayed their membership and their acceptance of its values by adopting distinctive forms of dress that differed sharply from those worn by peasants and urban workers. Machiavelli reported that clothing separated a soldier from his origins, as the soldier "changes not only his clothing, but he adopts attitudes, manners, ways of speaking and bearing himself, quite at odds with those of civilian life."[92] During the era of the aggregate contract army, apparel sported by common soldiers often exaggerated or parodied the appearance of their betters, and in the more regimented world of the state commission army, uniforms of enlisted men blurred class lines by incorporating elements of upper class garb in a regulated fashion.

From the late Middle Ages into the early modern era, municipal and state governments tried to prescribe people's attire through sumptuary laws, so that their appearance accorded with their class, wealth, and function. A Zurich law of 1650 announced: "We commend with great earnestness and under heavy penalty that every person in city or country, whether cleric or layman, high class or low, woman or man, young or old, burger or peasant, attend to and use the clothing befitting his class both at home and abroad."[93] As the historian of consumption and

---

[91] Johann Jakob Christolffel von Grimmelshausen, *Simplicissimus*, trans. Mike Mitchell (Sawtry, Cambs: 2005), p. 53. Popular woodcuts carry on the story of the soldier who returns with nothing. In two drawings, ca. 1520, Urs Graf portrayed Reisläufers returning from the wars with little. One shows a thin purse hanging on this two-handed sword; the sword bears the legend "Al mein gelt verspilt" – all my money has been wasted. The other shows a sturdy soldier presenting his pursed to his disappointed pregnant wife. J.R. Hale, *Artists and Warfare in the Renaissance* (New Haven, CT: 1990), p. 1, Pls. 1 and 2.

[92] Machiavelli in Hale, *War and Society in Renaissance Europe*, p. 128.

[93] Alan Hunt, *Governance of the Consuming Passions: A History of Sumptuary Laws* (New York: St. Martin's Press, 1996), p. 253. Such regulations could set elaborate

sumptuary laws, Alan Hunt, concludes: "The most active period of sumptuary regulation occurred between the demise of feudalism and the rise of manufacturing capitalism."[94]

Sixteenth-century Landsknechts and Reisläufers turned out in multi-colored pants and jackets slashed to reveal the fabric beneath and in large hats with feathers, in mocking imitation of aristocratic fashion[95] (see Plates 1, 4, and 20). Early seventeenth-century Spanish infantry had its own style as well:

There has never been a regulation for dress and weapons in the Spanish infantry because that would remove the spirit and fire which is necessary in a soldier. It is the finery, the plumes and the bright colors which give spirit and strength to a soldier so that he can with furious resolution overcome any difficulty or accomplish any valorous exploit.[96]

J. R. Hale sees considerable significance in the soldiers' "sexually aggressive strut, the bulging codpiece, the suggestive sword hilt, the mixture of tousled peasant hairstyle with flamboyant costume that marked them as defying civilian morals and the every man-in-his-place social restrictions of the sumptuary laws."[97] These sons of peasants and workers transformed themselves from subservient sparrows to assertive peacocks.

Soldiers might also adorn their female partners in similarly showy apparel if they had the money to do so. Poet and historian Gustav Freytag, who collected and studied sixteenth-century works, observed of the Landsknechts: "It was the soldier's great pride to possess a beautiful prostitute, and many a one would spend all he had, his pay and booty, to

protocols for the wearing of expensive clothing by elites. See the elaborate table of permitted Elizabethan attire in Hunt, pp. 122–23.

[94] Hunt, *Governance of the Consuming Passions*, p. 142. See the comments of Ogilvie, "How Does Social Capital Affect Women?," p. 353, on sumptuary laws and communities.

[95] Here the original inspiration was aristocratic, but Landsknechts made it their own and kept it long after it had ceased to be the mode for the nobility.

[96] Parker, *The Army of Flanders*, p. 164. Parker identifies this only as a manuscript of 1610. Soldiers' attire was explicitly exempted from the Spanish sumptuary laws of 1623 and those that followed. Le Guzmán de Alfarache in Deleito y Pinuela, *El Declinar*, pp. 177–78, in Parker, *The Army of Flanders*, p. 164.

[97] See J. R. Hale, *War and Society in Renaissance Europe*, p. 127. Hale's emphasis on the role of clothing to display masculinity finds support in the complaints of Barnabe Rich, who complained that effeminate touches of men's styles threatened men's masculinity: "To be shorte, in England, Gentlemen have robbed our women of halfe their minds, and our women have robbed us of half our apparel." Rich in Barker, "*Allarme to England!*," p. 145.

adorn her and keep her in comfort."[98] Innumerable sixteenth-century woodcuts, such as Plates 5, 12, and 25 display overdressed women from the military camps.[99] Other illustrations demonstrate that camp women of the seventeenth-century could also be overdressed.[100] This is all the more jarring because European sumptuary laws often focused more on women's than on men's clothing.

For the soldiers themselves, military clothing that transcended the lower class origins of the troops survived even the introduction of uniforms in the mid- to late-seventeenth century. These uniforms were not patterned on the clothing of workers or peasants but on the more elegant styles of the nobility. Common soldiers wore simpler and cheaper versions of the richly adorned breaches, coats, and hats worn by their officers. They also carried swords, which had a double meaning, for the sword was a sign of aristocracy and a symbol of manhood. Common soldiers, as we have seen, could be as quick to resort to the blade as were their aristocratic officers.

Soldiers of common origins were often termed gentlemen, since they wore a sword. In his play *The Recruiting Officer* (1706), soldier and playwright Georges Farquhar has Sgt. Kite continually refer to would-be recruits as "gentlemen soldiers," a term that continued in use in Britain throughout the eighteenth century.[101] The *London Spy* observed in 1700: "A Foot Soldier is commonly a Man, who for the sake of wearing a Sword and the Honor of being term'd a Gentleman, is coaxed from a Handicraft Trade, whereby he might live Comfortably, to bear Arms, for his King and Country."[102]

As Sabrina Loriga points out, "Separation from family and community were sanctioned by the uniform, the military oath, and the change

[98] Freytag in Wilhelm Haberling, "Army Prostitution and Its Control: An Historical Study," in Victor Robinson, ed., *Morals in Wartime* (New York: 1943), p. 34.

[99] For representative views of Landsknechts see woodcuts by Wolfgang Strauch in Strauss, *The German Single-Leaf Woodcut*, vol. 3, pp. 1070–72 and 1074–76. Some of their women here are simply dressed and some have finery that would appear out of character with their tasks. For grandly dressed "whores" see, for example, two woodcuts presented by Moxey, *Peasants, Warriors, and Wives*, the first by Martin Weygel, p. 84, Pl. 4.12 and another by Urs Graf, p. 86, Pl. 4.15.

[100] For similarly over-dressed soldiers' women, sporting elaborate seventeenth century ruffs and finery, see Fishman, *Boerenverdreit*, Pls. 16–19 and 516.

[101] One recruit declares, "I take your money, sir, and now I'm a gentleman." George Farquhar, *The Recruiting Officer* (London: 1997), p. 33. The term was still there in 1795; a court case charged a sergeant with deceiving a lad and then ordering that he "must go for a gentleman soldier." Holmes, *Redcoat*, p. 144.

[102] *London Spy* in Holmes, *Redcoat*, p. 144. See also the term used by Deane, in Holmes, *Redcoat*, p. 142.

in name."[103] When soldiers entered armies such as the French or Piedmontese armies during the eighteenth century, they formally
adopted *noms de guerre*, sealing their new and distinct identities. These
could announce their new lives in ironic tones, such as "Bellerose" or
"Jolycoeur."[104]

Camp women attending such soldiers often wore cast-off uniform
jackets with their skirts during the late seventeenth and eighteenth-
centuries. Illustrations show them with military-style garments cut
down for their use.[105] The wearing of military dress in the field would
later be associated with *cantinières*, but it seems to have been more
generalized earlier. Wearing martial coats handed down from male
companions or taken from fallen soldiers marked the women's identity,
but may also have indicated their poverty, showing they could afford no
more than discarded clothing.[106] Edward Cotton, a Sergeant Major,
reported that after the battle of Waterloo, "Many women were found
among the slain ... as is common in the camp, the camp followers wore
male attire, with nearly as martial a bearing as the soldiers."[107] Yet
light-fingered camp women still stole female finery when they could.[108]

The War between the Campaign Community and the Peasantry

The campaign community not only marked itself as different from the
civilian world, but was hostile to that other form of existence. Soldiers of

---

[103] Loriga, *Soldats*, p. 125.

[104] See André Corvisier, *L'armée française*, vol. 2 (Paris: 1964), appendix 14, pp. 1049–58,
gives an extensive list of *noms de guerre* and their frequency among those who entered the
Invalides.

[105] For women wearing forms of military attire, see the illustration of a pretty British female
sutler, ca. 1700, in Forty and Forty, *They Also Served*, p. 61. For mid eighteenth-century
Prussian camp women or soldiers' wives in garrison wearing military jackets, see Engelen,
Soldatenfrauen in Preußen, p. 167, Pl. 2, and p. 362, Pl. 50.

[106] See the discussion of this in Noel T. St. John Williams, *Judy O'Grady and the Colonel's
Lady: The Army Wife and Camp Follower Since 1660* (London: 1988), p. 49, and in
Hagist, "The Women of the British Army in America."

[107] Cotton in Julie Wheelwright, "'Amazons and military maids:' An examination of
female military heroines in British literature and the changing construction of gender,"
Women's Studies International Forum 10, no. 5 (1987): 489.

[108] See commentary from J. Almon, *The Remembrancer or Impartial Repository of Public
Events* (London: 1775–83), vol. 5, p. 154, in Don N. Hagist "The Women of the British
Army in America," http://www.revwar75.com/library/hagist/britwomen.htm#110.
  "As to plundering, there is nothing so common as to see the soldiers wives, and other
women, who follow the army, carrying each three or four silk gowns, fine linen, etc. etc.
which have been stolen by the soldiers from different houses in their march. ... "

aggregate contract armies often regarded the working classes and particularly the peasantry as odious. Contempt for their victims helped soldiers to pillage ruthlessly. The disdain was mutual; as the historian Julius Ruff concludes, "most early modern Europeans feared and hated soldiers."[109] Victimized by soldiers, peasants took what vengeance they could, and war reigned between them.

Two common themes of popular literature and art during the sixteenth and seventeenth centuries were pillage by soldiers and subsequent peasant revenge. Grimmelshausen writes of both[110]; Jacques Callot gives us their images in his masterful series *Les misères et malheurs de la guerre* (1633). The text under his scene entitled Peasants' Revenge, (Plate 5) reads: "After the soldiers have committed much devastation, finally the peasants, whom they have treated as enemies, await them in a secluded place and by surprise ... put them to death."

Numerous other images of peasant revenge both precede and postdate Callot's classic rendering.[111] Historical documents tell the same grim tale. When Coligny's army crossed the Dordogne in 1569, peasants killed so many soldiers, that he sent a body of troops back "to teach them a lesson for their cruelties and slaughterings."[112] Soldiers separated from the Imperial Army in 1705 were killed by Piedmontese peasants; wounded Russians discovered by German peasants after the battle of Zorndorf in 1758 were buried alive.[113]

In the language of cultural history, the peasantry became the "other" to the campaign community. Each group defines itself as *not* being the other group, which is thus seen as separate and distinct and often in some way inferior. Military historians often reflect on the frequent, but not universal,

---

[109] Ruff, *Violence in Early Modern Europe*, p. 44.
[110] See Grimmelshausen, *Simplicissimus*, p. 46–47, for an account of peasants' revenge.
[111] For other scenes of peasant revenge and battles between peasants and soldiers see Fishman, *Boerenverdriet*, Pls. 14–15, 496–98, and 519, and Herbert Langer, *Thirty Years' War*, trans. C. S. V. Salt (New York: 1980), Pls. 100 and 101. So fundamental and seemingly so natural was the hostility between peasant and soldier, that it became a subject in the theme of inversion – the world turned upside down – in popular art. One of these engravings a frame shows a soldier pouring wine for a seated peasant with the legend: "Even the soldier angrily has to serve the p.easant." Die Verkehrte Welt, German engraving, first half of seventeenth century in David Kunzle, "World Upside Down: The Iconography of a European Broadsheet Type," in Barbara A. Babcock, ed., *The Reversible World: Symbolic Inversion in Art and Society* (Ithaca: 1978), pp. 80–81.
[112] Brantôme in Hale, *War and Society in Renaissance Europe*, p. 190.
[113] Ruff, *Violence in Early Modern Europe*, p. 58. See still other accounts of peasants' revenge in Ruff, *Violence in Early Modern Europe*, p. 58, and Parker, *The Army of Flanders*, p. 194.

Apres plusieurs degast par les soldats commis   Les guettans à l'écart. et par vne surprise   Et se vengent ayst. contre ces Malheureux
A la fin les Paysans qu'ils ont pour ennemis   Les tyans mis à mort les mettent en chemise.   Des perttes de leurs biens, qu'ne viennent que deux. 17.

PLATE 5. Jacques Callot, *Peasants' Revenge* from *Les misères et malheurs de la guerre*, Paris, 1633. Consider this view as the counterpoint to the pillage of the farmhouse in plate 2. Note the use of grain flails to bash soldiers to death.

49

phenomenon of dehumanizing an enemy, that is, defining that enemy as something other than a full human being. This dehumanization of the foe justifies the violence of war, but it also serves another purpose as well: It helps the soldier deal emotionally and ethically with the deadly acts that he or she must commit or witness. In other words, dehumanization of the enemy gives the soldier a means by which to cope with the necessary brutality of war. This is a subtle but immensely important difference.

Both aspects were especially important in the relationship between the campaign community and the peasantry. This dehumanization by the former of the latter was made even more important because soldiers and their women were children of the very peasants and town workers they victimized. In the midst of this disdain and violence, the mind and soul of the soldier must have been torn by conflicting feelings, as he saw his own family mirrored in those he robbed, raped, and killed. The line between soldier and peasant had to be drawn very sharply because the distance was actually so small.

Eventually, troops of the state commission army came to be viewed as protectors of the population they served, and the inherent animosity between the campaign community and the civilian world lost its bite. This would only emerge in the late-seventeenth and eighteenth centuries, however. For the French, Louis XIV would be the pivotal figure in this reversal, and other princes would follow the lead of the Sun King.

The campaign community was a military phenomenon, but it was also one of a variety of early modern European communities; its character and its interactions with other contemporary communities is a subject in itself. Women who formed part of the campaign community took on a special identity – assuming new loyalties, entering new hierarchies, performing new functions, and accepting new mores. Just as the campaign community must be compared to other European communities, the story of its women becomes a separate and necessary chapter in the history of early modern European women as a whole.

WOMEN AND THE BOUNDARIES OF IDENTITY, PROPRIETY, AND OPPORTUNITY

The more important the role of women is to the history of war and the campaign community, the more important these subjects become to the history of women and gender. This is more than simply a step in the direction of the gendering of the field of military history, although that is significant in itself. Though little-explored previously, the lives of camp women tell us a great deal. Several of the topics to be discussed in this volume relate to the boundaries that circumscribed feminine identity, moral propriety, and economic opportunity. Granted, these matters of definition and delimitation affected a special environment, the campaign community, but special though it may have been, it was nonetheless an important community, both in its size and its impact upon European society.

Related to this central issue of boundaries, the diminishing presence and participation of women in the campaign community also invites reference to the long-debated assertion that the relative independence, status, and power of women declined during the early modern era.[114] Ideas about the degeneration of women's power and status in early modern Europe have special relevance when discussing women within the campaign community for two reasons. First, the presence and roles of women did, in fact, decline within the campaign community over this era. Second, the diminishing presence of women accompanying early modern armies has already been explained in terms of a more general restriction of women's options and a fall in their status, and this explanation must be confronted.

Gender Overlap and the Border Zone between Masculinity and Femininity

Nothing is more fundamental to the history of gender than the definitions of masculinity and femininity that apply within the contexts of culture, time, place, and class. The early modern campaign community deserves particular attention in a discussion of gender.[115] Camp women chose to appropriate certain masculine traits to better deal with the physical and

---

[114] The thesis of decline has been criticized and rejected by much of the community of historians of women and gender. Although it still enjoys the status of textbook wisdom among many, the most prominent general works treating the history of women in gender in early modern Europe deal with the decline thesis either as questionable, Olwen Hufton, or wrong headed, Merry Wiesner-Hanks. Hufton, *The Prospect Before Her*, and Merry E. Wiesner, *Women and Gender in Early Modern Europe*, 2nd ed. (Cambridge: 2000).

[115] A number of books deal with issues of gender and war, including Jean Bethke Elshtain, *Women and War* (Basic Books, 1987); Joshua Goldstein, *War and Gender: How Gender Shapes the War System and Vice Versa* (Cambridge: 2001); and Leo Braudy, *From Chivalry to Terrorism: War and the Changing Nature of Masculinity* (New York: 2003). See as well Nobert A. Nye, "Western Masculinities in War and Peace," *American Historical Review* 112, no. 2 (April 2007), pp. 417–38 for a discussion of the literature.

psychological demands of life on campaign. This co-option of masculinity by women within the campaign community makes it a complex, and perhaps revealing, theater of gender tension and malleability.

The theoretical and historical literatures on gender are extensive, and I do not pretend to be well-versed in these deep and dense discussions. Frankly, I admit to being ill-at-ease with intensely theoretical approaches to history, a trait which might stem from my experience as a military historian.[116] I will therefore try to keep my comments modest. Still, certain aspects of the gender definitions of camp women are intriguing, and, I believe, important. Let me be clear on this; my primary interest does not concern cross-dressing women of the past who adopted entirely masculine identities and who excite such considerable interest among gender historians today.[117] The focus here is the more common but ambiguous and conflicted gender identities of camp women.

Gender is not simply about identities, for gender identities also establish hierarchies of status and power. As Joan Scott insists, "Gender is a primary way of signifying relationships of power."[118] Hierarchies are often contested in real life, and the military camp, with its hyper-masculine soldiers and necessarily masculinized women, must have been rife with the possibilities for conflict. Within the violent environment of the early modern military camp, power could quickly translate into physical force. The contemporary version of the battle of the sexes, to be discussed in Chapter II, could literally materialize as combat, with physical force used to enforce male dominance.

In a wonderfully phrased insight, Judith Butler argues that gender is a copy without an original.[119] Concepts of masculinity and femininity are not based on absolute reality; they are ideas in search of themselves, copies of copies. This opens the door for adaptation to special circumstances. Judith Halberstam, a feminist and queer theorist, advances

---

[116] See the commentary on my work and approach in Robert M. Cition, "Military Histories Old and New: A Reintroduction," *American Historical Review* 112, no. 4 (October 2007): 1086–87.

[117] The recent literature on Catalina Erauso, who will be discussed in Chapter IV, exemplifies how gender historians become fascinated with cross-dressing women soldiers. See Sherry Velasco, *The Lieutenant Nun: Transgenderism, Lesbian Desire, and Catalina de Erauso* (Austin, TX: 2001) and Nerea Aresti, "The Gendered Identities of the 'Lieutenant Nun': Rethinking the Story of a Female Warrior in Early Modern Spain," trans. Rosemary Williams, *Gender and History* 19, no. 3 (November 2007): 401–08.

[118] Joan Wallach Scott, *Gender and the Politics of History* (New York: 1989), p. 42.

[119] Judith Butler, *Gender Trouble: Feminism and the Subversion of Identity* (New York: 1990) is her classic work.

the idea that masculinity is not inextricably tied to physically being male.[120] Although she concentrates this "female masculinity" in "butch" women from the lesbian community, her ideas have value beyond the specific focus of her work, and may help us understand the camp women who maintained their identities as heterosexual women, but exemplified certain strong masculine virtues.

It seems that the campaign community required that women function within an area of overlap between contemporary conceptions of masculinity and femininity.[121] By this I do not mean a blurring of gender boundaries because, while feminine women adopted certain masculine traits to survive their hard lives, masculine men did not cross into the feminine. This overlap created a border zone for women consisting of particular characteristics and abilities that might normally be labeled as masculine, but that could be adopted by camp women without eroding their basic feminine identity, at least while they were part of the camp. Women bore heavy burdens and did hard labor (see Plate 6). Certain kinds of hard labor were expected of all plebian women, of course, but as Merry E. Wiesner points out, even in peasant life, "Agricultural tasks were highly, though not completely, gender specific."[122] The demanding shovel work required of camp women would not usually be considered women's work. However, it was not just the hard labor that demonstrated this gender overlap; women in the campaign community also needed to combine this physicality with being psychologically tough and personally assertive to manage successfully in the hard-scrabble existence they chose. Certainly, in this life full of dangers, they also had to be brave[123] and hardened to violence

---

[120] Judith Halberstam, *Female Masculinity* (Durham, NC: Duke University Press, 1998). Halberstam argues that female masculinity does not merely copy male masculinity but has actually been a force in construction masculinity per se. She does not convince me that this was the case before 1900, but I am very drawn to the notion of women possessing a variation of masculinity even when those women are heterosexual. Scarlet Bowen, "The Real Soul of a Man in Her Breast": Popular Oppression and British Nationalism in Memoirs of Female Soldiers, 1740–1750," *Eighteenth-Century Life* 28, no. 3 (Fall 2004): 20–45, tries to build on Halberstam's argument for the early modern era, but without great success, in my opinion. Bowen is more prone to assertion than proof.

[121] In another sense, Nye argues that "War thus both sharpened and blurred the lines between the sexes." Nye, "Western Masculinities in War and Peace," p. 432.

[122] Merry E. Wiesner, *Women and Gender in Early Modern Europe*, 2nd ed. (Cambridge: 2000), p. 106.

[123] Nye states "The indispensable masculine qualities of the combat soldier have altered little over the long run of modern history: personal courage, the willingness to sacrifice for comrades, the fear of shame or dishonor." Nye, "Western Masculinities in War and Peace," pp. 419–20. Such traits were also displayed by camp women.

PLATE 6. Pierre Bontemps, bas-relief on the tomb of François I, circa 1547, showing heavily burdened women on the march with the army.
Musée des Monuments Français, Paris. Giraudon/The Bridgeman Art Library.

and its effects. To survive, therefore, women had to be much like men and yet somehow remain defined as feminine. This gives a twist to the observation by Gayle Rubin, "Far from being an expression of natural differences, exclusive gender identity is the suppression of natural similarities."[124]

---

[124] Rubin in Merry E. Wiesner, *Women and Gender in Early Modern Europe*, p. 3.

There were limits, of course, to the masculine characteristics a woman could assume. Camp women were to comport themselves as women and choose male sexual partners, defer to their male companions or husbands, perform certain gender-defined tasks, and concern themselves with their children, if they had any. Camp women could fight, but they had to refrain from the deadly violence employed by men – feminine women poked, punched, and pulled, but they did not draw swords as a rule.

As Chapters II and III illustrate, this overlap was essentially one-sided. Women were expected to display a masculine hardiness and to perform certain hard physical work such as digging trenches and mounting cannon. Not only were these forms of masculinity accepted, but a woman who fell short in performing hard camp labor could be beaten by military authorities. However, a man who performed characteristically feminine tasks such as washing clothes risked ridiculed. The military environment of the camp required women to take on some mannish ways, but would not allow men to compromise their own masculinity.

Observing the modern-day military, feminist commentator Cynthia Enloe asserts, "Taking women in male-dominated and/or masculinized settings seriously yields significant explanatory rewards."[125] Of course, early modern camp women were not soldiers in the sense of today's uniformed women, and we must recognize the different standards of the community they lived in. These stalwart women, imbued with masculine virtues, still lived in an age that believed in the need for men to impose their mastery over women in an unavoidable struggle for dominance. The potential for gender-based tensions within individuals, relationships, and the campaign community as a whole must have been great in the male-dominated environment of the military camp. Nonetheless, the study of women in the early modern military environment may also yield the kinds of rewards Enloe expects.

Religious Reform and Practical Morality

The more invasive moral principles of the Protestant Reformation and the Catholic Counter-Reformation are credited with lowering the status of women by restricting their options and confining them in more patriarchal marriages. The rationale for this stems from institutions such as convents, seen as bastions of female autonomy, but these are beyond

---

[125] Cynthia Enloe, "Afterword," in *One of the Guys: Women as Aggressors and Torturers*, ed. Tara McKelvey (Emeryville, CA: 2007), p. 231.

our scope. The two focuses of the new practical morality, however, that strongly influenced women of the campaign community were the suppression of prostitution and the elevation of marriage. Prostitution, which had previously benefited from official toleration, came under fire in the sixteenth century; reformers condemned the oldest profession with righteous fury in the hopes of abolishing it. This abolition would eventually extend to the armies. New moral emphasis was placed on the family and marriage, advocating a strong but restricted domestic role for women as wives and mothers. The higher status accorded to marriage created strong and contradictory dynamics in the camps. While insisting that women who marched with armies be good and honorable wives, regulations at the same time controlled the number of troops who could marry and the number of wives who could accompany troops on campaign.

Medieval towns officially allowed and controlled prostitution, as exemplified by a fifteenth-century Nuremburg regulation forming a municipal brothel, "for the sake of avoiding worse evils in Christianity, low women will be tolerated."[126] Prostitution was regarded as a way of venting the sexual appetites of men to forestall "evil to wives and virgins"[127] and, it should be added, to shield family honor and protect husbands from being cuckolded.[128] Marriage came late for common men – on average, men married at age twenty-six to twenty-eight – so it was a long span from puberty to the conjugal bed.[129] Even some men of the church, including the Dominicans, were known to accept prostitution as necessary in an imperfect world.[130] And, during the period when the

---

[126] In Herman Heinrich Ploss, Max Barthels, and Paul Barthels, rev. Ferd. F. von Reitzenstein, *Woman in the Sexual Relation: An Anthropological and Historical Survey* (New York: 1964), p. 98. See as well Ruth Mazo Karras, *Common Women: Prostitution and Sexuality in Medieval England* (Oxford: 1996), p. 32. See Mary Elizabeth Perry, *Gender and Disorder in Early Modern Seville* (Princeton: 1990), pp. 45–47, as well on prostitution as a necessary evil.

[127] Wording of a Munich ordinance on prostitution in Karras, *Common Women*, pp. 32–33.

[128] Thomas Coryate reported Venetian opinion concerning brothels in 1611: "First, they think that the chastity of their wives would be the sooner assaulted, and so consequently they should be caricornised [cuckolded] ... were it not for these places of evacuation." Evans, *Harlots, Whores & Hookers*, p. 66.

[129] While nobles married early to ensure the family line, common folk waited to establish themselves in life. The average marriage age for common men in this period was twenty-six to twenty-eight, and for women twenty-four to twenty-six, Hufton, *The Prospect Before Her*, p. 13.

[130] Hufton, *The Prospect Before Her*, p. 304. The cardinal archbishop of Spain also seemed to tolerate prostitution in the sense that he gave prostitutes legal recourse against their customers. Ibid., p. 324. Women from brothels could be required to

Popes resided in Avignon, that town supported an officially recognized brothel, complete with medical inspections and specified clothing for the young women it employed.[131] Although such practices were less common in England, Scandanavia, and the Netherlands, legalized prostitution still was practiced in those countries as well.[132]

The new moral rigor typical of the Reformation and Counter-Reformation rejected prostitution. These moral values were expressed via efforts to rescue and reform prostitutes, which included supplying them with modest dowries to secure husbands.[133] While there was a definite trend toward reform, standards and values varied through Europe, and fluctuated between tolerance and suppression in the same area or town.[134] Easy generalizations, as we know, are almost sure to suffer exceptions. Concerns over public health reinforced the more demanding moral imperatives, when syphilis, also known as the French disease, struck Europe hard at the end of the fifteenth century.[135] Prostitutes and soldiers were quickly feared as carriers of virulent venereal disease. This fear cut two ways; it led some to want all prostitutes contained in legal brothels where they could be inspected by doctors, while it inspired others to close brothels and criminalize prostitution.[136] The French crown had tolerated and regulated prostitution before 1565, but it banned prostitutes from Paris that year and renewed the prohibition in 1614.[137] French righteousness slacked for some time, but Louis XIV renewed the fight against prostitution with an ordinance of 1684, and by the end of the century licensed brothels were a thing of the past in

attend mass and to refrain from working on Sundays and Feast Days. Perry, *Gender and Disorder in Early Modern Seville*, pp. 140–41.

[131] Hilary Evans, *Harlots, Whores & Hookers: A History of Prostitution* (New York: 1979), p. 58.

[132] Hufton, *The Prospect Before Her*, p. 290, Hilary Evans, *Harlots, Whores & Hookers*, pp. 60–63; and Karras, *Common Women*.

[133] See, for example, Perry, *Gender and Disorder in Early Modern Seville*, p. 49.

[134] Merry E. Wiesner, *Women and Gender in Early Modern Europe*, 2nd ed. (Cambridge: 2000), p. 122–24.

[135] There is a good discussion of syphilis, or the pox in Cunningham and Grell, *The Four Horsemen of the Apocalypse*, pp. 247–70.

[136] Perry, *Gender and Disorder in Early Modern Seville*, p. 137. A law of 1570 there required that doctors visit brothels every week to inspect the women. Perry, *Gender and Disorder in Early Modern Seville*, p. 49.

[137] Philip F. Riley, *A Lust for Virtue: Louis XIV's Attack on Sin in the Seventeenth Century* (Westport, CT: 2001), p. 55. In 1623 Philip IV outlawed brothels in Spain. Perry, *Gender and Disorder in Early Modern Seville*, p. 150; Hufton, *The Prospect Before Her*, p. 310.

Europe.[138] Of course, the criminalization of prostitution did not mean its end, merely that it was driven underground. As will be seen, declining official tolerance of prostitution in the campaign community paralleled that in European towns.

Although marriage was a common and old institution, the importance of the family and of a woman's role in it were not static constants. The Protestant Reformation preached that the family was the moral center of the community; this was a powerful concept as the institutional church was no longer seen as an essential intermediary between God and mankind, and celibacy lost its holy status. Luther himself, originally a monk, married an ex-nun and became an archetypal *pater familias*. The Counter-Reformation maintained religious communities and celibacy, harnessing them more securely to the papal will, but it too awarded greater emphasis to marriage and the family.

Customs varied throughout medieval Europe; however, in general marriage practices were not very formal. The consent of bride and groom sufficed, so that published bans, witnesses, and official ceremony were not required. However, during the sixteenth century, the demand increased for regular procedures to sanctify marriage. The great reforming cardinal and bishop, Gian Matteo Giberti (1495–1543), proclaimed "Let no one afterwards presume that engagements or marriages were contracted unless they were done in churches or public places or homes of relatives, and in the presence of their parish priest and the fathers and mothers of the contracting parties."[139] Condemnation of irregular, or clandestine, marriages multiplied, and they were finally not recognized at all. The emphasis upon marriage affected the lower as well as the upper reaches of society, as witnessed by its growing importance within the campaign community.

Concubinage, which was legally recognized in parts of Europe during the late Middle Ages, lost its status. While some men, particularly men of wealth and status, could flout the prohibitions and continue to keep concubines, it formally disappeared as an option for less wealthy individuals. Men and women might live in "free unions" and have liaisons, but concubinage disappeared as a legal state.[140]

---

[138] The French relaxed the policy of locking up prostitutes in the mid-eighteenth century. Riley, *A Lust for Virtue*, p. 169.

[139] Giberti, Constitutiones, in Eisenach, *Husbands, Wives, and Concubines*, p. 97.

[140] See Donald Weinstein, *The Captain's Concubine: Love, Honor, and Violence in Renaissance Tuscany* (Baltimore, MD: Johns Hopkins University Press, 2000), and Eisenach, *Husbands, Wives, and Concubines*.

The growing status of marriage and the family in the eyes of the Church provided women with increased domestic responsibilities and importance, enough so that it won women to the Church.[141] However, the woman was not defined as the head of this more essential family; that was the man's honor. Along with literature stressing family propriety came literature stressing the man's obligation to enforce his will within the family, if need be by physically disciplining his wife.[142]

Peter Wilson argues that this new family morality undercut the status of women and that the efforts of church and state to control women led to their exclusion of from camps.

[This article] will also question the prevailing view that the exclusion of women from armed forces came with the militarization of the support services in the later eighteenth century, arguing instead that this occurred ... after about 1650, and is a reflection of the growing confidence of church and state after the upheavals of the Reformation and the Thirty Years War ... *This process was accompanied by a general decline in their status in the eyes of both civil and military elites and "respectable" society.*[143]

Thus Wilson argues that women were removed from armies not because they were needed less after 1650, but because they were disparaged in Reformation and Counter-Reformation moral teachings. So Wilson's important article relates their falling numbers in the campaign community to the theory of a general erosion of women's standing in society. I take exception to his conclusion, as I regard changing military utility as explaining the decline in participation of camp women. Nonetheless, the moral dimensions of the campaign community must be taken seriously. Military authorities conducted campaigns condemning prostitution and privileging marriage. And, within the male-dominated military

---

[141] Hufton, *The Prospect Before Her*, p. 400.

[142] This matter of physical discipline will be discussed in Chapters II and III.

[143] Wilson, "German Women and War, 1500–1800," pp. 127–28. Italics are mine. I do not understand why he labels a misconception about the eighteenth century as the "prevailing view," and he seems to think that reforms for the mid-seventeenth century occurred in the mid- to late-eighteenth century. Ulinka Rublack, "Wench and Maiden: Women, War and the Pictorial Function of the Feminine in German Cities in the Early Modern Period," trans. Pamela Selwyn, *History Workshop Journal*, 44 (January 1997): 11, would seem to buttress Wilson when she writes: "Fears of the undermining of civic morality were countered, among other things, by a strict control of 'wanton' women. ... In 1674 the Konstanz town council ordered the expulsion of all 'loose wenches' who 'latched' onto soldiers – and most cities employed similar tactics." However, she is talking of women of the particular town, not women of the campaign community.

community, it would be odd if society's expectations for masculine authority were not accepted and exaggerated.

Women in the Economic Sphere

Women actively played a number of economic roles in the campaign economy; they and their children were consumers, but women also engaged in small commercial ventures and, through pillage, produced their share of the wealth of the community. They seemed to have enjoyed a wide berth for their endeavors and makeshift scramblings to garner whatever they could. This was at a time when women in the civilian community faced censure and punishment for going outside the boundaries of allowed economic practice as defined by guild and municipal regulation. Economic practice restricted women in certain activities but permitted them to pursue other endeavors. Reformation and Counter-Reformation's emphasis on the patriarchal family and the more restrictive marriage laws mentioned above also confined women.

Recent historical studies debate the degree to which women's economic opportunities declined during the early modern era.[144] Merry E. Wiesner argues that while German guilds increasingly blocked women's contributions to production to the point of exclusion, capitalist production and retail sales provided other opportunities for women. Women were key figures in markets, for example, and certain kinds of retail sales, including beer, wine, and spirits. Clare Crowston stresses that through formal and illicit participation in guild work, French women apparently enjoyed significant access to a large labor market, particularly as witnessed in sources from the late seventeenth and eighteenth centuries.[145] French women also

---

[144] See the very useful paper by Clare Haru Crowston, "Women, Gender and Guilds in Early Modern France," presented at "The Return of the Guilds," a Conference of the Global Economic History Network, Utrecht, Utrecht University 5–7 October 2006, available on the web at http://www.iisg.nl/hpw/papers/guilds-crowston.pdf. She discusses the history of women's work and guilds over the last few decades. As always, I learn a great deal from my colleague Clare and am happy to follow her lead. Those who nuance but retain elements of the decline thesis in the crafts include Martha Howell, *Production and Patriarchy in Late Medieval Cities* (Chicago: 1986) and Merry Wiesner, *Working Women in Renaissance Germany* (New Brunswick, NJ: 1986), although Wiesner argues that while participation in craft production fell off, there were new openings in capitalist enterprises. Although Sheilagh Ogilvie adopts a new theoretical approach to buttress the thesis of decline, she denies a " 'pre-capitalist' golden age within the guild framework." Ogilvie "How Does Social Capital Affect Women?," p. 343.

[145] For example, the plates of the great mid-eighteenth-century compendium, Diderot's *Encyclopédie*, show women working in trades organized as male guilds, including

had their own guilds. In the early seventeenth century the linen drapers and the hemp merchants guilds were women's institutions, and the small grain-dealers guild included both men and women. In 1675, the French government chartered seamstress guilds in Paris and Rouen and fresh-flower sellers in Paris.[146] Such evidence has not ended the debate over women's economic opportunities, if for no other reason than patterns varied in Europe. There were no women's guilds in England and only five throughout all of German-speaking central Europe.[147]

Camp women engaged in market and retail sales, as did their civilian sisters, and they also displayed considerable initiative in improvising ways to make money. Because the campaign community had particular needs, remained outside the jurisdiction of guilds or municipal regulation, and depended heavily on plunder, its economic life may be considered as a case apart. Yet it was still a venue for commerce and craft-work performed by women, so limiting the number of women in that community after 1650 may be seen as a special instance of the shrinking economic alternatives for women.

One facet of the civilian economy that I believe translated into the campaign community was the role of women as business and financial managers. In the world of shop and guild, women demonstrated commercial ability. Market and shop sales were standard women's responsibilities. Even if guilds restricted women in craft production, masters' wives played a very active role behind the counter or in market stalls. Women regularly made sales, tended the till, and did the bookkeeping, and they often knew enough of the trade to assist journeymen and judge their work.[148] Artist's portrayals of shops give graphic evidence of women's active participation in managing the business.[149] In addition,

stocking-makers, fan-makers, enamelers, paper-makers, wigmaker-barbers, and saddlers. Crowston, "Women, Gender and Guilds," p. 12, makes this point.

[146] Clare H. Crowston, *Fabricating Women: The Seamstresses of Old Regime France, 1675–1791* (Durham, NC: 2001).

[147] Ogilvie, "How Does Social Capital Affect Women?," p. 334.

[148] Hufton, *The Prospect Before Her*, p. 242, and James R. Farr, *Hands of Honor: Artisans and Their World in Dijon, 1550–1650*, (Ithaca: 1988), pp. 8–9.

[149] Three seventeenth-century French images present a market where women sell bread from their stalls, a pastry shop with men working while a woman takes money from a customer, and a shoemakers shop graced by a well-dressed women, apparently the master's wife, who undertakes a light task as workmen make footwear. An eighteenth-century engraving shows a woman weighing bread for a customer in a bakery. But the most interesting view for our purposes comes out of a book describing the bakers' trade. In this engraving, a woman serves as bookkeeper, noting credit accounts in her ledger. Kaplan, *The Bakers of Paris and the Bread Question*, pp. 92 and 95; Farr,

women were responsible for the well-being and moral propriety of the shop.[150] If the business maintained a market stall, this was the wife's preserve, for the husband was needed back at the shop.[151] In fact, it was so difficult for a master to run his business without a wife, that a widowed master really had to find new wife.[152] Women were regarded by the guilds as competent enough in business affairs that master's widows were allowed to continue running the family shop until remarried.[153]

The fact that women were often the custodians of the books and the money in small businesses is of particular interest.[154] In his journal, the French eighteenth-century glazier, Jacques-Louis Ménétra, compliments his wife on her business head and her ability to get a good price; however, he also criticizes her for squirreling away money without telling him, implying she had control of accounts. To his surprise and consternation, she was able to produce a tidy sum as a dowry for their daughter from her clandestine savings.[155] An intriguing study by Jacob Melish draws its evidence from records of legal actions in Paris during the 1670s and early 1680s. He demonstrates how the sexual division of labor "led husbands to become dependent on wives for a number of tasks, one of which was the daily management of accounts and earnings."[156] In one extreme case that Melish uncovered, a frustrated artisan complained to the police commissioner in 1683 that his wife held all the money and refused to give him any!

Hands of Honor, pp. 33 and 71; Paul-Jacques Malouin, *Description des arts du meunier, du vermicelier*, new edition (Neufchâtel: 1771) in Kaplan, *The Bakers of Paris and the Bread Question*, p. 141.

[150] Hufton, *The Prospect Before Her*, pp. 64 and 164.

[151] Hufton, *The Prospect Before Her*, pp. 164–67.

[152] Hufton, *The Prospect Before Her*, pp. 140 and 223.

[153] Farr, *Hands of Honor*, p. 20. In 1727, among the 927 bakers who ran their own bakeries in Paris were 131 women, of whom 100 were widows. Some of these women ran illicit bakeries and were culled out by 1733. Steven Laurence Kaplan, *The Bakers of Paris and the Bread Question, 1700–1775* (Durham, NC: 1998), pp. 123–26. For examples of widows running their own bakeries see Kaplan, pp. 110, 146–47, 112, 213, and 324–25.

[154] See Olwen Hufton's summation on this reality in *The Prospect Before Her*, pp. 152–53. Also see examples of women keeping accounts in Kaplan, *The Bakers of Paris and the Bread Question*.

[155] Jacques-Louis Ménétra, *Journal de ma vie*, (Paris: 1998), pp. 244, 250, and 258.

[156] Jacob Melish, "Cash and Relations Between Working Spouses in Late-Seventeenth-Century Paris," paper delivered at the April 2006 meeting of the Society for French Historical Studies, held at the University of Illinois at Urbana-Champaign. Used with permission.

As a reflection of this civilian practice, camp women seemed to have managed the goods and money in the family economy of production and pillage that powered the campaign communities of the sixteenth and seventeenth centuries. This will be a subject explored further in Chapter III.

Women, War, and State Formation

Women of the campaign community exerted a special influence over the course of war, and their fates were linked with military and political reform. Consequently their stories need to be put in the context of debates over the public roles of women. Almost all of the discussion of women as influences over the grand affairs of state concern female rulers, consorts, or those elite women who played some military role defending their estates. Yet beyond pointing out plebian women's roles in demonstrations and riots concerning food and politics – definably rare upraisings – few historians have suggested that the daily lives of such women helped determine the shape of states or the course of wars. In contrast, this volume insists on camp women's importance to these aspects of the public sphere.

During the Middle Ages and the early modern period, elite women often did grand things. Of course, women rulers stood at the head of state militaries – witness the likes of queens Elizabeth I and Anne of England; tsarinas Catherine I, Anna, Elizabeth, and Catherine II of Russia; and Habsburg empress Maria Theresa. Women from powerful families transmitted power as brides and mothers, but they also exercised it when the men who headed families were absent, incapacitated, or too young to assume command. Land owners and town leaders possessed political authority and military power on the local level, and, although these diminished over time, they would still be significant well into the seventeenth century. When the state was unable to muster an adequate defense during episodes of invasions, internecine warfare, and marauding, local elites were forced to take to the walls and to the fields at the head of whatever forces they could command. Although men most commonly assumed command, women also did when circumstances demanded.

The story of women who found themselves engaged in combat often stops with the upper class, but women of the lower classes also fought in defense of their homes and towns. It was commonplace that women worked alongside men in constructing and repairing fortifications. Additionally, a small number of women also wielded arms alongside men or banded with other armed women. Fighting may have diverged from normal gender-defined roles, but it was seen as proper that a woman would defend her family, her home, and her religion. Women on the walls received praise as heroines rather than rebuke as contradictions of society's norms.

The early modern period provides numerous examples of another kind of women at arms – the woman who assumed the appearance of a man and served as a soldier. Popular culture celebrated such cross-dressing women in song and story. Although society looked askance on transvestitism, authorities were relatively tolerant of women soldiers when they were revealed as women, as long as they committed no other transgression such as active homosexuality. Many women soldiers even petitioned for military pensions after they left the armed forces. Although such women were celebrated in European culture, there were only a few who actually served at any one time.

Chapter IV will deal with elite women commanders, working-class women defenders, and cross-dressing women soldiers. They all share something in common: they were extraordinary in one way or another. Women commanders took charge in the absence of men, but almost always relinquished this role to males when they reemerged on the scene. Women-defenders from the working class fought when required by the immediate threats the community faced; their combat was an exceptional event in their ordinarily routine existences. Cross-dressing women soldiers were noteworthy but rare exceptions; such individuals may have served for many years, but they lived outside the conventions of society.

But what of the ordinary rather than the extraordinary? This volume aims at exploring the great number of camp women whose daily activities intersected with and influenced the great issues of war and state formation. The interest here is in the mundane, the matter of simply getting through the day, the week, the month. If war was the ultimate public and political act, then the needs and actions of women in the campaign community inescapably became part of the public as well as the private sphere. As mouths to be fed, women accompanying armies helped to determine their logistical requirements, and women's actions in finding sustenance and support for themselves and others helped to supply these greater needs. Because logistics determined the movements of armies, women also exerted influence over the conduct of wars and the shaping of strategy.

Military and state reform would eventually lessen the need for women to accompany armies into the field; therefore, women's lives were caught up in these major processes. But women need to be seen not simply as victims of reforms but as causes of them as well. The problems, limitations, and excesses of European armies before 1650 were not simply the result of soldiers' actions; they were a product of the entire campaign community, with its large noncombatant contingent, including considerable numbers of women. Therefore, the disciplinary, logistical, and operational issues that inspired reforms involved camp women as well as their male companions.

* * *

A contemporary account describes an interesting incident that occurred in 1710, during the War of the Spanish Succession.[157] A sergeant in the British infantry, "my Lord Hartford's Regiment," arranged for his sister, who he learned was in the French camp, to visit him. She is referred to in the account as "in the French service," and the British sergeant is described as "getting his sister into our Army." Thus, it was accepted that a woman in the campaign community was de facto in the army, even though she could not be a soldier. The reunion of brother and sister was open and jolly, as she had brought with her a bottle of brandy: "They were a jovial Crew, and drank round the Table like Sons of Bacchus." The sergeant's officers did their best to persuade his sister to join them by boasting of the better conditions of camp life among the British, but she counted that she preferred French provisions, "that all the world allow their Bread to be better than that of any other nation." But she could not stay for long; the French sent a drummer to fetch her and she crossed the lines back to the enemy camp, leaving her brother desolated. This particular woman lived in the three contexts discussed in this chapter. She was "in the French service," living in a world regulated by command and ordinance; she was an inhabitant of the campaign community, sharing its life; and the brandy she brought suggests that she was a sutler, but in any case she was a woman living by her labor in the relative economic freedom of the campaign community.

[157] Bishop, *The Life and Adventures of Matthew Bishop*, pp. 222–24.

II

Camp Women: Prostitutes, "Whores," and Wives

On 4 June 1759, Mary May petitioned Colonel Henry Bouquet to pardon her for her breach of military discipline. When she saw her husband seized for an infraction, she had flown into a rage that caused her own arrest. In her appeal we see her affection, her history, and her toughness:

I beg and hope you'll take it into Consideration that it was the Love I had for my Poor husband and no [bad] will to Y^r Honour, which was the cause of abusing so good a Colonel as you are. Please to Sett me at Liberty this time & I never will dis-oblige y^r Honour nor any other Officer belonging to the Army for the future as I have been a Wife 22 years and have Traveld with my Husband every Place or Country the Company Marcht too and have workt very hard ever since I was in the Army I hope y^r honour will be so Good as to pardon me this time that I may go with my Poor Husband one time more to carry him and my good officers water in hottest Battles as I have done before.[1]

This durable and devoted woman was no stranger to camp or battlefield. According to her testimony, she even carried water to her husband and others during combat.[2] She seems to have been formidable to a fault, which landed her in the Carlisle jail. Mary was no saint, but she possessed the virtues of the campaign community.

Mary exemplified the thousands upon thousands of women who accompanied the troops and who were denizens of the early modern

---

[1] Letter of Martha May to Bouquet, Carlisle, 4 June 1758, in Henry Bouquet, *The Papers of Henry Bouquet*, eds. S.K. Stevens, Donald H. Kent, and Autumn Leonard (Harrisburg, PA: 1951), Vol. II, p. 30.

[2] In *The Life and Adventures of Christian Davies*, pp. 112–14, Davies similarly reports bringing broth and meat to her husband and his officers in siege trenches in 1706. There she also took musket in hand and killed an enemy soldier.

combat zone. What differentiates this zone from the "rear" or the "home front"? The combat zone is best defined by the intensity and immediacy of danger and by the ability to do direct harm to the enemy. It is where adversaries collide, where the enemy is in striking distance. The full reality of war lives here, including fear and the sights, sounds, and smells of death, as does the opportunity for victory or the possibility of defeat. It would be ridiculous to claim that only those who bear weapons endure the rigors of war. For women like Mary May who lived within the sound of the cannon, it was not simply a question of *supporting* the fighting individuals but of *sharing* much of what the men on the firing line experienced, including the danger of injury and death.

Modern armies regard it as an innovation to send *some* women into combat, but in the campaign community, *all* women stood in harm's way. Danger, fatigue, and toil were not exceptions in their lives, but their daily fare. This chapter concentrates on the personal lives of these redoubtable women—the relationships they formed, the challenges they negotiated, and the dangers they faced. Chapter III will focus specifically on their labors within the campaign community.

PROSTITUTES, "WHORES," AND WIVES

Camp women populated a complex hierarchy that we can only partially reconstruct. Much of this female hierarchy, which determined function, respectability, and status, concerned women's relationships with men. To help understand women's lives within the campaign community we must differentiate among the three sexual and partnership relationships summed up in the categories of prostitutes, "whores," and wives. Women who had sex with many customers for compensation, whatever their other duties in camp, will be termed prostitutes. Those that were exclusive to one partner without the sanction of a formal marriage will be called "whores" here, as they often are in contemporary discussions. Lastly are those such as Mary May that were soldiers' legal wives. Throughout the early modern period, wives almost always received some special recognition from military authorities, and as the support from church and state for marriage increased, armies privileged wives even more and formally excluded prostitutes and "whores."

Before beginning this discussion, however, it should be noted that many historians who are indifferent or even hostile to the discussion of women in militaries before the twentieth century assume that women were little more than abased camp followers, selling sex to survive like parasites on the body *militaire*. However, a woman's sexual activity is rarely the most important thing that can be said about her. To assume so is to adopt a double standard: men can be sexually promiscuous and still be good soldiers in the face of the enemy, but should a woman sleep with a man or men, that is all you need to know about her. Yet a camp laundress who had multiple sexual partners still could wash clothes as clean as could a devoted wife and thus be a necessary part of the military project, and still face the toil and danger of campaigning in the combat zone.

Prostitutes

Prostitution in military camps benefited from tolerance and regulation during the sixteenth century, but suffered increasing restrictions that climaxed in complete prohibition in the late seventeenth century. Situations varied and no absolute rule applied, particularly during the earlier period. On the whole, however, the fate of prostitution within the campaign community paralleled its course within contemporary civil society. Although this varied across Europe, and could fluctuate between tolerance and suppression in the same area or town,[3] in general, a more stringent sexual morality generated by the Reformation and the Counter-Reformation privileged marriage and pressured rulers to ban prostitutes and "whores" from military camps. It would seem that the ban on prostitution within the campaign community was more absolute and consistent over time than were civilian regulations. The Reformation/Counter-Reformation ethical reform cut into the libertine lifestyle that flourished with the aggregate contract army. Particularly before 1650, sexual opportunity was both a lure and a compensation for soldiers, so the assault on prostitution signaled an effort to change camp dynamics.

Not surprisingly, attempts to ban prostitutes met with uneven success, and demand tended to ensure supply. In all probability, declarations against prostitution had greater effect when troops were in the field than in winter quarters and garrisons. In the campaign community, troops lived separate from civilian society and under the direct supervision and control of their officers; however, when garrisoned or quartered in towns, soldiers lived among civil communities with their own practices and pitfalls.

---

[3] Merry E. Wiesner, *Women and Gender in Early Modern Europe*, 2nd ed. (Cambridge: 2000), p. 122–24.

From the late Middle Ages through the mid-seventeenth century, military writers and commanders often defended prostitution, advancing familiar arguments that the presence of prostitutes prevented worse problems, particularly in a community populated by so many young men. Writing in the mid-sixteenth century, Sancho de Londoño defended prostitutes because they occupied men who might otherwise pose a danger to local women.[4] According to Mathieu de la Simonne, writing in the 1620s, "It is good for the local inhabitants, it is said, because their wives, daughters, and sisters will be more in security."[5]

Different field commanders followed varying practices regarding prostitutes, from regulating their numbers and working conditions to hounding them out of camp. In 1465, Captain Mignon's company of mounted archers was accompanied on its passage through Paris by eight prostitutes. These *filles de joi*, or "daughters of joy," even brought their own father confessor with them.[6] A Burgundian military ordinance issued in 1473 by Charles the Bold prohibited soldiers from bringing their own women but allowed each company of 100 lances, perhaps 500 men, to have as many as thirty prostitutes.[7]

During the sixteenth century and into the seventeenth, many commanders readily accepted and regulated the presence of prostitutes, usually called "public women," "women in common," or "common women." Depending on time and place, Spanish authorities permitted different numbers of prostitutes per company of troops, ranging from three to eight per company. The duke of Alba, who commanded in the Spanish Netherlands from 1567 to 1573, established price controls of

---

[4] Sancho de Londono (1589) in Barton C. Hacker, "Women and Military Institutions in Early Modern Europe: A Reconnaissance," *Signs: Journal of Women in Culture and Society* 6, no. 4 (1981), p. 651. See also the 1524 treatise by Michael Ott and Jacob Preiss that advocated that each small garrison have "two or three women who are every man's wife." Treatise in Baumann, Landsknechte, p. 156, in Peter H. Wilson "German Women and War, 1500–1800," *War in History*, vol. 3, no. 2 (1996): 130–31.

[5] Simonne, *L'Alphabet du soldat* (1623), p. 230, in Babeau, *La vie militaire*, 1:200–01. Grimmelshausen's female anti-hero, Courage, makes the same case in Johann Jakob Christoffle von Grimmelshausen, *The Life of Courage, the Notorious Thief, Whore, and Vagabond*, trans. Mike Mitchell (Sawtry, Cambs: 2001), p. 151.

[6] Barante in Wilhelm Haberling, "Army Prostitution and Its Control: An Historical Study," in Victor Robinson, ed., *Morals in Wartime* (New York: 1943), pp. 27–28.

[7] Hale, *War and Society in Renaissance Europe*, p. 162. Charles's army before Nuess was said to be accompanied by 1,600 prostitutes and 900 priests, and a year later he brought 2,000 prostitutes to the field. Ploss et al, *Woman in the Sexual Relation*, p. 98. A "lance" was a tactical unit, the size of which varied by country, time, and losses suffered, but at this time it could be counted as five or six men.

five solds per session for such women.[8] Charles III of Lorraine, leading troops in the French Wars of Religion, ordered in 1587:

No military man entering the service of this army shall bring with him any special woman, unless she is his legitimate wife having been married or affianced to him; all other women present with this army shall be public women and the common property of all and that in each company there shall be no more than eight women under penalty of flogging and the men shall be deprived of his effects; and if it is proved that soldiers or officers of our military forces have, or bring into our army such woman for their own privacy, they should be driven off and henceforth declared incapable of carrying on the war, and be further chastised at our pleasure.[9]

Writing in the early seventeenth century, Simonne reported that prostitutes were quartered like soldiers when a unit was sedentary, but that the prostitutes would be lodged in some out-of-the-way place and be subject to inspection by army surgeons, because infectious disease, particularly venereal disease, was such a problem.[10] This all seems relatively tolerant and rational, but it was not always so.

Acceptance was far from universal, even during the sixteenth century. An English broadside of 1513 forbade that any "common woman presume to come within the King's host, nor nigh the same by the space of three miles, upon pain if any so be taken to be burned upon the right cheek."[11] The earl of Leicester's disciplinary code of 1585 barred any women but lawful wives on campaigns, and this became the basis for Essex's later codes.[12] It may be said that, in general, the British were less inclined to accept prostitution as necessary, however, Dutch articles of war dated 1580 also criminalized prostitution: "all common whores

---

[8] Parker, *The Army of Flanders*, pp. 175–76, text and notes. Alba in Haberling, "Army Prostitution and Its Control," p. 37.

[9] In Haberling, "Army Prostitution and Its Control," p. 39. A German document, ca. 1524, listed women needed specifically for garrisoning a small castle: "In addition to one seamstress, there are to be two kitchen maids, and two or three other females who shall be everybody's women and regarding whom there must not be any rivalry. The captain shall take these poor women under his protection and care, and no one must think that he can have them alone." However, just as was often the case in civil regulations, men "who have wedded wives must have no share in the common property under the punishment of God." The women were to receive "suitable women's money of two Kreutzer." In Haberling, "Army Prostitution and Its Control," p. 38–39.

[10] Mathieu de la Simonne, *L'Alphabet du soldat* (1623), p. 230, in Babeau, *La vie militaire*, 1:200–01.

[11] *Tudor Royal Proclamations*, cit., p. 113, in Hale, *War and Society in Renaissance Europe*, p. 161.

[12] Code in Cruikshank, *Elizabeth's Army*, p. 298.

shall for the first offense be shamefully driven from camp, and for the second offense, being found in the camp, shall be heavily flogged and banished."[13] Punishments for prostitutes varied, but their fate could be dire. In command of French troops during the sixteenth-century Wars of Religion, Philippe Strozzi is said to have ordered that the 800 prostitutes following his army be thrown off a bridge at Pont-de-Cé; all of these unfortunates drowned.[14]

Regulations banning prostitutes appeared more frequently during the Thirty Years' War, and they became universal afterwards. The Protestant champion, Gustavus Adolphus, promulgated stringent regulations in 1621: "No Whore shall be suffered in the Leaguer: but if any will have his own wife with him, he may. If any unmaried woman be found, he that keepes her may have leave lawfully to marry her; or else be forced to put her away."[15] These influenced later German articles of war, such as those issued by Duke George of Braunschweig-Lüneburg in 1636.[16] Frederick William, the Great Elector of Brandenberg (r. 1640–88), also banned prostitutes in 1656.[17]

Armies in the new state commission form assaulted prostitution with greater vehemence. Louis XIV, despite his own lust for women, adopted a moralistic attitude toward prostitution in the army that suited his times. Older regulations had sporadically prohibited prostitution in Paris or the army, but in 1684 Louis took up the crusade in earnest, when he banned prostitutes from within two leagues of Versailles where large numbers of troops were encamped, because soldiers were fighting over the women and some men had been killed.[18] Prostitutes caught within the restricted area were to be disfigured by having their ears and noses

---

[13] John R. Hale, *War and Society in Renaissance Europe 1450–1620*, (1998), p. 162.

[14] Brantome, *Couronnels françois, Oeuvres* in Babeau, *La vie militaire*, 1:201.

[15] Article 88 in the 1621 Swedish Articles of War. It can be found on the internet at http://www.icrc.org/Web/eng/siteeng0.nsf/html/57JN8D.

[16] These reproduce Article 88 above almost word for word. See Duke George's article in Haberling, "Army Prostitution and Its Control," p. 46.

[17] Article quoted in Haberling, "Army Prostitution and Its Control," p. 46.

[18] Philip F. Riley, *A Lust for Virtue: Louis XIV's Attack on Sin in the Seventeenth-Century* (Westport, CT: 2001), p. 55. SHAT, Bib., Col. des ord., vol. 25, #70, 31 October 1684, "Ordonnance du Roy pour faire condamner les Filles de mauvaise vie qui se trouveront avec les soldats, à deux lieues aux environs de Versailles, à avoir le nez et les oreilles coupées." See other ordinances against prostitution: SHAT, Bib., Col. des ord., vol. 25, #93, 1 March 1685; Col. des ord., vol. 25, #123, 20 May 1686; and Col. des ord. vol. 25, #149. For an earlier, 1644, regulation against *filles de joi* in a French army, see SHAT, Bib., Col. des ord., vol. 16, #160, 1644, "Forme de la justice militaire de l'infanterie de France," in André, *Le Tellier*, 589.

cut. In 1687, Louis extended these provisions to the army as a whole. Women without gainful employment found in the company of soldiers within two leagues of a camp or garrison were to be whipped and disfigured. Fear of spreading venereal disease among the troops would lead to further French laws against prostitution in 1713, 1724, 1734, 1776, and 1777.[19] Military historian Fritz Redlich speaks of a policy of "restricting soldiers' copulations" by the end of the seventeenth century.[20]

Official attempts to ban prostitution apparently met with incomplete success. André Corvisier, the noted French military historian, comments that when war broke out again, the restrictions imposed by Louis and his war minister, the marquis de Louvois, relaxed: "There was no longer a question of depriving Mars of Venus."[21] Towns could supply ready women even if they were banned from camps. The major garrison town of Berlin was known to be notoriously thick with prostitutes.[22] Across the Channel, Hogarth's well-known painting, "March of the Guards to Finchley," shows troops assembling to fight against the Scottish rising of the 1745. Soldiers pile out of a brothel as others in the streets are surrounded by women of apparently differing standards of virtue.[23] Yet it would be inaccurate to say that military officials simply reverted to a permissive policy. Prostitutes could be punished with permanent or temporary disfigurement, or worse. They were still driven out of camp if discovered; they might even be drummed, or "beaten" in the terms of the day, through town to a "whores' march."[24]

[19] Olwen Hufton, *The Prospect Before Her: A History of Women in Western Europe, vol. 1, 1500–1800* (New York: Vintage Books, 1998), p. 310. Hilary Evans, *Harlots, Whores & Hookers: A History of Prostitution* (New York: 1979), p. 58. An interesting American regulation of 1776 barred prostitutes from camps or barracks: "No Woman of Ill Fame Shall be permitted to Come into the Barricks on pain of Being well Watred under a pump, and Every Officer or Soldier who Shall Bring any Such woman will be tryd and Punished by a Court Martial." Holly A. Mayer, *Belonging to the Army: Camp Followers and Community during the American Revolution* (Columbia, SC: 1996)., p. 111.

[20] Fritz Redlich, *The German Military Enterprizer and his Workforce, 13th to 17th Centuries, Vieteljahrschrift fur sozial- und Virtschaftsgeschite,* Beihelft XLVII, 2 vols. (Wiesbaden: 1964), 1:208.

[21] Philippe Contamine, *Histoire militaire de la France, vol. 1, Des origines à 1715* (Paris: Presses Universitaires de France, 1992), 1:403.

[22] Christopher Duffy, *The Army of Frederick the Great* (Newton Abbot, Devonshire: 1974), p. 45.

[23] J. R. Western, "War on a New Scale: Professionalism in Armies, Navies and Diplomacy," in *The Eighteenth Century: Europe in the Age of Enlightenment,* ed. Alfred Cobban (New York: 1969), pp. 190–91.

[24] An interesting, naïve British drawing of 1780 shows a prostitute being drummed out of a military camp set up in Hyde Park as "respectable" women look on. These range from

During the 1790s, French Revolutionaries would incongruously charge that prostitution was a monarchist plot: "Remember that despots favor debauchery and corrupt men in order to debase them and bring them into the most sordid servitude." Prostitutes "not only enervate the courage of the warriors but also corrupt the most pure source of French blood."[25]

Certain medical arguments against prostitution remained constant throughout the period from 1500 to 1815. Moralists usually frowned on fornication and adultery and, in general, disapproved of the libertine life soldiers were thought to enjoy. The prevalence of venereal disease raised a more practical argument against prostitutes. Syphilis and gonorrhea struck Europe at the close the fifteenth century, and were particularly obvious in military camps. At the time, the two diseases were considered to be one and the same and were not clearly differentiated until 1837. As early as 1530, the medical poem, *Syphilis sive Morbus Gallicus* by Girolamo Fracastoro, advised the use of mercury as a cure, and it remained the favored treatment for three centuries.

By the late sixteenth century, military codes that accepted prostitution often stipulated that the women be inspected for disease. Infected women might display lesions or rashes, but we now know that half of women infected with gonorrhea are asymptomatic and that the initial signs of syphilis can be minimal; therefore, inspection could not really halt the spread of venereal disease. In any case, prostitutes were feared as disease-carriers (see Plate 7).

Prostitutes were also seen as a source of disorder, causing men to fight over their favors. Both written and graphic sources argue that the two most pernicious causes of deadly disputes within the campaign community were gambling and women.[26] Drinking probably played a role in the disputes concerning women, as would the heightened state of carnal desire in an environment of possible imminent death. However, notions

officers' ladies to what appear to be the wives of common soldiers with children in tow. One of these wives brandishes a stick, as if to threaten the prostitute. Forty and Forty, *They Also Served*, p. 214. Across the Atlantic, prostitutes could be paraded through the town to the whores' march. Alfred Young, *Masquerade: The Life and Times of Deborah Sampson, Continental Soldier* (New York: 2004), p. 7.

[25] Warning to the soldiers of the Armée du nord in January 1794, in Bertaud, *La Révolution armée*, p. 198.

[26] See, for example, Wallhausen's account in Haberling, "Army Prostitution and Its Control," p. 35. It appears on page 106 of this chapter.

PLATE 7. Martin Weygel, *The Landsknecht's Whore*, with verse, mid-sixteenth century; as elaborately dressed as she is, she is nonetheless burdened with a pack on her back. The accompanying verse reads:

> If you're not into gluttony and boozing
> I don't want to follow you for long.
> If I stay near you for any length of time
> I'll certainly let you have the "French disease."
> You'll wish you had stayed at home.

She is with one man, so she qualifies as a "whore," but her lack of commitment and her demand for reward give her much the spirit of the prostitute as well. Note the rooster on her shoulder. The rooster symbolizes masculinity and virility. This docile rooster perched on her shoulder suggests that she has tamed and commands the masculinity of her partner(s). For other visual references to a rooster on a woman's shoulder see Plates 12 and 24. The fate of a chicken, rooster, or hen that was pillaged was quite different; see Plate 25. For another use of the rooster as male symbolism, see Plate 9.

Germanisches Nationalmuseum, Nürnberg.

of aggressive masculinity *vis-à-vis* other men and ideals of male dominance and male protection of women were almost certainly factors as well.

"Whores"

Many women in the campaign community were often called prostitutes, whores, or some other disparaging synonym, when they really did not sell sex to multiple partners. Such pejorative words were used as unspecific terms of abuse, for example, a German woodcut depicting a baggage train carried the legend: "Armed in this way, the pitiless soldiers sally forth accompanied by their horses, whores, wagons, and camels."[27] Here it was simply a dismissive term for any woman who followed the camp. However, we need to differentiate between true prostitutes and those women who might not have been married, but who still maintained exclusive relationships with particular men.

Unmarried women having but a single partner made up a very important segment of the campaign community, particularly during the sixteenth and seventeenth centuries, and they deserve to be considered at length. For want of a better term, they will be labeled here as "whores"— expressly enclosed in quotation marks to highlight that this is a special and specific use of the word.[28] To a certain extent, calling them "whores" reflects language usage at the time, as in Plate 7; however, classifying a woman as "whore" in this study does not depend on the evolving meanings of language during the early modern period, but on the actions and relationships of the women discussed.

It could be argued that this label is overly harsh. Other alternatives might be "companion" or "partner," but such terms are too sterile and miss the hard edge of the camp. Besides, prostitutes and wives both could

[27] Johann Theodore de Bry, "Baggage Train with Death," in Keith Moxey, *Peasants, Warriors, and Wives: Popular Imagery in the Reformation* (Chicago: University of Chicago Press, 1989), p. 87, Pl. 4.16.87. See Peter H. Wilson, "German, Women and War, 1500–1800," *War in History*, vol. 3, no. 2 (1996), p. 130, on the common use of derogatory words for camp women.

[28] I am not the first historian to make this kind of differentiation; see, for example, Linda Grant De Pauw, *Battle Cries and Lullabies: Women in War from Prehistory to Present* (University of Oklahoma Press:1988), p. 99, and comments in Hacker and Vining, "The World of Camp and Train: Women's Changing Roles in Early Modern Armies." However, De Pauw seems to imply that the use of the term "whore" for a kind of common law wife was implicit in the language, but the use of contemporary words was looser, and we should not be tied to it. It is enough to define "whore" by what a woman did and thus free oneself from the contemporary meanings of words and the tastes of translators.

be companions and partners in several senses of the word. Still another choice might be "concubine," but this seems too grand for the circumstances, and in the context of both reality and historiography, "concubine" better suits the kept mistresses of wealthy men.[29] The relationship outside formal marriage between a common soldier and his female partner might be called a "free union." While this may serve as a useful term to describe the relationship, it does not supply a handy label for the woman. "Whore" suits the irreverent existence of the camp.

The key point here is that a "whore" attached herself to one man for the long haul or for a shorter, but not fleeting, period of time; Little Ursula of Plate 1 or the Landsknecht's whore of Plate 7 are examples. In this sense, "whores" were not hired; they were possessed, and they had reciprocal claims on their men as well. For example, the articles of war for the German artillery promulgated by Emperor Maximillian II in 1570 stipulated that "no man may possess a whore."[30] A German reformer who wanted to cut down the number of women in the train of an army argued, "A soldier who is without a wife or whore at the time of his induction in the army, [should be] enjoined from acquiring one afterwards."[31] These varied quotations demonstrate that such women were not literally women in common. In the rough world of the camp, such women might choose to change partners in a set of serial relationships, but they focused on one man at a time.

A longer-term relationship between a soldier and a woman provided more than sex, and some soldiers formed *Mainehen*, "May Marriages," which were pragmatic arrangements meant to last for the campaign. Because aggregate contract armies were often dismissed as rapidly as they were formed, a campaign-long agreement would likely be all a

---

[29] Consider such works as Donald Weinstein, *The Captain's Concubine: Love, Honor, and Violence in Renaissance Tuscany* (Baltimore, MD: 2000) and Emlyn Eisenach, *Husbands, Wives, and Concubines: Marriage, Family, and Social Order in Sixteenth-Century Verona* (Kirksville, MO: 2004). However, we find some use of the term in the armies. An imperial code of 1668 banished "mistresses and concubines" from the army. Peter H. Wilson, "German Women and War, 1500–1800," *War in History*, vol. 3, no. 2 (1996), p. 131. Frederick the Great gave long-term relationships between unmarried partners the legal status "Liebsten-Konkubinate" but in Potsdam and Berlin only. This replacement for marriage was seen as a way of preventing prostitution. Beate Engelen, *Soldatenfrauen in Preußen. Eine Strukturanalyse der Garnisonsgesellschaft im späten 17. und 18. Jahrhundert* (Münster: 2004), pp. 114–17.

[30] Haberling, "Army Prostitution and Its Control," p. 40.

[31] "Discourse Pertaining to the Present German Army," in Haberling, "Army Prostitution and Its Control," pp. 41–42.

soldier needed. Dionysius Klein, writing at the end of the sixteenth century, described such liaisons:

[T]he German soldiers, no sooner an expedition arrives, saddle themselves with frivolous and loose women with whom they contract 'May Marriages' whom they drag here and there just as millers do their sacks. The soldiers enhance the situation by pretending that in war they cannot get along without women; they are needed to take care of clothes, equipment and valuables; and in cases of illness, injury or any other personal harm, the women are needed to nurse and take care of them.[32]

However, what Klein dismisses as flimsy rationales when soldiers argue "that in war they cannot get along without women" turn out to be serious matters, as we shall see in Chapter III.

"Whores" could enjoy legal status in the army. Earlier regulations awarded the right of inheritance to soldiers' female partners. "Whores" with the army might even have precedence over legal wives left at home.[33] But the status of "whores" declined over the decades. Regulations and ordinances technically directed against prostitutes were often phrased to effect "whores" above all. The 1656 "Brandenberg Military Law and Article Letter" issued by the Great Elector stated: "No whores are to be tolerated in camp or garrison, but should there be an individual who wants to keep his with him, he must marry her honorably and he will then be on the same free footing as a man who wishes to have his lawful wife with him."[34] In 1673, the Great Elector took another tack to eliminate "whores," ordering that any woman who lived with a soldier and participated in a campaign with him became his wife de facto; thus, he simply declared long-term "whores" to be wives.[35] An imperial code of 1668 banished "mistresses and concubines," and a Württemberg code issued in 1700 branded all unmarried women as *gaile Dirnen*, or lascivious prostitutes.[36]

When faced with the alternative of leaving their "whores" or marrying them, many soldiers chose marriage. Wallshausen told a story of a commander of the early seventeenth century who tried to rid his army of its female camp followers by announcing that he would flog any man

---

[32] Klein in Haberling, "Army Prostitution and Its Control," p. 32. See also the discussion of May Marriages in Baumann, *Landsknechte*, pp. 157–59; Wilson, "German Women and War," p. 134.

[33] Reinhard Baumann, *Landsknechte* (Munich: 1994) pp. 154–56, 161–62; Wilson, "German Women and War," p. 130.

[34] In Haberling, "Army Prostitution and Its Control," p. 43.

[35] Engelen, *Soldatenfrauen in Preußen*, p. 112.

[36] Wilson, "German, Women and War, 1500–1800," p. 131.

who was accompanied by a woman who was not his wife. In response, his soldiers dispersed to find churches and willing clergy, because the women were too useful to the men to be abandoned. "In two days 800 prostitutes, including some most miserable creatures, became duly wedded wives."[37]

Wives

Debates over soldier marriage revolved around two criteria: propriety and efficiency. Marriage won out as the more moral type of relationship between men and women, and because military authorities condemned prostitutes and "whores" and excluded them from camps. This movement toward propriety increased markedly during the seventeenth century, as Reformation and Counter-Reformation views on women and marriage led military authorities to privilege wives. Yet although camps were eventually open to soldiers' wives alone, this did not necessarily mean that armies encouraged their troops to marry or that all wives were allowed to accompany their husbands on campaign. The number of soldier marriages varied from army to army, as some regimes were far less tolerant than others. Adoption of permissive or prohibitive standards came down to the good of the army and the state. But every major army, whatever its policy toward soldier marriage, limited the number of wives that could accompany the troops on campaign after 1650; this was a matter of sheer military efficiency.

Sixteenth- and early seventeenth-century military writers and field commanders took a variety of stands on soldier marriage and the presence of wives in camp. In 1585, the earl of Leicester's disciplinary code may have excluded "vagrant idle women" from the army and permitted only lawful wives, but Leicester was no fan of soldier marriage. In fact, he pleaded with Walsingham in 1586 not to send him any more married soldiers.[38] Yet certain military commentators during the era of the aggregate contract army, with its reliance on mercenary soldier bands, accepted that troops should come equipped not only with weapons but with wives and "whores." Marshal Fabert, who practiced his trade during the French war with Spain (1635–59), advised that when hiring foreign troops, it was best to have them bring their wives with them "in

---

[37] Wallhausen, *Defensio patriae* (1621), in Haberling, "Army Prostitution and Its Control," p. 43.
[38] Hale, *War and Society in Renaissance Europe*, p. 107.

order that they will not desert to go rejoin them."[39] As stated at the start of this study, Walhaussen warned that German bands were likely to bring with them more women and children than fighting men. By all accounts, Germans were the most likely to be accompanied by large numbers of women. As one would-be contemporary reformer commented, "Other nations ... than the Germans such as Italians, Spaniards, French do not have so large a woman-load."[40]

Yet there was no denying that large numbers of noncombatants posed problems for efficiency in movement and supply. Those who might favor a small number of women "in common" could advocate prostitutes precisely to avoid the problems imposed by carrying along numerous wives and "whores." Thus, Simonne advised: "Let the captain do whatever he can to keep his men from marrying ... because of the great impediments that [women] bring both on campaign and in garrison."[41]

Some writers speculated on whether the presence of wives made soldiers fight harder, or if they were a distraction. The idealistic Thomas More hypothesized that in his ideal society, wives were encouraged to go to war with their husbands because this would cause men, and their women, to fight harder, driven by "the greatest zeal for assisting one another."[42] The immensely practical and successful Hapsburg commander, Raimondo Montecuccoli (1609–80) also believed that that married men fought better so as not to be dishonored in their wives' eyes.[43] In contrast, Blaise de Montluc (1502–77) argued that married

---

[39] Fabert, *Mémoires* in Babeau, *La vie militaire*, 1:201. Vauban would later share Fabert's belief that marriage could limit desertion. Albert Rochas d'Aiglun, *Vauban, sa famille et ses écrits*, 2 vols. (Paris: 1910), 1:340–41. Yet, in one Prussian case, after the battle of Zorndorf, widespread desertion thinned the ranks of East Prussian troops who had left their wives and children back home. Christopher Duffy, *Russia's Military Way to the West: Origins and Nature of Russian Military Power, 1700–1800* (London: 1981), p. 90.

[40] "Discourse Pertaining to the Present German Army" in Haberling, "Army Prostitution and Its Control," pp. 41–42.

[41] Mathieu de la Simonne, *L'Alphabet du soldat* (1623), p. 53, in Babeau, *La vie militaire*, 1:203–04. Robert Monro, a Scottish mercenary officer who wrote in the 1630s, also argued that wives should not accompany their husbands on campaign, because they would be a distraction. Mary Elizabeth Ailes, "Camp Followers, Sutlers, and Soldiers' Wives: Women in Early Modern Armies (c. 1450–c. 1650)," *A Companion to Women's Military History*, Barton C. Hacker and Margaret Vining, eds. (Leiden: 2010). I benefited much from this paper and followed several leads that it gave me.

[42] More, *Utopia*, Book II, Chapter 7, "Of their Military Discipline," on line at http://www.constitution.org/tm/utop2-7.htm.

[43] Tallett, *War and Society*, p. 133.

PLATE 8. Louis-Joseph Watteau, *Un grenadier prenant congé de sa maitresse,*
1766. The sentimental tenderness between man, woman, and child, as well as the
child's age, speak of marriage. Characteristically, the grenadier must leave his
woman behind as the marches off with his regiment. For another sentimentalized
view of soldiers' family life in the eighteenth century, see Plate 13.

> Bibliothèque National de France, Estampes et Photographie.

men were less likely to risk themselves in battle than were their single
comrades, and his was the more common opinion.[44] Montluc cautioned
that the pursuit of women was ill-suited to life on campaign: "Leave love

---

[44] Tallett, *War and Society*, pp. 133, and 274, n94.

hanging when Mars is on campaign. You will have enough time for it later."[45]

Taking all these arguments and counter-arguments into consideration throws into question Barton Hacker's assertion that "[M]ilitary policy had not much to do with marriage before 1650."[46] It might be more accurate to say that until the formation of the more regularized state commission army, it is hard to identify any general state military policy at all in the modern sense, but it is evident that soldier marriage was a matter of concern among military practitioners and commentators well before 1650. Military reforms after that date explicitly regulated the relationships between soldiers and their women. Writing in 1670–71, the experienced Scottish soldier, Sir James Turner, reflected the now universal insistence on marriage. Turner divided the women following armies into three classes and then concluded that "Among all these kinds of Women in well order'd Armies, there are none but those who are married. If there be any else, upon examination made by the Minister, Priest, or Consistory, they are put away with ignomity, at least should be conformable to all Articles of War."[47] As states and armies criminalized camp prostitution, rejected free unions, and privileged marriage in the era of the state commission army, they asserted greater control over their soldiers' lives.

Beate Engelen provides the most extensive study of early modern soldier marriage in her *Soldatenfrauen in Preußen*.[48] In his 1656 articles of war, Frederick William, the Great Elector of Brandenberg, allowed soldiers to marry and bring wives into the field and reside with them in garrison, but he formally excluded prostitutes and "whores." Later, in 1669, he instituted support payments to wives left behind when their husbands went on campaign. As mentioned previously, in 1673 he converted long-term "whores" into wives. But in the early 1680s, he began to restrict soldier marriage, limiting the number of soldiers per company who could marry to a total of thirty or forty and giving captains authority to decide who could marry in their companies. His son, Frederick I (r. 1688–1713), increased the

---

[45] Blaise de Montluc, *Commentaires de Messire Blaise de Montluc*, ed. P. Corteault (Paris, 1964), p. 29. Tallett, *War and Society*, p. 274, n94, states that in this passage Montluc argues that married men fight with less courage, but Montluc warns that men fight too much over women, and that is the problem.

[46] Hacker, "Women and Military Institutions," p. 659.

[47] Sir James Turner, *Pallas Armata: Military Essayes of the Ancient Grecian, Roman, and Modern Art of War* (New York: Greenwood Press, 1968; facsimile reproduction of 1683 edition published by Richard Criswell), p. 277. See page 110 of this volume concerning the three classes of women.

[48] Engelen, *Soldatenfrauen in Preußen*, pp. 42–65.

difficulty of soldier marriage by allowing only a few married men per company unless a soldier paid his captain the equivalent of three months' pay to gain permission to marry. Frederick William I (r. 1713–40) moderated the soldier marriage policies of his father, guided by Pietist beliefs in the importance of the family and by the realization that soldiers' offspring could be a source of recruitment for the army. Frederick II, the Great (r. 1740–86) reduced restrictions on soldier marriage and praised it "so as to populate the country, and to preserve the stock, which is admirable."[49] Frederick II's army thus multiplied the population of the state while preparing to defend it. This fit particularly well with the Prussian canton system established in 1733, which created a native reserve force that could be mobilized in wartime.[50] During peacetime, these troops stayed at home to work the land except for two months of the year when they drilled with their regiments. Such men were encouraged to raise families.

Several lesser German states mirrored the evolving Brandenberg-Prussian policies. In 1682 Hessen-Kassel stipulated that common soldiers must get the permission of their officers to marry, and by 1700 most German states had adopted similar restrictions.[51] Soldiers who married without permission could suffer severe penalties. By the mid-eighteenth century, the majority of German armies required such culprits to run a gauntlet of 200 soldiers twelve to twenty-four times, while being beaten by the troops forming the gauntlet. The unfortunate brides were to serve a minimum sentence of one year in a workhouse.[52] Yet as the eighteenth century progressed, German states tended toward more liberalized marriage policies and adopted versions of the canton system.

It is still important to realize that marriage policies varied, and that among them, the French marriage regulations were quite restrictive.[53] The

---

[49] Frederick the Great, *Political Testament* (1768), p. 86 in Duffy, *The Army of Frederick the Great*, p. 60. Interestingly, Frederick did not discourage officers from marrying. Marriage distracted officers from their duties, and officers' widows could request pension, p. 46.

[50] The latest interpretation of the canton system is Martin Winter, *Untertanengeist durch Miliärpflicht? Das preussiche Kantonverfassung in brandenburischen Stäten in 18. Jahrhundert* (Bielefeld: 2005).

[51] Wilson, "German Women and War, 1500–1800," p. 136. In the Austrian service, the colonel had extensive rights dating back to 1508, and these included his right to sanction marriages for soldiers and NCOs through the mid-eighteenth century. Christopher Duffy, *The Army of Maria Theresa: The Armed Forces of Imperial Austria, 1740–1780* (New York: 1979), p. 32.

[52] Wilson, "German Women and War, 1500–1800," p. 136.

[53] See as well the more restrictive regulations in the Piedmontese army, and the way in which soldiers could and did subvert them. Sabina Loriga, *Soldats – Un laboratoire disciplinaire: l'armée piémontaise au XVIIIe siècle* (Paris: 2007), p. 46–47.

reformed army of Louis XIV limited the ability of soldiers to marry and treated marriage almost as crime. Besides demanding that private soldiers gain the officers' permission to wed, the ordinances of 1685, 1686, and 1691 also imposed penalties. Even with permission, a soldier lost all his seniority, which would begin to accrue again only from the moment of the marriage.[54] The 1686 ordinance condemned marriage because "the needs of their wives and of their children inhibit" soldiers, and it particularly railed against those who married young.[55] In contrast to regulations, Vauban argued for allowing soldiers to marry if they were stable men with a profession to help augment their military pay.[56] Authorities did not want troops to become too attached to the local population, either because troops might be required to repress civil disorder or because local contacts made desertion easier; therefore, regulations forbade soldiers to marry women from the towns in which the troops were garrisoned. This restriction applied to officers as well.[57]

Statistics show the decline of marriage in the French army from the mid-seventeenth century through the early eighteenth. According to research by Chaboche, among *invalides* who had served in the Thirty Years' War and who listed their family condition, 45.9 percent had been or were married.[58] But of the men admitted to the Hôtel des invalides between 1674 and 1691, only 21 percent were married, and of those admitted in 1715, 16 percent had wives. These figures probably overstate the average, since veterans with many years of service and sergeants, the very men most likely to marry, were also more likely to gain the highly valued places at the Invalides. The same statistical sample reveals that those who married were most likely to choose women from their own regions, that is, a girl from home rather than someone they met while in the army.[59] The royal government would

---

[54] Babeau, *La vie militaire*, 1:205; Contamine, *Histoire militaire*, 1:403; *Ordonnances militaires du roy de France*, 2 vols. (Luxembourg: 1734–35), 171–72.

[55] Ordinance of 6 April 1686 in Corvisier, *L'armée française*, 2:757.

[56] Albert Rochas d'Aiglun, *Vauban, sa famille et ses écrits*, 2 vols. (Paris: 1910), 1:340–41.

[57] A 15 December 1681 ordinance forbade army chaplains to marry any soldier to any woman who lived in the town where his regiment was in garrison, and a 1 February 1685 ordinance denied any officer the right to marry any woman who resided in or within ten leagues of his garrison without the express approval of an inspector. *Ordonnances militaires*, 171–72.

[58] Chaboche, "Les soldats français de la Guerre de Trente Ans," p. 18. Vauban reported that in earlier times, i.e., the Thirty Years' War, the La Ferté regiment contained 700 to 800 married men. Rochas d'Aiglun, *Vauban, sa famille et ses écrits*, 1:340–41.

[59] Contamine, *Histoire militaire*, 1:446.

continue to restrict soldier marriages until the French Revolution over-turned that policy.

In contrast to French practice, the more permissive Prussian policies under Frederick the Great resulted in much higher percentages of married soldiers.[60] The Knobloch regiment had 1,077 women and 1,925 children in 1751, meaning that 61.5 percent of its soldiers were married.[61] Roughly one-third of the soldiers in the Berlin garrison were married during peacetime from the 1770s into the early 1800s with about 7,000 to 9,000 children. Considering the entire electorate of Brandenberg, this proportion stood higher, at 38.8 percent of 34,861 troops in 1790 and 43 percent of 28,163 in 1800. The pattern of marriage in the Prince Heinrich Regiment indicates that soldiers married less during wartime years and rushed to the altar almost immediately when peace returned, as they did in 1748 when 148 soldiers married, 1764 when 188 soldiers married, and 1780 when 123 soldiers married.[62]

Lesser German states mirrored the Prussian experience to some extent. For example, the percentage of married troops in Württemburg notably increased after the War of the Austrian Succession, and in Frankfurt the portion of married troops doubled from one- third in 1733 to two-thirds in 1753.[63] Interestingly, German states were likely to oppose the marriage of officers, because the cost of pensions to their widows would have been prohibitive.[64] It is often stated, as Ulinka Rublack comments,

[60] See the tables concerning soldier marriage and wives in Engelen, *Soldatenfrauen in Preußen*, pp. 79, 89, 90, 155, 175, 176, 177, 263, 462, 494, 496, 566, 567, and 571. The figures used in this paragraph come from p. 90, "Percentage of married soldiers of all those living in the electorate"; p. 566, "Number of marriages in the Prince Heinrich Regiment"; and p. 569, "Military population in several garrisons and regiments." The great majority of her figures come from the late eighteenth century.

[61] Wilson, *German Women and War*, p. 144, gives different figures for the Knoblock regiment in 1751, concluding that 79.2 percent of the soldiers were married. He gives the same number for wives, but must figure a lower number of soldiers for the regiment. He also differs on some other calculations. I have used the Engelen tables here because they are more recent scholarship. However, it is valuable to consult Wilson's tables, pp. 141–44.

[62] Owing to incomplete numbers for the Wars of the Austrian Succession and the Seven Years' War, the clearest contrast comes from the minor War of the Bavarian Succession, 1778–79. The regiment saw seventy-two marriages in 1776 and 85 in 1777 before the war, but these numbers dropped to 36 and 43 during the conflict, spiking up to 123 in 1780 only to decrease to a pre-war level of 87 in 1781. Engelen, *Soldatenfrauen in Preußen*, p. 566–67. There is also a rise in marriage from 1791 to 1793 which does not fit this pattern.

[63] Wilson, "German Women and War," p. 145.

[64] Wilson, "German Women and War," pp. 137–38.

"soldiers were almost never permitted to marry," but the percentage of German married troops does not support such a conclusion across the board.[65] Of course, the above figures on the prevalence of soldier marriage impacted garrison and rural life, not the campaign community, which restricted the number of accompanying women.

Although often restrictive through the eighteenth century, British regulations became more generous toward soldier marriage during the Napoleonic Wars. From the mid-1600s, English regulations required that soldiers gain permission to marry from their officers, who were to inquire into the suitability of the women in question. Many a commander echoed the sentiments of James Wolfe, the hero of Quebec, who cautioned his regiment garrisoned in Scotland, "The Officers are desired to discourage Matrimony amongst the men as much as possible." But his rationale, that "the Service suffers by the multitude of Women already in the Regiment," admits that marriage was still common.[66] As late as 1795, British cavalry regulations still insisted "Marriage is to be discouraged as much as possible. Officers must explain to the men of the many miseries that women are exposed to, and by every sort of persuasion they must prevent their marrying if possible."[67]

The reform era associated with the Duke of York, who became commander-in-chief of the British Army in 1798, brought a change in attitude within British regiments. The 1801 article regulating marriage and wives with the Corps of Riflemen at Shorncliffe began by affirming: "The Marriage of soldiers being a matter of benefit to a regiment."[68] However, a more open policy toward allowing soldiers to marry did not increase the number of wives allowed to accompany the troops. Because the British fought overseas, wives who shipped out with troops were carried on the books at state expense; they were "wives on the strength"

---

[65] Ulinka Rublack, "Wench and Maiden: Women, War and the Pictorial Function of the Feminine in German Cities in the Early Modern Period," trans. Pamela Selwyn, *History Workshop Journal*, 44 (January 1997), p. 12. In fairness, I should say that, because my studies were centered on France for much of my career, I reached and stated the same conclusion.

[66] Wolfe, in Noel T. St. John Williams, *Judy O'Grady and the Colonel's Lady: The Army Wife and Camp Follower Since 1660* (London: 1988), p. 12. See as well the advice offered by Bennet Cuthbertson, *A System for the Compleat Interior Management and Oeconomy of a Battalion of Infantry* (Dublin: 1768), pp. 192–94.

[67] Regulation in Carol Whitfield, "Tommy Atkins' Family," *Bulletin of the Association for Preservation Technology* 5, no. 4 (1973), p. 65

[68] Riflemen regulation in Hacker, "Women and Military Institutions," p. 660. This order has been oft-quoted; see St. John Williams, *Judy O'Grady*, p. 19, and J. F. C. Fuller, *Sir John Moore's System of Training* (London: 1924).

and British practice was to limit this number. This was an old policy. In 1703, the Lord Lieutenant of Ireland explained that he had to dispatch four women per company with troops sailing for Portugal, "which is the least that has been permitted and cannot be avoided."[69] Numbers could be more, or less, restrictive depending on circumstances. In his 1764 American campaign, Henry Bouquet cut the number of women who could march with his column to one woman for each unit and two nurses for the column's hospital.[70] Although the number permitted to go with their men on campaign varied, six wives per hundred men was a common standard.[71] This was, in fact, the number set for all British troops by the duke of York in his order of 29 October 1800; women not permitted to sail with their regiment were to be given funds to return home.[72] This led to the painful matter of choosing which wives could accompany their husbands. Selection could be made by lot, throwing dice on a drumhead. Once a woman shipped over, she was likely to remain in the married state one way or another as long as she survived— in other words, widows did not stay widows for long. Lieutenant William Gratton reported, "When a man was shot, and his wife was a capable and desirable person, she would receive half a dozen proposals before her husband was 48 hours in the grave."[73] Women were wise to remarry in order to retain their regimental rations and support.

In all armies, the necessity of choosing only a restricted number of regimental wives to accompany the troops on campaign was the natural product of the moral policy of privileging marriage and the dictates of military efficiency that limited the number of women with a state commission army in the field. Vauban wrote of marriage as a way of limiting desertion, because soldiers would want to return to their wives in winter quarters, but he argued that the wives would not be a hindrance in war,

[69] Lord Lieutenant of Ireland to the Secretary of State in St. John Williams, *Judy O"Grady*, p. 11.

[70] Scott Hendrix, "In the Army: Women, Camp Followers and Gender Roles in the British Army in the French and Indian Wars, 1755–1765," in *A Soldier and A Woman: Sexual Integration in the Military*, ed. Gerard J. DeGroot and Corinna Peniston-Bird (New York: 2000), p. 33.

[71] For a survey of counts of women with the British Army serving in America during the War of the American Revolution, see Don N. Hagist, "The Women of the British Army in America," a series of four brief articles published in *The Brigade Dispatch* (1993–95), now available on the internet at http://www.revwar75.com/library/hagist/britwomen. htm#110.

[72] St. John Williams, *Judy O'Grady*, p. 17.

[73] Gratton in David Cordingly, *Heroines & Harlots: Women at Sea in the Great Age of Sail* (London: 2002), p. 105.

since "one took along on campaign only three or four women per company," which in a standard fifty-man company meant six to eight wives per hundred men.[74] Frederick the Great only permitted five to twelve wives per company to accompany the troops in the field, even though the number of married Prussian troops was very high.[75] During the mid-eighteenth century, the Austrians allowed three to five wives per company, but later they would adopt the most restrictive policy of all, when a 1775 regulation banned all soldiers' wives from accompanying the army in the field.[76] Such a restriction could not have eliminated women who performed functional duties, such as sutlers.

A painful irony arose as armies banned prostitutes but privileged wives—these same wives could slip into prostitution. Because soldiers earned such meager salaries, wives in garrison were forced to supplement family income through their own labor, usually in low-paying jobs. Hard times compelled some to turn to prostitution, as was the case among some Prussian soldiers' wives.[77] This phenomenon occurred elsewhere as well; Loriga states that Piedmontese soldier wives also did so when in garrison.[78] Army wives that were left behind when the troops went on campaign found themselves particularly vulnerable. In 1714, the last year of the War of the Spanish Succession, complaints were lodged against nine soldiers' wives who were brazening soliciting by a Paris city gate. Authorities did not arrest them, however, out of consideration for their circumstances, because their husbands were away on campaign.[79] It is perhaps even more unfortunate that daughters of soldiers were all too likely to turn to prostitution as well, at least in Prussia. A 1717 inspection of the Berlin prostitution section and brothels revealed that the largest percentage of girls working the trade were actually the daughters of soldiers in this garrison town.[80]

When on campaign, desperation and starvation could drive army wives and widows to offer sex for food. After the battle of Talavera in 1809 the British forces were in bad straits to provision themselves.

---

[74] Rochas d'Aiglun, *Vauban, sa famille et ses écrits*, 1:340–41.
[75] Duffy, *The Army of Frederick the Great*, p. 59.
[76] Duffy, *The Army of Maria Theresa*, p. 57.
[77] Engelen, *Soldatenfrauen in Preußen*, pp. 156–58.
[78] Sabina Loriga, *Soldats – Un laboratoire disciplinaire: l'armée piémontaise au XVIIIe siècle* (Paris: 2007), p. 46.
[79] Philip F. Riley, *A Lust for Virtue*, p. 66.
[80] Haberling, "Army Prostitution and Its Control," p. 53, and Duffy, *The Army of Frederick the Great*, p. 60. Obviously the closing of Berlin brothels by Frederick I was short-lived.

A commissary officer reported that soldiers' wives dressed in rags were offering themselves to any man who would give them a half a loaf of bread.[81] Women who lost their soldier husbands on campaign were particularly vulnerable, which explains their willingness to marry again soon after their husband's death.

Marriages for soldiers and their brides most probably followed patterns typical of poorer couples in civilian communities. Camp women could find precedent in practices that were common among their plebian sisters. Women from the countryside who were without the means to supply themselves with dowries often migrated to towns in search of employment, in order to survive and also to accrue the necessary dowries.[82] Such women lived outside their parents' control and chose their own lives and partners, as would most women who married husbands from the campaign community.

There is some amusing but very scanty evidence of special soldier marriage customs among the British. This interesting ceremony attaches the word "whore" to a bride in an English camp wedding. In Farquhar's play, *The Recruiting Officer*, the heroine Silvia, masquerading as a soldier, describes such an event: "our sword, you know, is our honour, that we lay down, the hero jumps over it first, and the amazon after—leap rogue follow whore, the drum beats a riff, and so to bed; that's all, the ceremony is concise."[83] The same brusque kind of marriage is described in *The Life and Adventures of Mrs. Christian Davies*, except that she stipulates that two crossed swords were used, over which the couple leaped at the command "Jump rogue, follow whore."[84]

---

[81] August Schaumann, *On the Road with Wellington. The Diary of a War Commissary in the Peninsular Campaigns* (1924), p. 102, in St. John Williams, *Judy O'Grady*, p. 52.

[82] Hufton, *The Prospect Before Her*, p. 125, and Eisenach, *Husbands, Wives, and Concubines*, p. 75.

[83] Farquhar, *The Recruiting Officer*, p. 79.

[84] *The Life and Adventures of Mrs. Christian Davies, Commonly Called Mother Ross* (London: 1740), p. 261. The authenticity of this work is challenged. Some ascribe it to Daniel Defoe. Should it be in part or in whole invented, the wedding custom may be copied from the Farquhar play. Interestingly, Moxey, *Peasants, Warriors, and Wives*, pp. 36–37, 40–41, and 54, Pls. 3.1, 3.2, and 3.10 presents and discusses three sixteenth-century German woodcuts by Sebald Beham, Barthel Beham, and Johann Theodor de Bry that portray a peasant festival day. Part of the day's activities involve a couple vaulting swords while holding hands. Moxey describes this as "a test of skill" as "a barefoot man leaps over upturned swords," but close inspection shows it to be an act by couples. Perhaps this is meant to be a kind of rough peasant custom to be contrasted with the more formal church wedding also shown in the woodcut. One can only wonder what the relationship between the military and,

Wives generally enjoyed higher status in camp than did prostitutes and "whores," but the higher status of the man to whom a "whore" attached herself could raise her over legitimate wives of lower-status soldiers. In any case, officers' wives were at the top of the hierarchy where her husband's rank determined her position. Mary Elizabeth Ailes demonstrates that officers' wives served as intermediaries between their husbands and other members of the community.[85] They also answered pleas from the plebian men and women of the camp who approached the elite women with the expectation of finding a sympathetic ear. The wife of Swedish commander, Johan Baner, earned the love of her husband's soldiers by accepting and acting on petitions for assistance. Officers' wives could also negotiate with local communities. Such grand roles were beyond the plebian women who are the subjects of this study. Even for them, however, hierarchy and status in camp were matters of concern, and as the partners of soldiers became legal wives, they gained a greater degree of respectability.

WOMEN WITH MEN: UTILITY, AFFECTION, SUPPORT, AND ABUSE

While it is a valuable statistic to tally the numbers of prostitutes, "whores," and wives accompanying early modern military forces, there is more to the story of women in the campaign community. As we try to understand the complex layering of their lives, we see that a major aspect of that complexity lay in their relationships with the men of the community. These relationships were, to a large degree, mutually beneficial in a practical sense, as women and men together faced the challenges of survival on campaign. But they were emotional relationships as well; affection and caring bound these men and women together so they could offer each other psychological support to overcome the hardship and brutality of war. There was also a darker side, for women often faced the threat of violence at the hands of their partners and from military authorities.

That women clearly were of utility to the campaign community and to the men within it is the central argument of this volume. In a sense, the

---

perhaps, peasant ceremony has to do with jumping the broomstick in African-American weddings.

[85] See the discussion of the roles played by officers' wives in Ailes, "Camp Followers, Sutlers, and Soldiers' Wives."

bargain between a prostitute and her customer was the ultimate pragmatic accommodation. Of greater interest, however, were the contributions of women to mutual welfare and to the exchanges of aid and service. These contributions are the focus of Chapter III where they will be more fully explored. Yet to reduce relationships to *quid pro quo* arrangements robs them of their human richness.

Women within the campaign community were certainly sexual partners, but many were also life partners, in short-term arrangements or long-term commitments. It would be foolish and arrogant to deny the roles of affection, dependence, dominance, and possession in their lives. Men and women in the campaign community were attracted to one another and raised families during wartime just as during peacetime. Sixteenth-century woodcut artists frequently displayed Landsknechts and Reisläufers accompanied by their women. Such portraits of pairs, as shown in Plates 1 and 20, often express mutual support and affection of the couples, such as one in which a Landsknecht and woman walk hand-in-hand.[86] Historian Geoffrey Parker argues that the prevalence of marriage among Spanish troops in The Netherlands during the early seventeenth century helped to form "a self-contained, inward-looking, almost inbred military society in the Spanish Netherlands, independent of the local population."[87]

In his diary, Peter Hagendorf repeatedly wrote of his wife and family with great feeling. He entered service in 1625, first with the Venetians, then with Papenheim's imperial cavalry on the Catholic side, then with the Protestant Swedes, and finally back with the imperials. He eventually rose to company commander in 1636, after being a soldier, corporal, and sergeant. His first wife and their four children were in the combat zone, and he was very shaken by their deaths: the children passed away in

---

[86] Georg Hirth, *Picture Book of the Graphic Arts, 1500–1800 (Kulturgeschichtliches Bilderbuch aus drei Jahrhunderten, hrsg. Georg Hirth)*, 6 vols. (New York: Benjamin Blom, 1972), vol. 2, Pl. 728. In addition see three versions of what one source presents as "Ursula and the Cobler": Hirth, *Picture book of the graphic arts*, vol. 1, Pl. 203; Walter L. Strauss, *The German Single-Leaf Woodcut, 1550–1600*, 3 vols. (New York: 1975), vol. 3, p. 1072; and Moxey, *Peasants, Warriors, and Wives*, p. 91, Pl. 4.19. See also field cook and wife in Walter L. Strauss, *The German Single-Leaf Woodcut, 1550–1600*, 3 vols. (New York: 1975), vol. 3, p. 1071; one-legged Landsknecht and wife in Strauss, *The German Single-Leaf Woodcut*, vol. 3, p. 1076; Landsknecht and sutler, in Walter Markov and Heinz Helmert, *Battles of World History*, trans. C. S. V. Salt (New York: 1979), p. 179; Landsknecht tailor and seamstress, Strauss, *The German Single-Leaf Woodcut, 1550–1600*, vol. 3, p. 1075; and baker and woman, in Strauss, *The German Single-Leaf Woodcut*, vol. 3, p. 1079.

[87] Parker, *The Army of Flanders*, p. 175.

succession and his wife died in 1633. He remarried in 1635 and again was emotionally invested in his new family. His diary contains repeated and tender commentaries on his family life in the army. At one point he uses the Flight to Egypt of Joseph, Mary, and Jesus as a biblical metaphor, explaining that in 1641, his second wife was so ill that he "led her on the horse. I came here like Joseph traveling into Egypt."[88]

Drawings by the Antoine Watteau and his nephew Louis-Joseph Watteau echo this reference to the Flight from Egypt.[89] Although this exemplifies the practice by artists to use common and familar motifs, the portrayal of a military family in this way, analogous to an idyllic family, is still illuminating. Endowing the lives and actions of contemporary soldiers with positive religious imagery may illustrate the rising status of soldiers. As will be seen in Chapter III, artwork portraying seventeenth-century pillage referenced the massacre of the innocents to demonstrate the depravity of the soldiery. Depicting a soldier and his woman and child in a scene equated with the Holy Family represents a different attitude, particularly when one takes into account the emphasis on the Holy Family as a moral guide in the literature of the Counter-Reformation.[90]

The sentimentality of the mid- and late-eighteenth century was also reflected in representations of affectionate soldier families (see Plates 8 and 13 for idealizations of family life). This may have also resulted from the fact that by that time, the women permitted by regulations to be with soldiers were more likely to be wives than casual liaisons. Mary May, whose petition began this chapter, pleaded that she loved her "poor husband," and who can doubt her testimony?[91]

[88] Hagendorf, *Ein Soeldnerleben im Dreissigjaehrigen Krieg*, p. 99, in Mortimer, *Eyewitness Accounts*, p. 34. He used another Biblical metaphor to describe getting his son and taking him off to be schooled: "Until Munich I carried him, from Munich I let him ride ... he was five years and nine months as I fetched him out of Egypt." Peter Hagendorf, *Ein Soeldnerleben im Dreissigjaehrigen Krieg*, in Mortimer, *Eyew itness Accounts*, p. 241.

[89] See a graphic interpretation of the Flight from Egypt theme applied to a soldier family by Louis-Joseph Watteau, *La Conduite d'une vivanière*, which portrays a soldier leading a donkey bearing a woman who wears a broad-brimmed hat that mimics a halo as she cradles a baby. Maës, *Les Watteau de Lille*, p. 175, Pl. LP 6. I have seen another form of this drawing and engraving attributed to both Jean-Antoine Watteau and to his nephew, who may simply have copied it. The common artistic theme of a man leading a woman and child on a donkey or horse appears again in Louis-Joseph Watteau's, "Soldats en marche," ca. 1770–80. Maës, *Les Watteau de Lille*, pp. 50, Pl. LD 52 and 328, LD 52.

[90] See, for example, the brief discussion in Perry, *Gender and Disorder in Early Modern Seville*, p. 60, and Hufton, *The Prospect Before Her*, p. 41.

[91] See also a poignant scene of British camp life in 1707 drawn by Marcellus Laroon, a valuable witness because he was a soldier. Corelli Barnett, *The First Churchill: Marlborough, Soldier and Statesman* (New York: 1974), pp. 230–31. A soldier is hung in

Other touching instances come from the British experience in the Napoleonic Wars. As already demonstrated, the quota of wives allowed to accompany their husbands left many behind. Joseph Donaldson of the 94th Regiment tells of a fellow soldier's pregnant wife who, after being excluded, attempted to march the six miles from the barracks to the wharf, hoping to be allowed to go with him, but she and her newborn child "never made it." The grief-stricken husband rarely spoke again and perished in the Penninsula.[92] Rifleman Harris tells another sad tale concerning the retreat to Coronna in 1808–09:

> Toward the dusk of the evening of this day I remember passing a man and woman lying clasped in each other's arms, and dying in the snow. I knew them both; but it was impossible to help them. They belonged to the Rifles, and were man and wife ... [A]s he had not been in good health previously, himself and wife had been allowed to get on in the best way they could in the front. They had, however, now given in, and the last we ever saw of poor Sitdown and his wife was on that night lying perishing in each other's arms in the snow.[93]

Camp women also offered their soldier partners another dimension of psychological support as well. Although the historical sources of this information do not permit any more than speculation on this, it seems reasonable to assume that the presence of women and families helped soldiers cope with the stress of early modern campaigning. The horrors of warfare as conducted by aggregate contract armies arose not only from battle but also from pillage, which seems to have reached its brutal apogee during the Thirty Years' War. As hardened as they may have seemed, many troops must have engaged in acts that filled them with revulsion and anguish.

Recent studies of twentieth- and twenty-first century veterans pose an important question for historians of earlier eras. We now know that the

---

camp for desertion; among the small crowd gathered for the execution stands a woman with two children, her head bowed in grief and tears. One can imagine that she was the condemned soldier's friend, perhaps even his partner. The sketch displays both the brutality and the compassion of life within the campaign community.

[92] Donaldson, *Recollections of the Eventful Life of a Soldier* (1845) in St. JohnWilliams, *Judy O'Grady*, p. 19. See as well the touching parting scenes as Hessian troops left home to journey to fight for George III and the revolutionary Americans. "Disconsolate mothers, lamenting wives and weeping children followed the regiment in the crowds, and impressed on us most sensibly the whole of this sad scene." Rodney Atwood, *The Hessians: Mercenaries from Hessen-Kassel in the American Revolution* (Cambridge: 1980), pp. 37–38.

[93] Benjamin Harris, *Recollections of Rifleman Harris, as Told to Henry Curling*, ed. Christopher Hibbert (Hamden, CT: 1970), pp. 82–83.

trauma of warfare imposes destructive short- and long-term stress on combatants. During the American Civil War, the psychological crises associated with combat went by the name of "soldier's heart"; "shell shock" was the term used during World War I and "combat fatigue" during World War II. Today the immediate effects are called "combat stress reaction," while those that plague veterans some time after the event are called "post-traumatic distress syndrome" (PTSD). Critics of the Vietnam War saw a specific link between PTSD and the contentious political environment of that war; however, that seems much too narrow a view.

Australian military studies of veterans who fought in a much broader range of twentieth-century conflicts suggest that PTSD is a product of military conflicts themselves, not the special circumstances of the Vietnam War.[94] World War II veterans displayed the same symptoms, although they were loath to admit such "unmanly" reactions to combat. Aussies who fought in Korea may have suffered from PTSD in higher percentages than those who fought in Vietnam, and even soldiers committed to the high-minded tasks of peacekeeping deployments experienced the same problems.

One researcher, Kristy Muir, goes even further arguing that the most important causes of PTSD were not the political circumstances or the violence of actual combat *per se*, but "the level of fear and the potential threat which affected service personnel."[95] Such a statement has great implications for the study of military history across time. During the early modern era, living conditions for soldiers and their companions were appalling, medical treatment rudimentary at best, and the specter of death everywhere. In fact, death was a common theme of commentaries and art of that period. Monro, the Scottish mercenary wrote, "Here we needed no dead mans pawe before us, to minde us of Death, when Death

---

[94] Rosalind Hearder, "The Legacy of Memories: the Australian Military and Post-Traumatic Stress Disorder," paper delivered at the meeting of the Australian Historical Association, July 2006; Kristy Muir, "Uncovering the hidden consequences of the war: oral histories of Australian psychiatric casualties," paper delivered at the meeting of the Australian Historical Association, July 2006. I would like to express my thanks to Ros, Kristy, and Damien Fenton for sharing their knowledge with me and for sending me materials. Recent works by the Australian government include *Australian Gulf War Veterans' Health Study*, 3 vols. (2003) and *Australian Veterans of the Korean War Health Study* (2005). See also George Kearney *et al.* (eds.), Military Stress and Performance: *The Australian Defence Force Experience* (Melbourne: 2003).

The Australians will soon produce a new health study of their Vietnam War veterans which will greatly revise the 1997 study.

[95] Kristy Muir, "The Hidden Cost of War: The Psychological Effects of The Second World War and Indonesian Confrontation on Australian Veterans and their Families," Ph.D. dissertation, University of Wollongong, 2003, p. 344.

it selfe never went night or day with his horror from our eyes, sparing none, making no difference of persons, or quality, but *aequo pede*, treading alike on all came in his way, whose houre was come."[96]

There is some evidence that combat stress wore down men in the early modern era, much as we know it did later. Geoffrey Parker speaks of Spanish troops suffering from "*el mal de corazòn*," sickness of the heart, which he interprets as "a sort of shell-shock or deep despair" and a condition reported as "to be broken" which forced authorities to discharge the men.[97] If Kristy Muir's analysis is correct, women exposed to the dangers of the combat zone would also have been subject to similar reactions even if they did not carry weapons in battle. The campaign community had to deal with the suffering of its women as well as its men.

Women and men of the campaign community probably offered each other a depth of understanding and support that no civilian could provide. In formal and informal surveys, modern veterans make it clear that only someone who has been on campaign could truly know the stresses, fears, and horrors of that experience.[98] It is entirely reasonable to assume, then, that this argument is also applicable to those who campaigned in past centuries.

INVERSION, THE BATTLE FOR THE PANTS, AND VIOLENCE AS AN ARBITER

While it would be callous to deny affection and mutual support, it would be naïve to deny the presence of gendered violence within the campaign community. Consider a working hypothesis that women were very likely the targets of violence from their partners and from military authorities for three related causes. First, the women of the camp by necessity had to adopt masculine traits to survive; that is, their values and actions had to overlap with contemporary concepts of masculinity. Living in the border zone of masculinity, they raised the specter of the kind of gender inversion pictured so commonly in popular culture. Second, while their

---

[96] R. Monro, *Monro, His Expedition with the Worthy Scots Regiment Called Mac-Keys*, ed. William S. Brockington (Westport, CT: 1999), p. 79.

[97] Parker, *The Army of Flanders*, p. 169

[98] For example, after his return home in 2005, a U.S. Marine from a reserve company that had suffered horrendous casualties in Iraq insisted that only men who endured what he had endured could understand him: "Right now, I need to be with people who have the experience. You know, all three of us who live in our house are combat vets, and, ah, you know that's what's helping me, having them around, having them close." Lance Corporal Travis Williams, 3/25 Marines, in the documentary *Combat Diary: The Marines of Lima Company*.

hard life demanded that camp women demonstrate masculine virtues, this did not win them power. They certainly had agency as women, but this did not flow from their largely impotent masculinity. Third, the popular culture of the sixteenth and seventeenth centuries counseled men to use violence against their female partners to maintain proper dominance. Violence would be all the more justified when large numbers women posed a threat to proper order and deference. Gender is about power, and physical force became a tool of male dominion and honor.

Gender stereotypes must have determined many dynamics of relationships and life within the campaign community in a unique way. I use the speculative language of "must have" because we lack significant data here, and must construct a case based on impressionistic evidence glued together with reasonable supposition, and I emphasize "reasonable." Concepts of femininity by nature had to diverge from stereotype in the campaign community. Women on campaign lived both inside and outside the accepted parameters of womanly propriety and activity. They necessarily exemplified certain masculine characteristics and inhabited a masculine sphere, even when they performed gender-defined "women's work." The trying conditions of life on campaign demanded that women who accompanied the army possess and employ physical strength. The fact that plebian women could be strong would have come as little surprise to their contemporaries; therefore, it was expected that they could perform certain forms of hard labor, although the particularly demanding spade work that camp women performed would not have normally been within a woman's domain.[99] But the masculinity of camp women was not simply a matter of muscular work.

This chapter began with the story of one camp wife; let us now consider another, the formidable wife of Sergeant Stone, as described in *The Royal Gazette* of 25 September 1779. Here we see praise for her conduct at the siege of Louisbourg in 1758:

[She] accompanied him, though she was rather of a small and handsome make, through most of the hardships of our armies underwent in America during the last war; no consideration of fear could make her leave her husband's side, thro'

---

[99] See the comments on how Europeans expected plebian women to be capable of hard physical labor in Wiesner, *Women and Gender in Early Modern Europe*, p. 106, and Dianne Dugaw, "Balladry's Female Warriors: Women, Warfare, and Disguise in the Eighteenth Century," *Eighteenth-Century Life* 9.2 (1985), p. 3. Dugaw speaks of the late seventeenth and eighteenth centuries as an "age … which … not only recognized in but expected of women the same physical toughness and energy we find in the female warrior."

nine engagements in which he was concerned; in the course of which she twice helped to carry him off wounded from the field of battle; and it is a fact which can be testified by living witnesses, now in Dublin, that at the siege of Louisburg, at a time when many of our troops were killed, she supplied the living with the powder cartridges of the dead, and animated the men in the ranks next to her by her words and actions. Though a woman of the most surprising intrepidity, she was never known to be guilty of any thing that could impreach her delicacy, or violate the modest demeanour of her sex.[100]

The story makes her conventional femininity clear: her "small and handsome make," her "delicacy," and "modest demeanour." But she also bore "most of the hardships of our armies," even helping to carry off her wounded husband twice. Through it all she was not simply hard working but courageous in the face of enemy fire; unmoved by any "consideration of fear," she would not "leave her husband's side." In the thick of the fight, "she supplied the living with the powder cartridges of the dead, and animated the men in the ranks next to her by her words and actions." Her portion of masculinity derived not simply from being physically strong, but from being tough and courageous in the combat zone.

Troops drew the contrast between sex and gender with direct simplicity in the aftermath of the unsuccessful 1637 Spanish battle of Leucate, near Perpignan. When the fight was over, as the bishop of Albi administered last rites to the dying, he discovered the bodies of several women among the Spanish dead. Castillian soldiers praised the fallen women's courage to the Bishop as ultimately masculine: "They were the real men, since those who had fled, including certain officers, had conducted themselves like women."[101]

Camp women were praised for showing strength, toughness, and courage while on campaign; however, as Natalie Zemon Davis points out, European popular culture also portrayed the mannish woman as a perversion, or an inversion, of the natural order.[102] A late sixteenth-century broadsheet on the theme of inversions—of the world turned

---

[100] *The Royal Gazette*, 25 September 1779, in Holly A. Mayer, *Belonging to the Army: Camp Followers and Community during the American Revolution* (Columbia, SC: 1996), p. 9.

[101] The Bishop of Albi in Frank Tallett, *War and Society in Early Modern Europe, 1495–1715* (London: 1992), p. 133. Henri de Campion wrote of a cross-dressing woman officer, Captain Hendrich, found dead at the battle of Turin in 1640. Henri de Campion, *Mémoires* (Paris: 1990), p. 128, in Steinberg, *La confusion des sexes*, p. 43. The body of a seventeen-year-old woman, who had "served well for a year" in a Swiss regiment was discovered on the field during the fighting before Gibraltar in 1782. A. G., series A1, ms 3722, p. 196, in Steinberg, *La confusion des sexes*, p. 132.

[102] Natalie Zemon Davis, "Women on Top: Symbolic Sexual Inversion and Political Disorder in Early Modern Europe," in Barbara A. Babcock, *The Reversible World:*

upside down—suggests how much women of the campaign community bent gender norms and took on aspects of masculinity (see Plate 9). Such broadsides were meant to amuse as a kind of cultural play, but they also defined stereotypes by presenting reversals as ridiculous.[103] Among the several illustrations of inversion—rats attacking a cat, sheep killing a wolf, a child feeding its mother—are two that deal with women and war. One shows a seated man holding a distaff with a woman armed to go to war standing in front of him, and another shows an army of women besieging a town.[104] Women were not to go to war or take part in attacking fortresses; however, women of the campaign community did both, albeit not normally bearing arms. These two images are all the more threatening when seen in the context of another on the broadside: the hen mounting the cock, a potent image of not only gender but sexual inversion. The text with the image reads, "now the hen would be the cock, that is the experience of many men."[105]

Symbolic Inversion in Art and Society (Ithaca: Cornell University Press, 1978), pp. 147–90.

[103] In a far more serious form, John Knox reflected such negative images of inversion in his political tract, *The First Blast of the Trumpet Against the Monstrous Regiment of Women* (1558), directed against Mary Stewart and Mary Tudor. His words present the visions of the world turned upside down in popular broadsides:

And first, where I affirm the empire of a woman to be a thing repugnant to nature, I mean not only that God, by the order of his creation, has spoiled [*deprived*] woman of authority and dominion, but also that man has seen, proved, and pronounced just causes why it should be. Man, I say, in many other cases, does in this behalf see very clearly. For the causes are so manifest, that they cannot be hid. For who can deny but it is repugnant to nature, that the blind shall be appointed to lead and conduct such as do see? That the weak, the sick, and impotent persons shall nourish and keep the whole and strong? And finally, that the foolish, mad, and frenetic shall govern the discreet, and give counsel to such as be sober of mind? And such be all women, compared unto man in bearing of authority. For their sight in civil regiment is but blindness; their strength, weakness; their counsel, foolishness; and judgment, frenzy, if it be rightly considered.

For a discussion of "monstrous women" see Philip Benedict, *Christ's Churches Purely Reformed: A Social History of Calvinism* (New Haven, CT: 2002), pp. 158–59. Knox directed this 1558 appeal against the Catholic women rulers, Queen Mary of England and also Mary of Lorraine, the regent of Scotland. He would later apologize to Elizabeth I and to Mary Stuart, the daughter of Mary of Lorraine, for the *First Blast*, but with little effect.

[104] Four world-turned-upside-down broadsheets that picture women armed for war as part of the inversions are C. F. Van Veen, *Dutch Catchpenny Prints: Three Centuries of Pictorial Broadsheets for Children* (The Hague: 1971), Pls 36, 38, 39, 41. For other such broadsheets, see David Kunzle, "World Upside Down: The Iconography of a European Broadsheet Type," in Barbara A. Babcock, ed., *The Reversible World: Symbolic Inversion in Art and Society* (Ithaca: Cornell UP, 1978), Pl. 1.2 and 1.12.

[105] From *Die Verkehrte Welt*, a German broadsheet of the early seventeenth-century. Kunzle, "World Upside Down," p. 80, Pl. 1.12.

PLATE 9. Visions of the world turned upside down by Ewout Muller of Amsterdam, late sixteenth century. Note the panel on top row of the armed woman standing before the seated man with a distaff, titled "The wife goes off to war," and the panel in the sixth row showing women besieging a building, titled "The women storm the house."[106] In the same row, a hen mounts a cock, with the text "Now the hen would be the cock; that is the experience of many men."[107]

C. F. Van Veen, *Dutch Catchpenny Prints: Three Centuries of Pictorial Broadsides for Children* (The Hague: 1971). Library, University of Illinois at Springfield.

[106] Thanks to my friend Kelly DeVries for translating the Dutch.
[107] David Kunzle, "World Upside Down: The Iconography of a European Broadsheet Type," in Barbara A. Babcock, ed., *The Reversible World: Symbolic Inversion in Art and Society* (Ithaca: 1978), p. 80.

The image of the woman-at-arms retains the biting ridicule of inversion throughout the early modern period. A number of mid-eighteenth century drawings by the German artist Martin Engelbrecht portray women in uniform, complete with skirts, firing a cannon and mortar, holding a lighted grenade, and drilling with muskets before an encampment.[108] But these images were not advocating women in the ranks; they were in the tradition of using the warrior woman as a source of ridicule, both of her and of her man. One of the Engelbrecht images shows a uniformed woman seated at a table, drinking and smoking a pipe, as her male companion at the table rocks a cradle and works at a distaff. It is classic, satiric inversion. A later American print entitled *Cornwallis turned nurse, and his mistress a soldier* appeared in for *The Continental Almanac for 1782*. This plate humiliates the British general by showing him seated with a baby on his lap and holding a distaff, while his woman shoulders a flintlock musket.[109]

Another theme of gender inversion in popular culture stresses the struggle between men and women for dominance or, as it was often portrayed in popular prints, "the battle for the pants." This theme justifies the use of violence between the sexes to keep the world in proper order. In variations of this depiction of the dominant woman, she beats her mate with switches or with a distaff, rides him like a horse, or abuses him in other ways.[110] Surprisingly, the beaten husband is often shown wearing the distinctive clothing of a Landsknecht, so it is the hyper-masculine soldier who is shamed.[111] It is no stretch of the imagination to

---

[108] See the section in Engelen, *Soldatenfrauen in Preuße*, pp. 372–79, which deals with these images of uniform-wearing soldier-women, particularly the Engelbrecht Pls. 8–13.

[109] Print in Young, *Masquerade*, p. 89.

[110] For prints with the theme of women beating men, see Davis, "Women on Top," p. 158, Pl. 5.1, p. 159, Pls. 5.2 and 5.3. Also see p. 160, Pl. 5.4, for a 1690 scene of a man and woman fighting over who gets to wear the pants. Also see Moxey, *Peasants, Warriors, and Wives*, p. 105, Pls. 5.4 and 5.5, p.106, Pls. 5.6 and 5.7, and p. 115, Pl. 5.15. In an unusual woodcut by Abraham Back, *Recipe for Marital Bliss*, ca. 1680, the artist balances two scenes of a man beating a woman and a woman beating a man with the usual bundle of sticks. Transgressions that call for a man to be disciplined by his wife include drunkenness, laziness, and not supporting his family. Merry E. Wiesner, *Women and Gender in Early Modern Europe*, 2nd ed. (Cambridge: 2000), p. 23, Pl. 1.

[111] A playing card designed by Peter Flötner portrays a woman beating the bare bottom of a man who is bent over to receive the blows. She wields a switch of sticks bundled together. This is very much in the tradition of the world-turned-upside-down prints, as the man assumes the position taken by women in scenes showing them being disciplined. The scene is all the more ironic because the man is dressed as a Landsknecht. Max Geisberg, *The German Single-Leaf Woodcut, 1500–1550* (New York: 1974), III, p. 818, G. 869. This can also be seen in Davis, "Women on Top," p. 158. Also, see Pl. 10 for probable Landsknecht attire.

see the masculinized women of the campaign community as an implicit challenge to the masculinity of the soldiers whose lives they shared.

This theme of the "battle for the pants" peaked in the sixteenth and early seventeenth centuries, but it continued well into the eighteenth century. A marvelous French engraving of 1690 shows a woman and man, each with one leg in a disputed pair of breeches, tussling with each other to gain complete control of the pants and the power that implied.[112] An eighteenth-century engraving from the *Mirror of Female Fools* shows a woman attired as a man and grasping a sword as she takes the breeches away from her docile husband; a cock, the symbol of masculinity, stands at her feet, while a slinking dog cowers with her husband.[113]

Popular culture accepted violence as a means to maintain the proper order between the sexes, an order that prescribed male dominance. Civilian society supported the right of a husband to physically punish his wife; in fact, it raised such violence practically to the level of a social obligation. "Correction modérée" (moderate correction) included slaps, punches, switching, and clubbing.[114] In parts of France such wife beatings were allowed until blood flowed. If civilian society approved of such means, how much more common might it have been in the camps, a community founded on the use of violence?

The iconography of the battle of the pants shows the couple literally coming to blows, often with a cudgel wielded by one party or with both so armed[115] (see Plate 10). The cudgel, a punishing but not usually fatal weapon, was frequently represented as a weapon of control. Many discussions of the battle between the sexes in popular literature advise the man to cudgel his wife. A carnival play of 1533, Hans Sach's *The Angry*

---

[112] Davis, "Women on Top," p. 160, Pl. 5.4.

[113] Dekker and Van de Pol, *Tradition of Female Transvestism*, between pages 48 and 49, Pl. 23. If the woman has a cock at her feet, the man is accompanied by a dog slinking away with his tail between his legs. See as well Pls. 24–27 that pick up the theme of the world turned upside down as females play male roles in children's prints of the eighteenth century.

[114] See the section on domestic violence in Julius R. Ruff, *Violence in Early Modern Europe, 1500–1800* (Cambridge: 2001), pp. 131–40, and the discussions in Hufton, *The Prospect Before Her*, pp. 56 and 289, for example.

[115] For examples of cudgels used in the battle of the sexes, see Moxey, *Peasants, Warriors, and Wives*, Pls. 5.6, 5.16, and 5.17. I have seen one delightful contrast to this appeal for violence. Print artist N. Guérard (c. 1648–1719), who also did a series of military prints, offered in his Moralités, a print of a man and woman at peace as the man puts (back) on his pants. The top of the print reads, "Tout d'amitié, rien de force"—all friendship, no force. Joseph Harris, *Hidden Agendas: Cross Dessing in 17th-Century France* (Tübingen: 2005), p. 273.

PLATE 10. Martin Treu, woodcut showing a battle for the pants with the woman wielding a cudgel, ca. 1540–43. The clothing of the man suggests that he may be a Landsknecht.

Albertina Museum, Vienna.

Wife, advises the wise husband to "Go ahead and act like a man! Otherwise she'll end up riding you," so he should "take an oak cudgel and beat her soundly between the ears!"[116] A sixteenth- century ditty counseled:

> Her body be sure well pound
> With a strong hazel rod;
> Strike her head till it turns round,
> And kick her in the gut.

---

[116] Hans Sachs, *The Angry Wife*, in Moxey, *Peasants, Warriors, and Wives*, p. 117. See as well a woodcut by Hans Vogtherr the Younger, "Allegory of Marriage," in Moxey, *Peasants, Warriors, and Wives*, p. 84, Pl. 4.13. A cock, symbol of masculine control, boasts of keeping his hens in line, "Whatever man does not do the same, Is a hen not a cock, And will not be able to wear the pants."

With blows be every zealous,
Yet see you don't her kill.

Thus shouldst thou thy wife punish
If you wilt have her tame;
Car'st thou about thy honour
Then must thou beat her lame
Of hand and foot also
So she can't run away.
Thus must thou beat and damp her
So to no priest she'll scamper;
Then first she'll thee obey. [117]

The highly popular, imaginative tale of Long Meg of Westminster is particularly apropos concerning plebian notions of women's masculinity, dominance, and submission in the campaign community. This staple of pamphlet fiction first appeared in 1582 and was reprinted in somewhat different versions for two hundred years.[118] The character of Long Meg is a virago who bests many a man. In her most famous adventures she goes off to the wars with Henry VIII where she works as a camp laundress with the army at Boulogne. But, when the French break through the walls, she grabs a halberd and marshals other women to hold off the attackers until the English soldiers rally. Later, dressed as a man, she challenges a French champion to single combat, defeats him, and beheads his corpse. Only in her moment of victory is she recognized as a woman. Upon her return from France, she marries a tall soldier. The soldier proposes they fight: "Because he heard she was so Man-like as to beat all she meet with, he would try her Manhood and therefore bid her take which Cudgel she would." However, Long Meg now refuses combat even after "he gave her three or four Blows." Instead she falls to her knees in submission. She explains: "Husband ... whatsoever I have done to others it behoveth me to be obedient to you; and never shall it be said, though I cudgel a Knave that wrongs me, that Long Meg shall be her Husband's Master; and therefore, use me as you please."[119] The story of

---

[117] Ruff, *Violence in Early Modern Europe, 1500–1800* (Cambridge: 2001), pp. 36–37.

[118] The collection Eighteenth Century Collections Online, a Gale database, as purchased by the Library of the University of Illinois at Urbana-Champaign includes two editions from 1775 and 1780.

[119] All quotes from *The Life and Adventures of Long Meg* (Newcastle: ca. 1775). See the discussion of Long Meg in Simon Shepherd, *Amazons and Warrior Women: Varieties of Feminism in Seventeenth-Century Drama* (New York: 1981), pp. 70–74. The frontispiece to the Hans Sachs play, "The Evil Smoke," shows a man and a woman tussling over a pair of pants as the each raise cudgels to strike at one another. Moxey, *Peasants, Warriors, and Wives*, p. 120, Pl. 120.

Long Meg thus ends with an example to good wives, perhaps with particular relevance to the masculine women of the camps.

In a parody of such a fight, Grimmelshausen, writing in the seventeenth century, married his anti-heroine Courage to a soldier, who proposes a battle with cudgels between them to decide who will wear the pants. Predictably, Courage knocks him senseless. But this tale is told precisely to show that Courage inverted the natural order of things.[120]

It has been argued that folklore about dominance and submission exaggerate the reality. In particular, peasant households that were supposed to be male domains were, in fact, partnerships between husband and wife.[121] Perhaps this is so, but the camps were populated not by sensible, hard-working, and conservative peasants but by young men and women who were still forging their identities in an environment of physical power and violence.

In any case, the cudgel of cultural folkore as evidenced in prints, poems, and stories, gains credence from real world practice. The figure who controlled women on the march and in camp, the Hurenweible—literally a whore sergeant—and the provost employed wooden staffs, cudgels, to strike offending parties. As Leonhardt Fronsperger (1520–75) stated in his *Kriegsbuch*: "When he cannot make peace by other means, he has a conciliator about the length of an arm with which he is authorized by their masters to punish them."[122] Their "masters" were their male partners, husbands or others.[123] Fronsperger also describes the hard work expected of a camp woman, presenting it as if the testimony actually came from of one of these women who, after listing her many duties, reports: "And if we don't do it, beatings are ours."[124] Kirchhoff, writing in 1602, marveled at the heavy loads carried by women for their men, but noted, "With all that they are not well treated, and for the slightest reason mercilessly trampled on and beaten as their black eyes bear witness."[125]

---

[120] Grimmelshausen, *The Life of Courage*, p. 54.
[121] See the discussion of this in David Hopkin, "Female Soldiers and the Battle of the Sexes in France: The Mobilization of a Folk Motif," *History Workshop Journal*, 56 (2003): 99. Hopkin takes into consideration the works of Martine Segalen, Yvonne Verdier, and Susan Carol Rogers.
[122] Fronsperger in Ploss *et al.*, *Woman in the Sexual Relation*, p. 99.
[123] Even in the relatively enlightened world of late eighteenth-century America, camp husbands were expected to keep their women in line. Mayer, *Belonging to the Army*, p. 247.
[124] Fronsperger in Haberling, "Army Prostitution and Its Control," p. 32.
[125] Kirchhoff in Haberling, "Army Prostitution and Its Control," p. 33. Gustav Freytag called this staff an "equalizer." Haberling, "Army Prostitution and Its Control," p. 34.

A great intellectual of the nineteenth century, Gustav Freytag, who collected a large number of tracts from earlier times, told of another kind of violent punishment inflicted on women. If the man perceived that his "whore" had grievously wronged him, he might do worse than hit her: "according to the monstrous camp custom, [he could] turn her over to the stable boys and camp hirelings."[126] This meant abandoning his precious darling to be humiliated, molested, and even gang-raped in public. Grimmelshausen's Simplicissimus, when he was masquerading as a woman, was turned over to the camp boys: "As was the custom of these fiends when a woman was handed over to them like this, they hurried off to a thicket with me, where they could more easily satisfy their bestial lusts, and a lot of other men followed to watch the fun."[127]

The threat of violence may help to explain why some women chose to partner with men. In her hard-edged analysis of marriage, Susan Brownmiller argues that it derived from a survival strategy by which a woman gave herself to one man, allowing him to rape her, so that this man would keep other men from raping her as well, not out of concern for her but in order to preserve his exclusive ownership of her body.[128] This grim interpretation may well apply in the tough and violent world of the early modern camp. A woman may have turned to one abusive paramour or husband in order to be protected from abuse by other men.

WOMEN AS PRECIPITATORS AND PARTICIPANTS IN VIOLENCE

If women were the victims of men and authorities within the camp community, they also played active parts as aggressors and instigators of camp violence. Military commentators, all men, often condemned women as provoking fights between men. Such combat seems to have broken out over one of two issues: disputes over the favors of a woman and instances of men upholding their "manly" duties to their woman in arguments with other women or men.

---

[126] Freytag in Haberling, "Army Prostitution and Its Control," p. 34. This practice seems related to the ritual group violence committed by young men in civil society discussed by Ruff, *Violence in Early Modern Europe*, chap. 5.

[127] Grimmelshausen, *Simplicissimus*, p. 172.

[128] See Susan Brownmiller, *Against our Will: Men, Women, and Rape* (New York: Bantam, 1975).

Montluc, who counseled that warriors must not be lovers, seemed most concerned over the pursuit of women and the way in which it led soldiers to slight their duties:

Such men should have a distaff and not a sword. And in addition to the debauchery and loss of time, this pursuit leads to an infinity of quarrels, and sometimes with your friends. I have seen more men fight for this reason than for the desire of honor. Oh, what a villainy, that the love of a woman strips you of your honor and very often confronts you with loss of life and reputation.[129]

Montluc may have been referring to officers, but men in the ranks fought over women as well. His words deal with the particular problems of military life, but they also reflect contemporary civil preconceptions about the disruptive potential of women. As historian Emlyn Eisenach summarizes, religious reformers felt that "women's presence, which tempted men, constituted a primary cause of men's passionate and violent behavior."[130]

The hyper-masculine environment of military life on campaign and in quarters must have colored relationships, bringing out a crude chivalry toward women, a sense of possession, and a willingness to resort to violence. Montluc's focus on disputes over women seems valid, but it is better stated as a criticism of the men who fought than the women they fought about. Montluc attacks the men involved not for being too ready to fight but for being under the power of women, and he exploits the ultimate symbolic insult by saying that such men should exchange their swords for distaffs. The idea that women caused violence outlasted the aggregate contract army. In a backhanded recognition of female agency, an imperial mandate adopted by several German states in 1668 set out punishments for women who did not make efforts to keep their men from brawling or goaded their husbands into fights.[131] Battles between soldiers as portrayed in popular art show the sutler's tent or military tavern as a common venue for violent arguments, the cause of which seems to be implied by the presence of women, although once swords are drawn women frequently try to restrain the combatants.[132]

---

[129] Blaise de Montluc, *Commentaires de Messire Blaise de Montluc*, ed. P. Corteault (Paris, 1964), p. 29.
[130] Eisenach, *Husbands, Wives, and Concubines*, p. 16.
[131] Wilson, "German Women and War," p. 130.
[132] For example, Louis-Joseph Watteau, who loves camp and tavern scenes with soldiers, shows two fights in which soldiers draw swords. Gambling is clearly not the issue as it is in so many disputes, but it is unclear exactly what the nature of the fight is about. Women are present in both scenes and are trying to restrain the combatants. See "La

Men fought with each other in pursuit of women, but the far more interesting form of violence involved men called upon by their women to fight over the women's precedence in the camp community. Here the honor of both the women and the men were at issue. Wallhausen described a fascinatingly complex incident that highlights these dynamics. He told of a party composed of soldiers, women, and boys bent on plunder. Having pillaged a farmhouse, they loaded a wagon, and then fought over who got to ride on it:

> Then when the conveyance is ready to leave, women, children and prostitutes fall upon the wagon like a flock of ravens. The prostitute who gets into the wagon first, takes the best place, then follows her master's boy with his bundle so full of stolen articles that a horse could barely carry it. The prostitute quickly sits down on it. One crowds the other. When a soldier's wife can no longer find a place, then: "You miserable prostitute, you want to ride, and I am an honorable wife of a soldier who has made many campaigns with him, and you wretch you would lord it over me." The wives and prostitutes fall upon one another, sticks and stones are tossed around and after the contingent mauled itself for a while, the soldier's wife, hair streaming runs up to her husband crying: "Look, Hans, there is this or that one's whore; she sits in the wagon, wants to ride and I have to go on foot, I, your honorable wife." Whereupon, the soldier rushes up to the prostitute and tries to pull her off the wagon and put his wife in her place; when the prostitute's soldier comes along and says: "Leave my girl alone; I am as fond of her as you are of your own wife." And the two soldiers rush at each other, out come the sabers and they cut and stab themselves to death or permanent injury. This is no rarity, for when in transit, hardly a day passes in which three, four or even ten soldiers do not lose life or limb for the sake of their women.[133]

In this vignette, the struggle over status and rights between two kinds of camp women turned deadly. Clearly the wife believed that her standing as a wife who had served several campaigns with her husband gave her preference over the current "whore" of another soldier.

Wallhausen provides another, less lethal, case of violent competition by women:

> There were as many prostitutes and boys in the contingent as there were soldiers, and during the eight days the camp-followers stole so many horses from the warlord's subjects that practically every soldier was mounted. The colonel who was

---

querelle militaire" and "La dispute de soldats," in Gaëtane Maës, *Les Watteau de Lille* (Paris: Arthena, 1998), pp. 234 and 246. For examples of dueling over women in the literature of the time see Grimmelshausen, *The Life of Courage*, p. 94 and *The Life and Adventures of Mrs. Christian Davies*, p. 40.

[133] Wallhausen, *Defensio patriae* (1621), p. 172, in Haberling, "Army Prostitution and Its Control," p. 35.

PLATE 11. Brunswick Monogrammist, *The Loose Society* (Brothel Scene), ca. 1535–40.

Gemaeldegalerie, Staatliche Museem zu Berlin. Bildarchiv Preussischer Kulturbesitz/Art Resource, NY.

an able executive, personally pulled the soldiers down from the horses and by strict measures forced the men to return the horses to their owners. It was impossible, however, to stop the prostitutes from riding horseback; there was not one who did not have a stolen horse and if they did not ride, they would harness three or four horses together to a peasant's cart. The authority of the whore sergeant was powerless to tame the women, and at times it was quite amusing for the officers to watch how one prostitute would try to ride ahead of another; how they would rush by and ram each other's wagons; from forty to fifty wagons were thus hopelessly entangled and required hours to pull them apart. Loud cursing and swearing, pulling of hair and blows were included in the scene.[134]

With all this in mind, let us return to the instance of women fighting over a place on the wagon. Hans was being called upon to enforce his wife's claim of precedence. He may well have drawn his sword partly because of concern for her, but he certainly drew it because it was a test of his manliness and honor among his fellow soldiers. Had he not, his wife would have scolded him and those around him would have seen him as weak. His wife was his partner, but also an extension of himself, so he must fight over the apparently trivial matter of a place on the wagon. A wife might hold a more

---

[134] Wallhausen in Haberling, "Army Prostitution and Its Control," p. 44.

honorable position in the hierarchy, but without doubt, a man's honor was caught up in his "whore" as well as his wife. It is not surprising that a man would fight over a place in a woman's bed; it is more striking that he fought so readily for a place on a wagon for his woman.

Hans's duel at the wagon resulted from a physical fight between women, and there is no question that women also employed violence against each other. A work of art by a sixteenth-century Antwerp artist provides a statement of female violence just as revealing as those written by Wallhausen (see Plate 11). The tavern and brothel seem to be a soldiers' "hangout," judging by the illustrations of soldiers mounted on the wall. But the heart of the action is a fight between two women, one of whom is on her knees striking the other who lays prone, while a man stands above pouring water on the two combatants to stop the combat. The most interesting character, however, is not the brawlers but a woman who stands above the adversaries with a stern but unexcited face. Her male companion tries to restrain the winner of the fight, whose arm is coiled for still one more blow, but the stolid standing woman reaches out to keep her paramour from intervening. She is willing to let the fight follow its course, which will end in a thrashing rather than in death. She must have seen this before, and probably thought that the woman being beaten either deserved it or should have better defended herself. The painting ultimately centers on the naturalness of violence among women. Although the record is not rich on the subject, we do find other artistic portrayals of female-on-female violence.[135] (See Plate 15 for an example of a fight between women or a case of women attacking men.)

The examples above date prior to 1650, but after that date, women still took part in fights, sometimes joining their men in brawls. Regiments jostled for position in camp and quarters, and in one such incident the women of an Irish regiment in French service fought alongside their men against a regiment of *fusiliers de la montagne*; one Irishwoman wounded

---

[135] One shows a jealous wife attacking another woman who is marching at the side of a Landsknecht, the wife's husband. Walter L. Strauss, *The German Single-Leaf Woodcut, 1550–1600*, 3 vols. (New York: 1975), vol. 3, p. 1074. Another portrays an unexplained fight involving several women in a village or camp. Engraving by Hans Ulrich Franck in Georg Hirth, *Picture book of the graphic arts, 1500–1800 (Kulturgeschichtliches Bilderbuch aus drei Jahrhunderten, hrsg. Georg Hirth)*, 6 vols., (New York: Benjamin Blom, 1972), vol. 4, Pl. 2248. Also, one of the playing cards, the three of bells, designed by Peter Flötner, shows two women fighting, but not in an identifiable military situation. Max Geisberg, *The German Single-Leaf Woodcut, 1500–1550*, vol. 3, p. 817, G. 868.

a fusilier with a well-thrown rock.[136] The noted historian Char...
described British camp women during the Napoleonic Wars as "har...
nails, expert plunderers, furious partisans of the supreme excellence of
their own battalion, much given to fighting."[137]

Women could also instigate soldiers to desert or mutiny. During 1691,
one such provocateuse was sentenced to death by a court–martial held in
Ireland "for inciting to desertion while in the field."[138] A Württemberg
decree of 1700 charged that "roving foreign wenches" were undermining
discipline and encouraging theft and desertion.[139]

It is clear that women within the campaign community were tough,
but the level and form of violence seem to differ between men and
women. Men were more likely to escalate camp violence to deadly
force, quickly drawing swords. Women pulled each other's hair and
exchanged blows, but are rarely described as going much further. Not
surprisingly, however, there is evidence that a woman might use
deadly force to defend herself from a man. An unknown diarist from
the ranks recorded an attack by a woman: "On the 10th of July a
soldier's wife stabbed a corporal, who, so she claimed, tried to force
her to sleep with him. She was held prisoner for several days but
afterwards she was set free again."[140] The woman soldier turned
sutler, Christian Davies, is supposed to have deterred an amorous
colonel with a knife, broke the leg of a bullying lieutenant, and killed
an enemy soldier with a musket, all after she changed back from male
to female dress and duties.[141] But in general, deadly force seems to
have been a man's preserve. Of course, woman cross-dressing as
soldiers in the ranks acted as men, including fighting duels, as will be
seen in Chapter IV.

---

[136] Service Historique de l'Armée de Terre (SHAT), Archives de Guerre (AG), MR 1787, piece 50.

[137] Oman in St. John Williams, *Judy O'Grady*, p. 49.

[138] St. John Williams, *Judy O'Grady*, p. 14; see also the case of the women flogged for having inciting to mutiny in Tangers, 1664, pp. 14–15.

[139] Wilson, "German Women and War," p. 145. See as well 1727 law that also claimed that "various easy-going whores" were tempting soldiers into marriage or getting them to desert. See Mayer, *Belonging to the Army*, pp. 255 and 259 for cases in which women were charged with inciting men to desert the army. Found guilty, Mary Johnson was sentenced to 100 lashes and being drummed out of the army.

[140] Unknown soldier, "Bruchstück eines Tagebuches aus der Zeit des 30 jährigen Krieges," ed. R. Lehmann, Neues Archiv für Sächsische Geschichte und Altertumskunde, 40 (1919), p. 174, in Mortimer, *Eyewitness Accounts*, p. 38.

[141] *The Life and Adventures of Mrs. Christian Davies*, pp. 210–11, 114, and 113.

ıpanied the armies were subject to military law and ⟨ugh they were not soldiers.[142] This meant that camp ⟩rought before officers or court-martials for punishment, ⟨ay. Women accompanying the army were placed under the ⟨f military officers, usually those charged with maintaining orᴅ⟨ ⟩ baggage trains. The need to impose order among the women of the campaign community greatly increased when large crowds of women accompanied troops into the field. Therefore, the regulation of women on the march was most elaborate before 1650.

When women composed a major percentage of the campaign community, they were often arranged on the march in an order of precedence according to the status of the men who were their partners. Military authorities recognized a hierarchy among the women, just as the women themselves were concerned with matters of status and rights themselves. When the duke of Alva advanced his Spanish army from Italy to the Netherlands in 1568, the women were under a discipline of their own. "They ranged themselves under particular flags, marched in ranks and sections, and in admirable military order, after each battalion, and classed themselves with strict etiquette according to their rank and pay."[143] Sir James Turner described the march of a seventeenth-century army as similar, with women divided into "three ranks, or rather in Classes, one below the other":

The first shall be of those who are Ladies, and are the Wives of the General and other principal Commanders of the Army, who for most part are carried in Coaches; ... The second Classe is of those who ride on Horseback ... The third Classe is of those who walk on foot, and ware the wives of inferiour Officers and Souldiers; these must walk besides the Baggage of the several Regiments to whome they belong, and over them the several Regiment Marshals have inspection.

---

[142] For example, Article 23, Section XIII, American Articles of War, 20 September 1776: "All suttlers and retainers to a camp, and all persons whatsoever serving with the armies of the United States in the field, though no inlisted soldier, are to be subject to orders, according to the rules and discipline of war." This mimicked European practice. Mayer, *Belonging to the Army*, p. 236.

[143] Freidrich Schiller, *The Works of Friedrich Schiller: The Revolt of the Netherlands and the Thirty Years' War*, trans. E.B. Estwick and A.J.W. Morrison, ed. Nathan Haskell Dole (Boston: 1901), p. 278. See as well the comments on this army in Brantôme, *Oeuvres completes de Pierre de Bourdeille, Seigneur de Brantôme*, ed. Ludovic Lalanne, vol. 1 (Paris: 1864), p. 106.

Turner praised the conduct of the women on horseback: "I have seen them ride, keep Troop, rank and file very well, after that Captain of theirs who led them, and a Banner with them, which one of the Women carried."[144]

The primary military officer detailed to command the women of the baggage train was known in Germany as the Hurenweibel, or whore sergeant. Fronsperger described such a Hurenweibel: "for [which] post an old and experienced soldier is chosen and used, for in his power and under his command is the whole baggage train as well as whores and boys"[145] (see Plate 12). The Hurenweibel "should have his own lieutenant and second-lieutenant" and he was paid as a captain. This crew had the duty of making sure that the women and other camp followers "do not hinder the troops on the march" and that they perform a long list of duties.[146] (See Fronsperger's list of their duties in Chapter III, p. 162.) Wallhausen went into even greater detail:

If a man lost his hand, leg or eye in battle, the raw camp humor declared him fit for the post. When during mustering the colonel introduced him to the soldiers, he admonished them to treat the veteran with respect because he received his injury honorably and the whore sergeant, also called "woman" or "contingent sergeant" bowed, greeted the soldiers and begged them to instruct their wives, children and youngsters to allow themselves to be guided by him without resentment and not to take his scoldings in an evil way. He was an important personage for the common soldier, and it was advisable to be on good terms with him for he guarded the soldier's dependents and his booty. Along the march route, the contingent carried a special flag and proceeded in military order with the sergeant at the head, with the most attractive prostitutes close by to protect them against improprieties of the boys. On marching into an encampment, the sergeant was the last to enter because if the prostitutes and hirelings stormed in, they would steal the accumulated provisions, hay, straw, wood. It was the duty of the prostitutes and the boys to clean and sweep the streets and market-places as well as the drinking places; this meant compulsory labor, with dishonest guards in charge, and any prostitutes refusing to do such menial work could be reported by the other women.[147]

As women became less numerous, they did not require a special officer detailed to control them, and eventually the tasks of the Hurenweibel were absorbed by the chief disciplinary officer of a field army, the provost and his agents. During the eighteenth century, the Prussians also

---

[144] See page 81 of this volume for more on the three classes.
[145] Leonard Fronsperger, *Kriegszbuch* (Frankfurt, 1598), as quoted by Hiller and Osborne in their translation of Grimmelshausen, *Runagate Courage*, p. 144, in Hacker, "Women and Military Institutions," p. 651.
[146] Fronsperger in Ploss et al, *Woman in the Sexual Relation*, p. 99.
[147] Wallhausen in Haberling, "Army Prostitution and Its Control," p. 36.

PLATE 12. Jost Amman, illustration from Fronsperger, *Kriegsordnung und Regiment*, 1564. The context of this piece suggests that the Landsknecht is a Hurenweibel; the staff he carries indicates command. Note the rooster perched on the woman's pack; this must be akin to the rooster riding on the shoulder of the Landsknecht's "whore" in Plate 7.

Georg Hirth (1841–1916), *Picture book of the graphic arts, 1500–1800. Kulturgeschichtliches Bilderbuch aus drei Jahrhunderten*, reprint of 1st. ed, published in Liepzig and Munich, 1882-90, vol. 2 (New York: 1972), pl. 1033. University of Illinois at Urbana-Champaign Library, Rare Book and Manuscript Library.

broke down the large baggage train into smaller units, although the French were more conservative.[148] However, regulations still ordered the lives of women with the campaign community. In 1757 Bouquet ordered "no Women or Children are allowed to set upon the Waggons; & they

[148] Engelen, *Soldatenfrauen in Preußen*, p. 349.

shall follow upon the March the direction of that Officer [in charge of baggage]."[149] French ordinances from the Napoleonic Wars prescribed that women with military units wear an oval placard on their chests detailing their profession and registration number.[150] The duke of Wellington's orders of August 1809 forbade women from cornering bread rations, demonstrating the chain of command women had to respect and their liability to punishment by the provost:

The women of the army must be prevented from purchasing bread in the villages, within two leagues of the station of any division of the army: when any women wants to purchase bread, she must ask the Officer of the company to which she belongs, for a passport, which must be countersigned by the commanding officer of the regiment. Any women found with bread in her possession, purchased at any place nearer than two leagues, will be deprived of the bread by the provost or his assistants; as will any women who goes out of camp to purchase bread without a passport. Women, who will have been discovered disobeying the order, will not be allowed to receive rations.[151]

Women could also be subject to the most intimate invasions of their privacy, particularly in matters pertaining to health. An example from the American Revolution brings this home, when the commander of a Delaware regiment ordered in 1777:

That the Weomen belonging to the Regt. be paraded tomorrow morning & to undergo an examination [for venereal disease] from the Surgeon of the Regiment at his tent except those that are married, & the husbands of those to undergo said examination in their stead. All those that do not attend to be immediately drumed out of the Regiment.[152]

THE DANGERS OF LIFE IN THE COMBAT ZONE

On the march, in camp, or during the fighting, life on campaign was hard and dangerous for the prostitutes, "whores," and wives of the

---

[149] Bouquet directive in Hendrix, "In the Army," p. 37. For similar American regulations, including the proscription against women riding on wagons or marching with the troops, see Mayer, *Belonging to the Army*, pp. 47–48.

[150] Order of 7 thermidor, and VII in Haberling, "Army Prostitution and Its Control," pp. 57–58.

[151] http://www.geocities.com/THE_RIFLES/campfollowers.htm. Longford references this order as well in *Wellington: The Years of the Sword*, p. 201. The English General George Napier thought camp followers far more difficult to control than the troops and the only way to keep order "is to have plenty of provosts, to hang and flog them without mercy, the devils incarnate." Longford, *Wellington: The Years of the Sword*, p. 201.

[152] Regimental Orders, Lincoln Mountain, 1 July 1777, Kirkwood's Delaware Regiment Orderly Book in Mayer, *Belonging to the Army*, pp. 243–44.

campaign community. Turner portrayed the characteristic ardors of life in the field:

I was at the sieges of severall towns and castles, and at many brushes, encounters and ... all the time sufferd exceeding great want of both meate and clothes, being necessitated to [bide] constantly in the fields with little or no shelter, to march always a foot, and drinke water.[153]

On the march, women could bivouac in the open air, sleep in tents with the men of their company, or share improvised huts with their male companions. In addition to discomfort, fatigue, and suffering, disease plagued early modern armies. As members of the campaign community, women endured all this while they performed strenuous jobs, from washing laundry to digging entrenchments.[154]

As a burden particular of their sex, the hardships endured by women of the campaign community included pregnancy and childbirth. Monro reported a shipwreck when his regiment voyaged to join the Swedish forces in Germany:

Here, I did remarke as wonderful, that in the very moment when our ship did breake on ground, there was a *Sergeants* Wife a shipboard, who without the helpe of any women was delivered of a Boy, which all the time of the tempest she carefully did preserve, and being come ashore, the next day, she marched neere foure English mile, with that in her Armes, which was in her belly the night before.[155]

She was not the only camp woman to march with a newborn in her arms.[156] Such fortitude proves false the statement that women by nature lack carrying power and stamina.

---

[153] James Turner, *Memoirs of His Own Life and Times* (Edinburgh: The Bannatyne Club, 1829), p. 6. I thank Mary Elizabeth Ailes for this citation used in her "Camp Followers, Sutlers, and Soldiers' Wives."

[154] When working in groups, women were to maintain military discipline. At the siege of Nuess (1474–75), Duke Charles the Bold ordered several thousand camp women to cart earth for the siegeworks: "The Duke gave them a small flag showing the picture of a woman, and when they went to or from work, the flag, and drum-and-fife preceded them." Wilwort of Schaumburg in Haberling, "Army Prostitution and Its Control," p. 27. This source reported that Charles had 4,000 women in camp; another source, Johann Knebel, put the number at 1,600.

[155] R. Monro, *Monro, his Expedition with the Worthy Scots Regiment Called Mac-Keys*, ed. William S. Brockington, Jr. (Westport, CT: 1999), p. 131.

[156] Rifleman Harris tells a similar story of childbirth and remarkable endurance on the grueling retreat to Coruna in 1808–09: "One of the men's wives ... being very large in the family-way, towards evening stepped from amongst the crowed, and lay herself down amidst the snow, a little out of the main road. Her husband remained with her; and I heard one or two hasty observations amongst our men that they had taken possession of their last resting-place .... To remain behind the column of march in such

Beyond the trials of the march and of camp life, women braved the dangers of war. Even if they did not bear muskets in the firing line, they were nonetheless in the combat zone. Even in the baggage train, they were still exposed to injury, rape, and death.[157] Because armies used the hope of booty as incentive, a rich baggage train was a particularly attractive target. Once hostile soldiers had broken through their adversary's line, they were likely to head for the baggage, and on the road, trains and convoys were always at risk. There could be very brutal fights.[158] At the battle of Naseby (1645), the royalist cavalry, having slashed the left flank of Sir Thomas Fairfax's parliamentary army, raided its baggage train, removing them from the fighting. The tide of battle then favored Fairfax, and his victorious army took the enemy baggage and pursued the fleeing royalists. The royalist earl of Clarendon described the carnage: "The enemy left no manner of barbarous cruelty unexercised that day, and in the pursuit killed above one hundred women, whereof some were officers' wives of quality."[159] Even allied forces might attack a vulnerable baggage train, as the Saxons pillaged the Swedes when the former thought the battle of Breitenfeld had been lost: "And all this night our brave Camerades, the Saxons were making use of their heeles in flying, thinking all was lost, they made booty of our waggons and goods."[160]

Women also risked capture and the hardship and humiliation of imprisonment. Sydnam Poyntz, a mercenary who fought on the victorious

---

weather was to perish, and we accordingly soon forgot all about them. To my surprise, however, I, some little time afterwards (being myself then in the rear of our party), again saw the woman. She was hurrying, with her husband, after us, and in her arms she carried the babe she had just given birth to." Harris, *Recollections of Rifleman Harris*, p. 84.

[157] See the painting portraying an attack on a baggage train, showing a woman being attacked, most probably to be raped, judging from the pose. Viscount Montgomery of Alamein, *A History of Warfare* (Cleveland: 1968), p. 281.

[158] For examples of paintings featuring brutal attacks on baggage trains during the seventeenth and eighteenth centuries see the painting by Sebastian Vrancx in Jacques Bourdet, ed., *The Ancient Art of Warfare*, vol. 1 (Paris and New York, 1968), p. 495, pl. 51, and Louis Laguerre, sketch for Marlborough House in Corelli Barnett, *The First Churchill: Marlborough, Soldier and Statesman* (New York: 1974), pp. 174–75

[159] Clarendon in Alison Plowden, *Women All on Fire: The Women of the English Civil War* (Stroud, Gloucestershire: 1998), p. 127.

[160] R. Monro, *Monro, His Expedition with the Worthy Scots Regiment Called Mac-Keys*, p. 194. See as well the fate of the Swedish baggage train and the women with it at the battle of Jankow, 6 March 1645. William P. Guthrie, *The Later Thirty Years War: From the Battle of Wittstock to the Treaty of Westphalia* (Westport, CT: 2003), p. 140, in Ailes, "Camp Followers, Sutlers, and Soldiers' Wives".

Imperial side of the battle Nordlingen (1634) reports that among the booty taken from the Swedes "wee found such a number of Ladies and Commaunders Wives that I can not count them, and all of them taken Prisoners."[161] A poignant description from the late eighteenth century describes a Boston woman's reaction to seeing British prisoners taken at Saratoga:

I never had the least Idea that the Creation produced such a sordid set of creatures in human Figure—poor, dirty, emaciated men, great numbers of women, who seemed to be the beasts of burden, having a bushel basket on their back, by which they were bent double, the contents deemed to be Pots and Kettles, various sorts of Furniture, children peeping thro' gridirons and other utensils, some very young infants who were born on the road, the women bare feet, cloathed in dirty rags, such effluvia filld the air while they were passing, had they not been smoking all the time, I should have been apprehensive of being contaminated by them.[162]

Women of a defeated army could also suffer worse than imprisonment. Simply being part of the campaign community was dangerous to life and limb. Hagendorf tells a story of a man and woman mutilated by cannon fire when the army attacked the town of Corbie in 1636: "As we skirmished outside this fortress many stayed where they sat, both men and women. There was a cannon in there which we called the skirtchaser, and one day early in the morning they shot all four legs off a man and his wife with it, tight up to the arse, in the hut next to my tent."[163] When women went to

---

[161] Sydnam Poyntz, *The Relation of Sydnam Poyntz 1624–1636*, (London: 1908), p. 113, in Mortimer, *Eyewitness Accounts of the Thirty Years War*, p. 34.

[162] In Linda Grant De Pauw, *Four Traditions: Women of New York During the American Revolution* (Albany: 1974), p. 27, in De Pauw, *Battle Cries and Lullabies*, p. 120.

[163] Hagendorf, *Ein Soeldnerleben im Dreissigjaehrigen Krieg*, pp. 75–76, in Mortimer, *Eyewitness Accounts*, p. 35. A 1514 woodcut by Urs Graf, himself a Swiss Reisläufer, shows a young women who has lost her arms and who has one wooden peg leg. Hale, *Artists and Warfare in the Renaissance*, p. 35, Pl. 48. In this work, Hale surmises that she was "a horrifically abused camp-follower." In another, J. R. Hale, "The Soldier in Germanic Graphic Art of the Renaissance," *Journal of Interdisciplinary History* 17, no. 1 (Summer, 1986): 100, describes her as a woman first raped and then disfigured. To me, her injuries indicate someone ripped apart by a cannonball or explosion, not dismembered by the swords of sadistic soldiers. See the mention of a woman who lost her leg to a cannon shot at Mas-d'Azil in 1625, mentioned in by Jacques de Saint-Blancard in his *Journal du siège du Mas-d'Azil en 1625 écrit par J. de Saint-Blancard, défenseur de la place, contré le maréchal de Thémines*, edited by C. Barrière-Flavy (Foix: Veuve Pomiès, 1894), pp. 16–17, in Sandberg, "Generous Amazons," p. 673. Another woman, while working, lost both arms to a cannonball at a siege during the English Civil Wars. Alison Plowden, *Women All on Fire: The Women of the English Civil War* (Stroud, Gloucestershire: 1998), p. 66. However, an illustration entitled *A maide Ravished and after quartered* in P. Vincent, *The Lamentations of Germany* (1638) does

aid their men in the front lines, as did Mary May and Mrs. Stone, they obviously risked being wounded in battle.

* * *

Be they prostitutes, "whores," or wives, women in the combat zone were full participants of the campaign community. They integrated themselves into camp life, adopting its customs, values, and prejudices; they suffered its hardships and faced its dangers. They also turned their hands to the work of the campaign community, and their labor both maintained and defined the changing nature of warfare.

show a man cutting off the arm of a woman; so Hale may be entirely justified. Illustation in Barbara Donagan, "Atrocity, War Crimes, and Treason in the English Civil War," *American Historical Review* 99, no. 4 (October 1994): 1145.

III

Women's Work: Gendered Tasks, Commerce, and the Pillage Economy

Beyond their roles as sex partners, life partners, and mothers, women performed a series of tasks essential to the maintenance of early modern military forces. Sir James Turner pointed out their value in the campaign community: "As woman was created to be a helper to man, so women are great helpers in Armies to their husbands, especially those of the lower condition; ... they provide, buy and dress their husbands' meat when their husbands are on duty, or newly come from it, they bring in fewel for fire, and wash their linnens."[1] Turner's respect for women's participation emerges even through his thick layer of assumptions about the naturally subservient status of women. While some of camp women's contributions in the field conformed to societal definitions of "women's work," they also took on duties unique to the campaign community. The latter could make great physical demands on the women, or require them to cross conventional moral boundaries.

ESSENTIAL CAMP DUTIES: GENDER-DEFINED TASKS

In much of what they did in camp, women conformed to the societal norms that assigned certain kinds of work to women. They increased the well-being of the men by washing and repairing clothes, nursing the sick, and cooking meals. In performing such gender-defined tasks, they relieved soldiers of work thought to be demeaning to men. Explaining why he was sending women with a military expedition in 1754, the duke

---

[1] Sir James Turner, *Pallas Armata. Military Essayes of the Ancient Grecian, Roman, and Modern Art of War* (New York: 1968 – reprt. of London: 1683), p. 277.

of Newcastle, serving as Secretary of State, stated: "the soldiers would be disgruntled, if the women did not accompany them to do the cooking, washing, sewing, and to serve other purposes for which women naturally go with the Army."[2]

Washing and repairing clothing remained one of the primary responsibilities of women throughout the early modern era.[3] Written sources also make clear the gendered nature of this service that, in directives, is often tied to other women's work. Leicester's disciplinary code of 1585 forbid men to "carrie into the fielde, or deteine with him in the place of his garrison, any woman whatsoever, other than such as be knowen to be his lawful wife" except for "women to tende the sicke and to serue for launders."[4] In the mid-eighteenth century, a French military commentator advised that in each company there should be one man married to a "woman who washed and mended the linens of the soldiers and sold them eau de vie and vegetables."[5] This would have amounted to

---

[2] Newcastle in Noel T. St. John Williams, *Judy O'Grady and the Colonel's Lady: The Army Wife and Camp Follower Since 1660* (London: Brassey's, 1988), p. 11.

[3] In rejecting that women had an essential role in maintaining units, Peter H. Wilson, "German Women and War, 1500–1800," *War in History*, vol. 3, no. 2 (1996), p. 155, states with great authority, "Most soldiers did their own washing and mending or expected their female partners to do it as a household chore." He seems to be talking about German garrison life. Yet Ulinka Rublack, "Wench and Maiden: Women, War and the Pictorial Function of the Feminine in German Cities in the Early Modern Period," trans. Pamela Selwyn, *History Workshop Journal*, 44 (January 1997), p. 17, states that Swabian militiamen could only receive permission to marry if their brides promised to wash and sew for the unit on campaign. There is abundant information that women on campaign continued to serve as laundresses and seamstresses. In addition, Engelen lists washing, nursing, and cooking as basic gendered tasks fulfilled by Prussian soldier wives. Beate Engelen, *Soldatenfrauen in Preußen. Eine Strukturanalyse der Garnisonsgesellschaft im späten 17. und 18. Jahrhundert* (Münster: 2004), pp. 365–67 and 371–72.

[4] Article 5 of Leicester's code in Cruikshank, *Elizabeth's Army*, p. 298. For illustrations of women serving as washer women for soldiers during the sixteenth and seventeenth centuries, see Hans Mielich's view of Charles V's encampment at Ingolstadt, 1549, with women washing clothes in the river and drying them on the bank. Max Geisberg, *The German Single-Leaf Woodcut, 1500–1550* (New York: 1974), vol. 3, p. 902, Pl. 913. Also see Jaques Callot, The Siege of La Rochelle, ca. 1630, which shows laundresses washing and drying clothes along the coast. Howard Daniel, *Callot's Etchings, 338 Prints* (New York: Dover Publications, 1974), Pl. 224.

[5] Montaut, *Réflexions sur la manière de former bons soldats d'infanterie*, 1747, p. 3, in Naoko Seriu, "Faire un soldat Une histoire des hommes à l' épreuve de l'institution militaire," Ph.D. diss., Ecole des Hautes Etudes en Sciences Sociales, 2005, p. 104. Vauban argued that a certain number of wives would not hamper a regiment but rather, would be "a great convenience because of washing clothes." Albert Rochas d'Aiglun, *Vauban, sa famille et ses écrits*, 2 vols. (Paris: 1910), 1:340–41. In George Farquar's comic play, "The Recruiting Officer" (1706), Captain Plume orders his sergeant to marry

six to eight women per battalion who served as washerwomen and *vivandières*.[6] Incidentally, laundresses enjoyed a reputation for physical strength developed by handling heavy baskets of wet clothes and great dripping sheets, as well as plying heavy irons.[7] During the French Revolution, when the National Convention voted to exclude "useless" women from military camps in April 1793, it explicitly allowed four laundresses per battalion, assigning them to their own tent in a specified part of camp.[8] Although this was a meager number, it demonstrates that even the morally severe Convention could not imagine an army without washerwomen.

Needlework was also regarded as work suitable for women. Women repaired clothing and turned their skills to making shirts and personal linens,[9] but often were barred from making men's outer garments, which was a task reserved for male tailors. As Clare Haru Crowston demonstrates in her excellent study of French seamstresses during the seventeenth and eighteenth centuries, the seamstresses' guild was permitted to make simpler women's dresses, but not men's clothing or elaborate court dresses.[10] Eighteenth-century commentators listed tailors as tradesmen who should be within the ranks of the regiments.[11] In civilian life, when times were hard, the tailors might even exclude women from making shirts to ensure that the tailors had work.[12]

Washing and sewing were poorly paid crafts, and women who worked at them were among those who often would cross over into part-time prostitution in order to survive.[13] A sixteenth-century woodcut of a

a woman who the captain had impregnated, arguing for her usefulness "we'll take her with us, she can wash." Farquhar, *The Recruiting Officer*, p. 10.

[6] See as well the British general orders for America, 2 June 1775, that allowed six wives per one hundred men, "who will be employed in washing for the men, that they may be kept clean." Orders in Don N. Hagist, "The Women of the British Army in America." http://www.revwar75.com/library/hagist/britwomen.htm#110.

[7] Olwen Hufton, *The Prospect Before Her: A History of Women in Western Europe*, vol. 1, 1500–1800 (New York: Vintage Books, 1998), p. 85.

[8] Charavay, *Correspondence de Carnot*, 2:116–17; *RACSP*, 3:309–10.

[9] Hufton, *The Prospect Before Her*, p. 171.

[10] Clare H. Crowston, *Fabricating Women: The Seamstresses of Old Regime France, 1675–1791* (Durham, NC: 2001).

[11] See for example, SHAT, 1M 1703: Montaut, op. cit., p. 3, in Seriu, "Faire un soldat," p. 104. When cloth was available to make uniforms for an American regiment, the call went out to find tailors in the ranks. Women were also to take part, but it would seem only as assistants to male tailors. Holly A. Mayer, *Belonging to the Army: Camp Followers and Community during the American Revolution* (Columbia, SC: 1996), p. 139.

[12] Hufton, *The Prospect Before Her*, p. 171, 248, 493.

[13] Ruth Mazo Karras, *Common Women Prostitution and Sexuality in Medieval England* (Oxford: 1996), pp. 54–55, and Hufton, *The Prospect Before Her*, p. 98 and Pl. 14.

tailor and a seamstress with an accompanying poem portrays the tailor convincing the seamstress to prostitute herself.[14] He urges: "Cheer up you pretty seamstress," because "your suffering will be worthwhile"; if you make yourself "a willing dish ... you will make more money in a month than in a year as a seamstress." She agrees to the bargain, "I hope we will benefit from this." Prostitution was a possible response to hard times. As pointed out in the preceding chapter, some soldiers' wives slipped into prostitution to supplement their income in hard times, a situation made worse when their husbands were on campaign.

PLATE 13. British light dragoon barracks, 1788. This romanticized view of family life in garrison portrays three couples and what appear to be three women's roles in the military. The woman on the left devotes herself to motherhood, the woman in the center seems to represent a *vivandière*, while the pretty young woman laundering clothes at the right may well be earning money for her family, as what must be her son and baby-cuddling husband look on.[15]

National Army Museum, London

---

[14] Wolfgang Strauch, *Tailor and Seamstress* in Walter L. Strauss, *The German Single-Leaf Woodcut*, vol. 3, p. 1075. My thanks to Mary Elizabeth Ailes for translating the German for me.

[15] An interesting English illustration of the early nineteenth century shows camp women engaged in a similar set of activities: sutling, cooking, washing, and carrying a heavy cauldron. See W. H. Pyne, Women's Duties in Camp, in St. John Williams, *Judy O'Grady and the Colonel's Lady*, Pl. 2.

An unusually revealing statement concerning washing and needlework comes from rules set out for the British Corps of Riflemen, soon to be the 95th Regiment of Foot, in 1801. It provided for "employment and comfortable livelihood" for women permitted to travel with the regiment. "The Colonel requests that the officers will never give their linen to wash out of the regiment, and also that they will distribute it nearly equally among the sergeants' wives."

Soldiers' laundry was "to be distributed in equal proportions among the other women of the companies." Interestingly, it specifies the amount to be paid for the wash and that the money was to be paid by the "pay sergeant," making the laundresses army employees (see Plate 13 for a washerwoman of this period). Moreover, "The Quartermaster will never give any needlework out of the regiment which can be done in it, and officers are requested to do the same."[16] Needlework was also to be apportioned out to soldiers' wives in the eighteenth-century Piedmontese army in order to give these women a livelihood.[17]

The idea that needlework was particularly suited to women was enshrined by Jean-Jacques Rousseau in Book V of *Emile*, where he argued that for young girls "needlework and lessons are the business of the day," describing girls as eager students of "holding a needle, that they always learn gladly."[18] Not surprisingly, the *levée en masse* of 1793 called young men to arms, but summoned women to needles and nursing: "The young men shall go to battle; ... the women shall make tents and clothing and shall serve in the hospitals."[19]

Nursing, as the *levée en masse* signaled, was another task traditionally considered particularly suited to women. Evidence from throughout the early modern period also establishes the continuity of this assumption.[20]

[16] From E. W. Shepard, ed., *Red Coat: An Anthology of the British Soldier during the Last Three Hundred Years* (London: 1952), pp. 48–49, in Barton C. Hacker, "Women and Military Institutions in Early Modern Europe: A Reconnaissance," *Signs: Journal of Women in Culture and Society* 6, no. 4 (1981), pp. 660–61.

[17] Sabina Loriga, *Soldats – Un laboratoire disciplinaire: l'armée piémontaise au XVIIIe siècle* (Paris: 2007), pp. 48–49.

[18] http://www46.homepage.villanova.edu/wood.bouldin/06S-3007/emileVedgirls.htm.

[19] See the discussion of the Levée en masse in John A. Lynn, *The Bayonets of the Republic: Motivation and Tactics in the Army of Revolutionary France, 1791–94* (Boulder, CO: 1996) originally published in 1984, p. 56.

[20] Men contracting May marriages, expected such women to act as their personal nurses. Wilhelm Haberling, "Army Prostitution and Its Control: An Historical Study," in Victor Robinson, ed., *Morals in Wartime* (New York: 1943), p. 32. In a baggage train scene portrayed by Hans Sebald Beham, ca. 1530, a wounded soldier on horse back is attended by a woman. Andrew Cunningham and Ole Peter Grell, *The Four Horsemen of*

General Robert Venables, when censured for having brought his wife and some other women on an expedition to the West Indies in 1654–55, replied that experience in the Irish wars had demonstrated "the necessity of having that sex with an army to attend upon and help the sick and wounded, *which men are unfit for.*"[21] Peter Hagendorf reported how his wife cared for him after the siege of Magdeburg in 1631: "As my wounds had to be dressed, my wife went into the city, even though it was burning everywhere. She wanted to fetch a pillow and towels for bandaging and upon which I could lay."[22] Camp women were close at hand and therefore could give immediate care to the sick and wounded at the front.

Women were also generally considered to be more capable of providing nursing care in military hospitals; although they might be aided by men, women still provided the primary nursing.[23] An English regulation for military hospitals from 1644 stipulated that nurses "are to be chosen from the widows of soldiers so far as fit ones can be found."[24] The nineteenth-century historian Victor Belhomme states that circa 1690, army hospitals maintained one nurse for every five wounded or ten sick.[25] Nuns might also provide nursing care. Sir William Howe ordered that any women who were to accompany his British army in October 1776 be willing to

the Apocalypse: Religion, War, Famine and Death in Reformation Europe (Cambridge: 2000), p.105, Pl. 3.4.

[21] Firth, *Cromwell's Army*, p.262. Italics are mine. See also Leicester's disciplinary code mentioned above.

[22] Peter Hagendorf, *Ein Soeldnerleben im Dreissigjaehrigen Krieg*, ed. Jan Peters (Berlin: 1993), p.138.

[23] For a discussion of civilian women who took it upon themselves to provide medical treatment and nursing to soldiers in early modern Europe, see Mary Elizabeth Ailes, "Camp Followers, Sutlers, and Soldiers' Wives: Women in Early Modern Armies (c. 1450–c. 1650)," *A Companion to Women's Military History*, Barton C. Hacker and Margaret Vining, eds. (Leiden: 2010).

[24] 15 November 1644 regulation, Calendar of State Papers, Dom., 1625–49, pp.643, 668–69, in Firth, *Cromwell's Army*, p.263, n. 1. In 1704 after the assault on the Schellenberg, Marlborough ordered "that all the widows in the army should repair ... to serve as nurses, and must have some small subsistence allowed for them." Hacker, p.662, from David Green, *Blenheim* (New York: 1974), p.50. Historian Paul E. Kopperman concludes that "already by 1750 it was redundant to refer to "female nurses" in the army, because almost all nurses were female." Paul E. Kopperman, "Medical Services in the British Army, 1742–1783," *Journal of the History of Medicine and Allied Sciences* 34 (1979): 436. Kopperman also states that women also served as laundresses, cooks, and matrons in eighteenth-century British army hospitals.

[25] Victor Belhomme, *L'armée française en 1690* (Paris: 1895), pp.154–57. The French intendant Robert reported of the hospital he had set up at Bergues in 1667, "I have also established a chaplain [there] with the suitable number of women and valets to assist him." SHAT, AG, A1209, #35, 10 June 1667, Robert at Furnes.

undertake nursing chores: "The Commander in Chief is Determin'd not to Allow any woman to Remain with the Army That Refused to take a Share of this Necessary Duty."[26] Henry Bouquet, while in command of British troops, stipulated that there be "two nurses for the general hospital" as among the few women he would allow in his 1764 expedition.[27] Describing German armies, Peter Wilson claims that women were barred from caring for troops after 1648, but this seems strange.[28] Perhaps it applies to some of the German examples he studied, but it is certainly wide of the mark concerning England and France.

Cooking was not so clearly a gender-defined task at any point and, in most, if not all, armies it eventually became more a man's than a

---

[26] Headquarters, 15 October 1776, Sir William Howe Orderly Book, in Mayer, *Belonging to the Army*, p. 13. Henry Bouquet in command of British troops stipulated that in his 1764 expedition there be "two nurses for the general hospital" as some of the few women he would allow with the column. *Historical Account of Bouquet's Expedition against the Ohio Indians in the Year 1764*, in Scott Hendrix, "In the Army: Women, Camp Followers and Gender Roles in the British Army in the French and Indian Wars, 1755–1765," in *A Soldier and A Woman: Sexual Integration in the Military*, ed. Gerard J. DeGroot and Corinna Peniston-Bird (New York: Longman, 2000), p. 33. See the statement concerning the need for a nurse in Bennet Cuthbertson, *A System for the Compleat Interior Management and Oeconomy of a Battalion of Infantry* (Dublin: 1768), p. 53. In 1776, the Continental Congress would ascribe the suffering of patients at Fort George as being due to the "Want of good female Nurses and comfortable Bedding." Hacker, "Women and Military Institutions," p. 661, from Blumenthal, p. 61. For material on nursing in United States forces during the Revolution, see Mayer, *Belonging to the Army*, pp. 142–43, 221–23.

[27] *Historical Account of Bouquet's Expedition against the Ohio Indians in the Year 1764*, in Scott Hendrix, "In the Army," in *A Soldier and A Woman: Sexual Integration in the Military*, ed. Gerard J. DeGroot and Corinna Peniston-Bird (New York: Longman, 2000), p. 33. In 1776, the Continental Congress would ascribe the suffering of patients at Fort George as being due to the "Want of good female Nurses and comfortable Bedding." Hacker, "Women and Military Institutions," p. 661, from Blumenthal, p. 61. For material on nursing in United States forces during the Revolution, see Mayer, *Belonging to the Army*, pp. 142–43, 221–23.

[28] "From being regarded as valuable assistants, women were officially excluded from the care of sick and injured soldiers after 1648." Wilson, "German Women and War," p. 155. Brian Crim similarly states, "Once the job of supplying and providing medical care for armies became the state's responsibility, women lost their largest source of employment." Brian Crim, "Silent Partners: Women and Warfare in Early Modern Europe," in *A Soldier and A Woman: Sexual Integration in the Military*, ed. Gerard J. DeGroot and Corinna Peniston-Bird (New York: Longman, 2000), p. 31. This is wrong. Most women with the aggregate contract armies were not uniquely there to nurse the sick and wounded, and most of the nursing done in the campaign community would not have been a paid employment. Thus, Crim is missing the true sources of camp women's income. See Engelen, *Soldatenfrauen in Preußen*, pp. 371–72, on Prussians soldiers' wives and nursing.

woman's job. Characteristically, a late sixteenth-century German set of articles regulating the artillery denied that any soldier could bring with him a "whore" unless permission was granted by the colonel "and that the women are formed into platoons in the regiments and shall be assigned to nursing and cooking."[29] But even in the sixteenth century, men are shown cooking as well, and baking remained a man's job with the armies as it was in civilian society throughout the early modern era.[30] During the second half of the seventeenth century, as authorities decreased the number of women in the camps and subjected camp life to much more ornate regulations, cooking duties were explicitly assigned to the men. In a typical French camp circa 1680, each company's tents stood in a row, with ten paces between companies, and company kitchens were set up six paces behind the last tent.[31] Men ate in mess groups — in French regiments, called the *ordinaires*. As defined by field regulations from 1758 to the end of the century, the *ordinaire* included fourteen to sixteen men who prepared their food in a marmite, or large kettle, and ate in common.[32] Some illustrations still show women at the cooking fires, and this may be particularly true of British troops who officially were permitted a larger number of accompanying women.[33] Women sutlers continued to prepare food for their improvised field

[29] Quoted in Haberling, "Army Prostitution and Its Control," p. 40.

[30] See the sixteenth-century woodcut of a cooking scene, in which a man is cooking, assisted by two women, in Goerge Hirth, *Picture Book of the Graphic Arts, 1500–1800 (Kulturegeschichtliches Bilderbuch aus drei Jahrhunderten, hrsg. von Georg Hirth)* (New York, 1972), vol. 2, Pl. 875. See also a woodcut by Wolfgang Strauch, "Field Cook and his Wife" (1568) in Strauss, Walter L. *The German Single-Leaf Woodcut*, vol. 3, p. 1071.

[31] For a discussion and detailed diagram of a French battalion camp in 1683, see Victor Belhomme, *Histoire de l'infanterie en France*, 5 vols. (Paris: 1893–1902), vol. 2, pp. 234–36. In his *L'armée française en 1690*, p. 178, Belhomme states that the kitchens were located twenty paces behind the company tents.

[32] See Lynn, *Bayonets of the Republic*, chap. 7, concerning the *ordinaire* in the army during the Revolution; also see *Bayonets*, p. 314, fn. 3, for a field test of a marmite, ca. 1789. Men bore the main responsibility for field cooking in the Continental army. Mayer, *Belonging to the Army*, pp. 14 and 63.

[33] According to French regulations, the optimum size of an *ordinaire* was sixteen men, and cooking was done in the *ordinaire*. British regulations allowing six women per one hundred men would mean that there was one woman for every sixteen men. See the drawing of a woman cooking at the fire of an English encampment, in Jacques François Joseph Swebach, British camp scene from the Napoleonic Wars, David Armine Howarth, *Waterloo: Day of Battle* (New York: 1969), p. 1. Engelen, *Soldatenfrauen in Preußen*, p. 366, includes a somewhat muddled view of camp life showing women at caldrons. She identifies this as women cooking, but the large size of the pots may indicate that they are really boiling clothes.

taverns, but troops were generally expected to prepare their own daily rations in the state commission army.

Beyond washing, nursing, sewing, and cooking, women with early modern European armed forces in the field were supposed to make themselves useful in any way possible. In his *Kriegszbuch* of 1598, Leonhardt Fronsperger insisted that the Hurenweibel in charge of the camp's women:

> must see that whores and loose fellows keep clean the latrines, and further: That they wait upon their masters faithfully and that they are kept occupied when necessary with cooking, sweeping, washing and especially attendance on the sick; and that they never refuse either on the field or in garrison, running, pouring out, fetching food and drink, knowing how to behave mostly with regard to the needs of other and taking it in turns to do what is necessary according to orders.[34]

REAL MEN DON'T WASH CLOTHES: GENDER ROLES AND SOCIAL PARODIES

Within the campaign community, gender roles and the assignment of gender-defined tasks were weighted with a particularly heavy symbolic burden, owing to the composition and purpose of the community. The male-dominated military is usually exaggeratedly masculine in its codes and standards, and this was certainly true in early modern Europe. Consider that soldiering was, and is, a job for the young, and it was understood to be the ultimate of man's work. Men and women in the camp community were generally cast-offs from the economy and the society, and as a consequence were probably very concerned with maintaining whatever status and respect they had in their new world. And they lived at a time when there was a good deal of discussion about the battle between the sexes and the proper roles of women and the power of men.

The literature and graphics of the time portray the young soldiers of the campaign community as embodying a form of masculinity heavy on violent assertion and aggressive sexuality. The latter was expressed not only through the sexual act but also through speech, relationships, and the like.[35] The

---

[34] Fronsperger in Ploss et al, *Woman in the Sexual Relation*, p. 99, in Hacker, "Women and Military Institutions," p. 653.

[35] Strong, open, and advertised sexuality in military service may not be a universal experience, but it seems to be a facet of modern American military life for men and women in the ranks. Consider, for example, the account of sexualized masculinity as portrayed among U.S. Marines presented by Anthony Swofford in *Jarhead* (New York:

experienced Spanish military commentator, Sancho de Londoño, seemed to be saying exactly this when he argued in 1589 for allowing prostitutes in the camp: "[W]ell organized states allow such persons in order to avoid worse disorders, in no state is it as necessary to allow them as in this one of free, strong and vigorous men, who might otherwise commit crimes against the local people, molesting their daughters, sisters and wives."[36]

Complicating, and probably exaggerating, the aggressive masculinity of the camp, were popular themes of inverted gender roles and the battle between the sexes over dominance in relationships, particularly within marriage, as discussed in Chapter II. Part of the iconography dealing with the battle between the sexes defines the washing of clothes as such a feminine duty that the ultimate humiliation for a man is to be forced to do the wash as his woman threatens him with whip or switch. A woodcut of 1533 by Erhard Schön, bearing the banner "There is no greater treasure here on earth than an obedient wife who covets honor," shows a woman who has harnessed her husband to a cart and is whipping him[37] (see Plate 14). She holds the traditional symbols of male authority—a sword, a purse, and pants (underpants, in this case). The cart is burdened with a large laundry tub full of dirty linen topped with a paddle to beat the clothes clean. Another woodcut from about the same time shows a stout and resolute wife holding a switch to threaten her husband as he uses a similar paddle to wash linens. A biting poem, "Ho, Ho the Diaper-Washer," accompanied this second woodcut. Interestingly, this engraving portrays the man in the distinctive slashed pants usually worn by a Landsknecht.[38]

2005). See as well the public recourse to masturbation described in Mark Bowden, *Blackhawk Down: A Story of Modern War* (New York: 2000). For a description of the sexualized atmosphere from a woman's point of view, see Kayla Williams, with Michael E. Staub, *Love my Rifle More than You: Young and Female in the U.S. Army* (New York: 2005).

[36] Sancho de Londoño, *Discours sur la form et manière qu'on devroit user, pour rédruir la discipline militaire à meilleur et son ancient estat* (1589) in Hacker, "Reconnaissance," from Hale, Cambridge.

[37] Moxey, *Peasants, Warriors, and Wives*, p. 102, Pl. 5.1. Chapter 5 is an extended discussion of this woodcut.

[38] Hans Shäuffelein, *Diaper Washer*, ca. 1536, in Moxey, *Peasants, Warriors, and Wives*, p. 108, Pl. 5.9. Interestingly, a broadsheet of the world turned upside down shows inversion by a man doing wash in a tub while a woman beside him chops wood with an axe. The broadsheet is undated, but costume suggests the early nineteenth century. C. F. Van Veen, *Dutch Catchpenny Prints: Three Centuries of Pictorial Broadsheets for Children* (The Hague: 1971), p. 40.

PLATE 14. Erhard Schön, *Woman's Reputation*, 1533. The title of the plate reads "There is no greater treasure here on earth than an obedient wife who covets honor."

> *The Illustrated Bartsch*, vol. 13, commentary, ed. Walter L. Strauss (New York: Abaris Books, 1984), pl. 179 , p. 355. Used with permission from Abaris Books.

The masculinity of the soldier was a vital trait, and to challenge it was to shame the soldier. Decking him out with woman's clothing ridiculed him to all who had eyes. In 1669, a court martial sentenced a soldier who had ill-treated his wife to riding a wooden horse in public with a petticoat draped around his neck.[39] In their attempts to improve the battle performance of the French army after the disaster of the Seven Years' War (1756–63), certain reformers wanted to exploit this kind of shame. One advised that "the cowardly soldier will be put in a woman's dress."[40] Another treatise would condemn cowards to be exposed "in the main street of the camp, with their belts detached and in a weak and effeminate pose," and deserters were to be put in a public place "attired in a woman's dress."[41] Napoleon Bonaparte actually carried out such a

[39] St. John Williams, *Judy O'Grady and the Colonel's Lady*, p. 15.
[40] SHAT, 1M 1711: *Notes sur l'infanterie*, 1769, p. 15, in Seriu, "Faire un soldat," p. 103.
[41] SHAT, 1M 1709: *Refléxions militaires*, p. 48, in Seriu, "Faire un soldat," p. 103.

punishment when campaigning in Egypt. The order of the day for 8 January 1799 set out the punishment for a spineless surgeon:

Citizen Boyer, surgeon of the hospital of Alexandria, has been cowardly enough to refuse to treat those wounded soldiers who had been in contact with patients allegedly suffering from a contagious disease. He is unworthy of being a French citizen. He will be dressed in women's clothes and led, on a donkey, through the streets of Alexandria, with a sign on his back, reading, "Unworthy of being a French citizen; he is afraid of dying." Whereupon he will be imprisoned and sent back to France with the first outgoing ship.[42]

Such an appearance of effeminacy would cause the deepest shame.[43]

Doing work defined as feminine shamed a soldier's demanding masculinity so, consequently, such duties had to be reserved for women. This fact may have imposed gender-defined tasks on women, but it also dictated that the campaign community must include a sufficient number of them to take care of the workload. Thus, Grimmelshausen's Courage feels she must stay with her husband rather than go to more comfortable winter quarters: "I refused to let him stay in the castle without me for fear he would be eaten up by lice, as there were no women to keep the men clean."[44] Benjamin Thompson decried the pitiful condition of American troops during the Revolution and ascribed it to the lack of laundresses: "[N]ot being used to doing things of this sort, [they] choose rather to let their linen, etc., rot upon their backs than to be at the trouble of cleaning 'em themselves."[45]

---

[42] Order in J. Christopher Herold, *Bonaparte in Egypt* (New York: 1962), p. 209. My thanks to David O'Brien for pointing this out to me.

[43] Emma Edmonds, who fought as Frank Thompson in the U.S. Civil War poetically proposed giving women's clothing to men too faint-hearted to enlist:

We send you the buttonless garments of women
Cover your face lest it freckle or tan!
Muster the apron-string guards on the common
That is the corps of the sweet little man

Poem by Edmonds in Julie Wheelwright, *Amazons and Military Maids: Women Who Dressed as Men in Pursuit of Life, Liberty and Happiness*, (London: 1989), p. 125.

I once witnessed a sergeant running a group of future USMC officers through their paces in the ROTC program at the University of Illinois. He chided the cadets as they did pushups by yelling at them, "Give me some real pushups, Girls!" The paradox was that this group of cadets was composed of young women as well as young men, so the sergeant's gendered insult seemed ill-considered. To him, I guess, "girl" simply meant "weak."

[44] Johann Jakob Christoffle von Grimmelshausen, *The Life of Courage, the Notorious Thief, Whore, and Vagabond*, trans. Mike Mitchell (Sawtry, Cambs: 2001), p. 78.

[45] Benjamin Thompson in Hacker, "Women and Military Institutions," p. 661, from Walter Hart Blumenthal, *Women Camp Followers of the American Revolution*

It is true that later in the eighteenth century, we find some descriptions of soldiers washing their own clothes, but it is only their own clothes they cleaned and only at those times when there were no women around to do the task. Men did not turn into launderers; that was women's work.

CLOSING THE GAP BETWEEN SUPPLY AND SURVIVAL: PROFITABLE PARTNERSHIPS

Beyond their money-producing roles as prostitutes, laundresses, seamstresses, and nurses, women helped to fill gaps in the supply system and to supplement the incomes of their male partners through a variety of small commercial ventures in the campaign community. Troops who were irregularly paid and ill-fed and those who accompanied them found ways to secure other sources of money and necessities. Many hustled at side occupations or formed *ad hoc* businesses. Moreover, in the days of aggregate contract armies, everyone pillaged. Women commonly took part in this campaign economy, sometimes on their own and more commonly as partners of male companions and husbands. Although written about civilian economies, the assessment of Olwen Hufton applies to life with the army as well: "Indeed, we might offer as a working generalization that the more modest the family, the more essential both the labour and the ingenuity of the womenfolk. They are at the center of the economy of makeshifts."[46] Working-class women in civilian society would improvise economic expedients, even when prohibited from doing so.[47] Life within the campaign community of the aggregate contract army was similarly an "economy of makeshifts," a useful term that sums up the catch-as-catch-can expedients employed by the poor to cobble together a living.[48]

***

(New York: 1952, repr. 1974), pp. 61–62. See also the comment: "[M]any of the Americans have sickened and died of the dysentery, brought upon them in a great measure through an inattention to cleanliness. When at home, their female relations put them upon washing their hands and faces, and keeping themselves neat and clean; but, being absent from such monitors, through an indolent, heedless turn of mind, they have neglected the means of health, have grown filthy, and poisoned their constitution by nastiness." Hacker, p. 661 from Blumenthal, p. 83.

[46] Hufton, *The Prospect Before Her*, p. 500.
[47] See the examples of such economic hustling provided in Sheilagh Ogilvie, "How Does Social Capital Affect Women? Guilds and Communities in Early Modern Germany," *American Historical Review* (April 2004): 325–26. She is trying to show how established economic interests punished such entrepreneurial creativity, but what strikes me is that the impetus for coming up with some ad hoc economic scheme was there.
[48] See, for example, Alannah Tomkins and Steven King, eds., *The Poor in England, 1700–1900: An Economy of Makeshifts* (Manchester: 2003).

If campaign communities were marching cities, they were also mobile marketplaces.[49] We know that women were central to civilian markets and retail trade.[50] We also know that in garrison, soldier wives hawked goods and sold cooked food.[51] It should come as no surprise that they created small commercial ventures in military camps. Women in civil communities legally dominated many areas of commerce, such as the sale of agricultural produce in open markets. However, they might also peddle goods without regard to municipal regulation; as the statutes of Bologna complained in 1557 and 1588: "These women ... for some time have disturbed this order and have not wanted to stay in their proper and appropriate places."[52]

Camp women also scrambled to make whatever money they could in their particular economy of makeshifts, and men chose to partner with them based, to a greater or lesser degree, on the ability of these women to bring something to the table. Their labor and the promise of earnings seemed to have served as their dowries. Advice literature aimed at working-class women warned that "none but a fool will take a wife whose bread has to be earned solely by his labour and who will contribute nothing towards it herself."[53] Even servant girls were counseled to start early to think about starting small business.[54] The seventeenth-century mercenary captain James Turner defended the presence of women with armies because a woman was able to "gain money to her husband and herself."[55] Grimmelshausen portrayed soldiers seeking to survive through marrying useful women:

[49] See Brian Sandberg, "'The Magazine of All Their Pillaging': Armies as Sites of Second-hand Exchanges during the French Wars of Religion," in Lawrence Fontaine, ed., *Alternative Exchanges: Second-Hand Circulations from the Sixteenth Century to Today* (New York: 2007), pp. 76–96, for an intriguing description of armies as "mobile marketplaces"—his term.

[50] Merry E. Wiesner, *Women and Gender in Early Modern Europe*, 2nd ed. (Cambridge: 2000), pp. 117–19.

[51] Engelen, *Soldatenfrauen in Preußen*, pp. 149–70. See the table on p. 155.

[52] Evelyn Welch, *Shopping in the Renaissance: Consumer Cultures in Italy, 1400–1600* (New Haven, CT: 2005), p. 35. See the treatment of women as small-scale merchants and peddlers, pp. 32–55.

[53] Eliza Haywood, *A Present for a Serving Maid* (1743) in Hufton, *The Prospect Before Her*, p. 62.

[54] Hufton, *The Prospect Before Her*, p. 133.

[55] Sir James, *Pallas armata*, p. 277. Even after the number of women on campaign was limited, Vauban favored marriage for troops because wives left in garrison towns "would work even at the heaviest tasks" to earn money for the family. Rochas d'Aiglun, *Vauban, sa famille et ses écrits*, 1:340–41.

There were some who supplemented their pay in several ways, though none that I liked or thought honourable. The situation was so wretched that they took wives (whores who'd escaped from the brothel if need be) simply in order to be fed on the proceeds from their work, be it sewing, washing, spinning, hawking goods or even stealing.[56]

His heroes, especially Courage, always hatched up ways of putting their hands on extra money. Christian Davies was equally energetic in scheming to make money, even turning to smuggling goods into Ghent at one point.[57] French soldiers, too, were notorious for smuggling, although salt was their specialty.[58] As Brian Sandberg aptly argues, second-hand trade was another important aspect of camp commerce.[59] The goods traded included used clothing, armor, and arms, and various items seized in pillage. Weapons and other military goods could be shipped in or simply taken from prisoners and the dead. An order directed to British troops in Rhode Island in 1776 commanded, "No soldier's wife is upon any account to keep a shop, without permission in writing signed by the Commandant," which is good indication that women were, indeed, setting up their own shops.[60] In one of the most original gambits, women from the Bevern Regiment of the Prussian army, then engaged at the battle of Kolin on a hot June day in 1757, broke into an icehouse and sold chunks of ice to the soldiers.[61]

Many rankers practiced trades part time, as professionals or amateurs, and women worked with them. It was usual for soldiers to possess artisan skills to a greater or lesser degree. We see this in sixteenth-century woodcuts that portray Landsknechts as cobblers, tailors, bakers, and

---

[56] Grimmelshausen, *Simplicissimus*, p. 307.

[57] *The Life and Adventures of Mrs. Christian Davies, Commonly Called Mother Ross* (London: 1740), p. 153.

[58] See the discussion of smuggling and battles between soldiers and agents of the salt monopoly, the gabelle, in Roy L. McCullough, *Coercion, Conversion and Counterinsurgency in Louis XIV's France* (Lieden: 2007). The legendary Mandrin, captured in 1755, was a smuggler with a large band that included demobilized soldiers and deserters. He smuggled and fought those sent to control him, killing fifty-three soldiers in a single engagement. Ruff, *Violence in Early Modern Europe*, pp. 11–13.

[59] Brian Sandberg, "'The Magazine of All Their Pillaging': Armies as Sites of Second-hand Exchanges during the French Wars of Religion," in Lawrence Fontaine, ed., *Alternative Exchanges: Second-Hand Circulations from the Sixteenth Century to Today* (New York: 2007), pp. 81–86.

[60] Don N. Hagist, "The Women of the British Army in America."

[61] Christopher Duffy, *The Army of Frederick the Great* (Newton Abbot, Devonshire: 1974), pp. 59–60.

cooks[62] (see Plate 1). All came to fight and are shown bearing arms; however, some also regularly plied their trades in the ranks, while others did so only if the possibility arose. Tradesmen in the ranks seem to have been a constant. Eighteenth-century French troops frequently claimed an artisan profession in the *contrôles*, or personnel files, maintained after 1716. Interrogations of deserters from the same period often stated a soldier's profession immediately after his name; these ranged from shoemaker and tailor to wigmaker and hairdresser.[63] Corvisier found that 41.9 percent of enlisted ranks in 1716 claimed to practice an artisan skill or to have come from artisan families, and this percentage rose to 52.9 percent in 1763.[64] Similarly, Prussian and Russian troops worked at trades to supplement their incomes when in garrison.[65] Military writers of the time even advocated recruiting men from robust and manly trades, such as blacksmiths, masons, and butchers, but also trades that served the needs of other soldiers, such as tailors.[66]

Camp women often assisted their male partners in artisan work. Woodcuts portraying a Landsknecht or Reisläufer with his woman often define these pairs by profession, for example, a cook and his wife and a baker and his wife.[67] Interestingly, the men in each of these woodcuts is dressed as a soldier carrying only his weapons, and if the pair is on the march, the woman carries a heavy burden, which may include tools of their trade (see Plate 20). This testifies to the existence within the campaign community of varieties of family economy, in which men and their female partners worked together in a common enterprise. Peter Hagendorf supplies more direct evidence in his report that, when hunger

---

[62] For cobblers, see Moxey, *Peasants, Warriors, and Wives*, p. 90, Pl. 4.17 and p. 91, Pl. 4.19. For tailors see Moxey, *Peasants, Warriors, and Wives*, p. 90, Pl. 18 and Walter L. Strauss, *The German Single-Leaf Woodcut*, vol. 3, p. 1075. For bakers and cooks, see Strauss, *The German Single-Leaf Woodcut*, vol. 3, Pls. 1071 and 1079.

[63] Concerning the *contrôles* and what the information they supply, see Corvisier, *L'armée française*. Seriu found that the maréchausee reported that 45 percent of those arrested claimed professions. For a selection of soldiers' professions, see Seriu, "Faire un soldat," pp. 249, 250, 259, 262, 265, and 292. A draper pursued his work even after enlisting. Seriu, "Faire un soldat," p. 12.

[64] Corvisier, *L'Armée française*, vol. 1, p. 505, and Seriu, "Faire un soldat," p. 112., and Seriu found that the maréchausee reported that 45 percent of those arrested claimed such professions.

[65] See Duffy, *The Army of Frederick the Great*, p. 55, and Christopher Duffy, *Russia's Military Way to the West: Origins and Nature of Russian Military Power, 1700–1800* (London: 1981), p. 134.

[66] SHAT, 1M 1703: Montaut, op. cit., p. 3, in Seriu, "Faire un soldat," p. 104

[67] Walter L. Strauss, *The German Single-Leaf Woodcut*, vol. 3, pp. 1071 and 1079.

struck the camp of Fritzar in 1640, he and his wife "had enough bread. We even sold it, for we had dug an oven in the earth and had baked the bread."[68]

Given the popular cultural imperative that the man should be dominant in a marriage, what were women's roles in such campaign business partnerships? As explained in Chapter I, artisans' wives often kept accounts and managed the money. It is reasonable to expect that women held a similar position as partners within the family economy of the camps. In Grimmelshausens, *Life of Courage*, Courage controlled her own business affairs with a vengeance. The far more sympathetic figure of Christian Davies also was a strong business woman, whether she was single or married at the time.

It may be a small thing, but in woodcuts showing partnered teams of Landsknechts and women, the men carry their weapons as if ready for battle, but they have no visible purse; women are usually shown with fat purses (see Plate 20, for example).[69] It seems as if women, free from the immediate risks of fighting in the front rank, held the money for their men while on campaign, just as did the wives of artisans. We know women carried their men's clothing and other personal items, including their "valuables," according to the description of May Marriages,[70] as well as their "booty," as attested to in a sixteenth-century poem.[71] Therefore, it would seem reasonable that this would include a purse full of the couple's stash of money. In contrast, rare woodcuts depicting a man dressed as a soldier in a peaceful civilian environment show him with a purse.[72] One such woodcut shows a Reisläufer, who has just returned home, presenting his empty purse to his

---

[68] Hagendorf, *Ein Soeldnerleben im Dreissigjaehrigen Krieg*, p. 167.

[69] For other examples see Walter Strauss, Walter L. *The German Single-Leaf Woodcut*, vol. 3, p. 1075; Walter Markov and Heinz Helmert. *Battles of World History*, trans. C. S. V. Salt (New York: 1979), p. 179; Hale, *Artists and Warfare in the Renaissance*, p. 36; and Hans Sebald Beham, ca. 1530 in Cunningham and Grell, *The Four Horsemen of the Apocalypse*, pp. 105–06, Pls. 3.4 and 3.5.

[70] The description, given in full on page 77 of this volume, includes "they are needed to take care of clothes, equipment and valuables." Klein in Haberling, "Army Prostitution and Its Control," p. 32.

[71] The poem, which ends this chapter, reads in part: "And if some booty should be mine, You shall keep it safe and fine." Poem on a woodcut print in Max Geisburg and Walter Strauss, eds., *The German Single-Leaf Woodcut*, vol. 3, pp. 1158–1661 in Rublack, "Wench and Maiden," p. 17.

[72] See Landsknechts with purses in peasant holiday woodcuts in Moxey, *Peasants, Soldiers, and Wives*, pp. 36–37, Pl. 3.1, and p. 54, Pl. 3.lo; and Hale, *Artists and Warfare in the Renaissance*, p. 1, Pl. 2, for example.

pregnant wife.[73] The woman carries signs of a wife's authority, including keys, knife, and full purse. This woman would seem to be a good manager, judging from her purse, and she is not pleased with her husband's meager earnings. This is no inversion, no battle for the pants, as her husband is still the Landsknecht, still in arms and someone to be reckoned with, but he has fallen short of her financial expectations.

SUTLERS AND VIVANDIÈRES

A common business in the campaign community was that of sutler, selling food items, alcohol, tobacco, and small luxuries to troops. Sutlers could be male or female; women sutlers were also known as *vivandières*. Sutlers set up markets or mobile canteens under the supervision of the local military authorities, usually the provost marshal of an army and the regimental marshals who worked under his supervision. Formal disputes were handled by the judge marshal.[74] Sutlers filled part of the gap between what the state supplied and what the men in the ranks needed or wanted.

Christopher Duffy, a military historian of unusual breadth, has argued that modern beliefs that earlier armies were nearly all "teeth" with only minimal "tail" are "very deceptive," because such assumptions tend to forget the civilian logistic support that traveled with military forces.[75] During the era of the aggregate contract army, when troops were often expected to buy their own basic foodstuffs with their pay, markets traveled with the army or set up in camps. This was especially true during sieges. Later, troops might be expected to purchase their own food only during winter quarters, but received their rations directly from army suppliers on campaign. A fundamental premise of this entire study is that we must recognize that the campaign community was large—often far larger than the number of those who actually stood in the line of battle and included many women who performed some role, or several roles, in providing necessary supply or petty luxuries for soldiers. As well as being

---

[73] Urs Graf, *The Soldier's Return*, ca. 1520, in Hale, *Artists and Warfare in the Renaissance*, p. 1, Pl. 1. Urs Graf had served as a Reisläufer, so he is probably portraying one here. Hale discusses this woodcut in J.R. Hale, "The Soldier in Germanic Graphic Art of the Renaissance," *Journal of Interdisciplinary History* 17, no. 1 (Summer, 1986): 93.

[74] See Turner, *Pallas Armata*, pp. 207–08, for a description of the duties of provost marshals and judge marshals as they applied to sutlers.

[75] Duffy, *Army of Frederick the Great*, p. 138.

sources of supply, sutlers' tents became centers for soldiers' recreation in camps that offered little else; thus, they buttressed morale, hardly an inconsequential function.

Sutlers bought their supplies or accumulated them through foraging and pillaging as circumstances allowed. We gain our best insights on this and other details concerning the lives and work of female sutlers from two fictional or fictionalized accounts of life on campaign. Grimmelshausen provides the first with his invention, *The Life of Courage*, set during the Thirty Years' War. The second, the anonymous *The Life and Adventures of Mrs. Christian Davies, Commonly Called Mother Ross*, deals with the War of the Spanish Succession. Davies was a real person, but her story was almost certainly heavily embellished.[76] The lives of Courage and Mother Ross were written by authors who knew the military practices of their times on both sides of the divide between the aggregate contract army and the state commission army. Their tales indicate that the daily existence of sulters and *vivandières* did not alter much from the early seventeenth century to the first decades of the eighteenth, even if sutlers were more essential for the supply of basic foodstuffs before 1650 than afterwards. Both Courage and the Mother Ross relied on forage and pillage as much as they could to secure their stocks; after all, they turned a much greater profit by stealing their inventory.[77] Courage spoke of herself as a champion pillager, and Mother Ross boasted: "I never lost an Opportunity of Maroding."[78] She foraged for pigs, sheep, cocks and hens ("in the camp language, corporals and their wives"),[79] fruits, vegetables, and grain.

As *The Life and Adventures of Mrs. Christian Davies* reports, the profession of *vivandière* was not an easy life. Once found, animals had to be butchered and cooked:

Having made these Prizes, I cut up my Mutton, laid by a Shoulder to roast, the Neck and Breast to make Broth; dug a Hole with a Hatchet to boil my Pot in , which, the Fire being made, I set on with the Mutton and Sweet-herbs.... They [officers] called for a Gallon of Beer ... ordered the Shoulder of Mutton to be roasted, which I did by pitching two forked Sticks in the Ground, putting it on a jointed Spit, and setting a Soldier's Wife to turn it. I made four Crowns a-piece of

---

[76] Concerning the reality of her existence, see the discussion of Davies in Chapter IV.

[77] It is interesting that Frederick the Great even provided his sutlers with escorts to aid them in plundering enemy villages. Duffy, *The Army of Frederick the Great*, p. 137.

[78] *The Life and Adventures of Mrs. Christian Davies*, p. 69.

[79] *The Life and Adventures of Mrs. Christian Davies*, p. 139. For examples of her foraging, see pp. 169–70, 174–75, and 201.

my Sheep, besides the Fat which I sold to a Woman, who made mold Candles for the Men, and made a good Penny of my Fowls and Pigeons.[80]

Strong drink—brandy or eau de vie—was also central to the *vivan-dière*'s trade. In fact, dealing in beer, wine, and strong drink was a traditional occupation for women in civil society.[81] One uncomplimentary remark came from a British soldier with Wolfe in Canada in 1759: "The swarming flies, short rations, dysentery and scurvy were as plaguing as the painted Red Indians, prowling around the old posts with tomahawks and scalping knives. The only relief was in the almost lethal spirits provided by the women sutlers."[82] In representations of *vivan-dières*, alcohol is a constant prop.[83] Depending on the army and the situation, she also sold tobacco. During the reign of Louis XIV, smoking came to be regarded as a necessity of life by French soldiers.[84] *Vivan-dières* had to scramble to make a living. Simplicissimus describes hard times and the way in which soldiers' wives coped as best they could: "There were some who sold tobacco and provided the men with pipes when they needed them; others sold schnapps, and had the reputation of mixing it with spirits they had distilled themselves, which did not make it any the less strong."[85]

Men and women both served as sutlers, but available sources suggest that over time the job transferred from male to female. Courage says that she had to have a male front man to run her business as a sutler during the Thirty Years' War, and so she had her stooge, Tearaway: "It would be good-bye to the business the moment I lacked such a figurehead."[86] Mother Ross ran her own business with gusto seventy years later. Eighteenth-century comments on sutlers seem to refer primarily or exclusively to women, particularly when it came to distributing strong drink to the troops. As the duke of Cumberland's standing orders of 1755 allowed, "Soldier's wives may suttle."[87] These were formidable women. It is said that Frederick the Great once

[80] *The Life and Adventures of Mrs. Christian Davies*, p. 176.
[81] Wiesner, *Women and Gender in Early Modern Europe*, pp. 117–18.
[82] In De Pauw, *Battle Cries and Lullabies: Women*, p. 122.
[83] See the painting of an English sutleress in classic pose with brandy keg and raised glass, George Forty and Anne Forty, *They Also Served: A Pictorial Anthology of Camp Followers through the Ages* (London: Tonbridge, 1979), p. 61.
[84] Babeau, *La vie militaire*, 1:253.
[85] Grimmelshausen, *Simplicissimus*, p. 307.
[86] Grimmelshausen, *The Life of Courage*, p. 136.
[87] Orders in St. John Williams, *Judy O'Grady*, p. 238.

rode up a hill to observe his troops, but was shoed away from this vantage point by two women sutlers who had already set up shop there.[88]

Sutlers and *vivandières* lived under increasing military regulation and supervision. Sir James Turner stated that the Swedish army allowed one sutler to each infantry company and one or two to each company of cavalry.[89] So many sutlers accompanied the French army during the war with Spain during 1635–59, that a law of 1653 cut down their numbers to four per regiment.[90] Austrian field regulations of 1749 and 1759 provided for *vivandières* to march with the troops and not travel back in the baggage train: "No woman in the infantry may, in future, march side by side with the regiment except those having no children and those serving soldiers with brandy."[91] During the same era, the provost in French field armies assigned numbers to the *vivandières'* wagons and supervised them in the baggage train. If they encumbered the march, the provost's men cut their traces and left them.[92] Sutlers might wear some version of military dress and/or a badge, as did Prussian male and female sutlers who sported a blue cocade in their hats.[93] Women who sold drink to French troops were allowed to remain with the regiments during the Revolution, according to the law of April 1793; shortly thereafter they were better known as *cantinières*, instead of *vivandières*. During the Napoleonic era, the French attached *cantinières* to particular regiments. A regulation stipulated that: "No women shall accompany the corps

---

[88] Duffy, *The Army of Frederick the Great*, p. 137.

[89] Turner, *Pallas Armata*, pp. 274–75.

[90] Law of 28 April 1653 in Babeau, *La vie militaire*, 1:200.

[91] Haberling, "Army Prostitution and Its Control," p. 52, and Christopher Duffy, *The Army of Maria Theresa: The Armed Forces of Imperial Austria, 1740–1780* (New York: 1979), p. 57. This is a repeat of the 1749 field regulation in which Bouquet set the rules for sutlers with his army in 1758. As such he drafted a "Form for Sutlers' Licenses" in June 1758, which ordered that no "Spirits or other Strong Liquors" be sold to Indians and that "no soldier, or Women belonging to the Army is to have any Spirits or other Strong Liquors from you, without Leave in writing from the Commanding Officer of the Regiment they belong to." *The Papers of Henry Bouquet*, eds. S. K. Stevens, Donald H. Kent, and Autumn L. Leonard, vol. 2, *The Forbes Expedition* (Harrisburg: 1951), p. 114.

[92] Lee Kennett, *The French Armies in the Seven Years' War: A Study of Military Organization and Administration* (Durham, NC: 1967), p. 123. American sutlers were strictly regulated during the War of the American Revolution. Washington wanted to control drunkenness by controlling licensing and controlling sutlers. Some soldiers and their wives tried to profit from unlicensed liquor sales. For details, see Mayer, *Belonging to the Army*, chapter 3.

[93] Duffy, *The Army of Frederick the Great*, p. 137.

except those employed as washerwomen, vendors of victuals and drink."[94] These women, often the wives of sergeants, were appointed by the regimental *conseil d'administration*, a committee of officers headed by the colonel.[95] A very notable pair of this sort was the future Napoleonic marshal Pierre François Joseph Lefebvre, a sergeant in the French Guards before the Revolution, and the woman he married in 1783, Catherine Hübscher, who worked as a *vivandière/cantinière* and washerwoman. She would later become the subject of the play, *Madame Sans-Gêne* and movies by that name starring Gloria Swanson in 1923 and Sophia Loren in 1962. *Cantinières* were well known in their day; the *cantinière* of the 26th Regiment crossed to enemy lines to take care of brigadier Simon saying, "we shall see if the English will kill a woman," and another, Catherine Baland of the 95th Infantry Regiment, was said to have distributed goods for free during combat. She was said to have received the Legion of Honor in 1813, although, in fact, Napoleon did not distribute this award to women.[96] Her role in the battle of Chiclana (1811) is memorialized in a grand painting by Louis-François Lejeune. The institution of *cantinières* would survive into the Third Republic.[97]

Early modern sutlers and *vivandières* set up their tents or huts in designated areas set off from the more regular encampment of the troops.[98] These could be rather large market areas in the sixteenth and early seventeenth centuries, or smaller precincts at the fringes of the camp in the late seventeenth and eighteenth centuries. Courage speaks of being in the same area as the "staff from the regimental office," which

[94] Article 13 of the ordinance of 7 Thermidor VIII (25 July 1801) in Haberling, "Army Prostitution and Its Control," pp. 57–58.

[95] Rothenberg, *Art of Warfare*, p. 88

[96] Rothenberg, *Art of Warfare*, p. 88

[97] *Cantinières* served with the French army throughout the nineteenth century, enjoying a particular heyday during the Second Empire. After creation of the Third Republic in 1873, military reformers saw *cantinières* as symptoms of the old army's decay, and legislation gradually removed their recognition and privileges. A 1906 circular was designed to suppress *cantinières*, and by the onset of World War I there were hardly any left. See Thomas Cardoza, "Exceeding the Needs of the Service: the French Army and the Suppression of Female Auxiliaries 1871–1906," *War and Society*, 20 (Spring, 2002):1–22. Also see Gil Mihaely, "L'effacement de la cantinière ou la virilisation de l'Armée française au XIXe siècle," *Revue d'histoire du XIXe siècle* 30 (2005) in which he argues that the cantinières had to be eliminated because of their apparent threat to the masculine nature of the new army.

[98] See, for example, the description of a sutler's area in camp provided in Turner, *Pallas Armat*, pp. 291–92, and the "Ordre qui doit être observé afin que le camp de chaque bataillon soit alligné avec les proportions convenables," SHAT, AG, MR 1701, piece #7, which specifically allows for *vivandières*.

included chaplain, quartermaster, commissary, provost marshal, executioner, and whoremaster.[99] Mother Ross states that when she opted to be a sutler, she was given special treatment, apparently in recognition of her previous service as a soldier; she "was permitted to pitch my Tent in the Front, while others were driven to the Rear of the Army."[100]

Because sutlers' and *vivandières'* tents were such a favorite subject for artists, many engravings and paintings illustrate the life that went on around them.[101] In established camps, for example, at sieges, sutlers might set up in rough wood huts. On the march, their tents often seemed improvised, perhaps a sheet of canvas thrown over a rough frame of branches or wooden poles. These tents were usually marked by some sign; as early as the mid-sixteenth century one such emblem emerged for sutler taverns—a tankard was hung above the front of the establishment, often from the ridge pole of a tent[102] (see Plate 15). A wreath seems to

---

[99] Grimmelshausen, *The Life of Courage*, p. 137.

[100] *The Life and Adventures of Mrs. Christian Davies*, p. 107.

[101] For seventeenth-, eighteenth-, and early nineteenth-century illustrations of sutler's and vivandière's encampments and tents, see the following: Corelli Barnett, *The First Churchill: Marlborough, Soldier and Statesman* (New York: 1974), p. 145; Stéphane Faniel, ed., *French Art of the Eighteenth Century* (New York: 1957), p. 30; Forty and Forty, *They Also Served*, pp. 30, 59; Hirth, *Picture Book of the Graphic Arts, 1500*, vol. 5, Pl. 2314–2316; David Howarth, *Waterloo: Day of Battle* (New York: 1969), p. 13; Herbert Langer, *Thirty Years' War*, trans. C. S. V. Salt (New York: 1980), Pl. 49; Gaëtane Maës, *Les Watteau de Lille* (Paris: Arthena, 1998), pp. 59, 61, 63, 64, 65, 246, 254, 286, and 317; Pierre Schneider and the Editors of Time-Life Books, *The World of Watteau, 1684–1721* (New York: 1967), p. 48; Hugh Trevor-Roper, ed., *The Age of Expansion: Europe and the World, 1559–1660* (New York: 1968), pp. 156–57; J. R. Western, "War on a New Scale: Professionalism in Armies, Navies and Diplomacy," in *The Eighteenth Century: Europe in the Age of Enlightenment*, ed. Alfred Cobban (New York: 1969), pp. 190 and 191. A woodcut from 1577 also seems to show a sutler's tent with men and women eating, but it is hard to judge by the context. Corelli, *Britain and Her Army, 1509–1970: A Military, Political and Social Survey* (New York: 1970), p. 46, Pl. 9. Hacker, "Women and Military Institutions in Early Modern Europe: A Reconnaissance," pp. 643–71, used a great many illustrations as sources for his excellent article, and I have followed his footnotes, so I owe many of the above illustrations here and elsewhere to his article.

There is a wonderful painting of a Sutler's tent painted by Philip Wouerman in 1655. It shows the tent, adorned by wreath and tankard, set among other such tents. A pretty serving(?) woman and three jolly cavalrymen converse in front of the tent; one trooper has his arm around the young woman. What makes this image so outstanding is that it is at http://www.dia.org/the_collection/overview/full.asp?objectID=94753&image=1, the site of the Detroit Institute of the Arts. The image can be enlarged and navigated to show all the marvelous detail.

[102] The earliest use of the tankard as an emblem that I have found is in a fresco depicting the siege of Florence in 1529–30. This work in the Palazzo Vecchio is attributed to Vasari and dates from 1558. Later examples of the tankard abound; see, for example, Pl. 15.

PLATE 15. Jan Martszen the Younger, a camp scene with a sutler's tent, from *Battle Subjects*, mid-seventeenth century. Note use of tankard, orb, and flag as signs of sutlers' tents. Also notice the presence of women, the handsome sutler or sutler's assistant and the women fighting in the right background. The two combative women at another sutler's tent seem to be attacking two men, one of whom is prostrate on the ground with his hand raised to parry a blow from the woman's broom. *The Illustrated Bartsch*, vol. 5 (formerly volume 4), *Netherlandish Artists*, ed.Walter L. Strauss (New York: Abaris Books, 1979), pl. 1(49), p. 68. Used with permission from Abaris Books.

have been an even more common emblem, sometimes combined with the tankard or a flag. But other emblems might be employed, including placards of one kind or another.[103] A miniature model of a camp circa 1614 was described: "The huts and offices of the sutlers who sell victuals are also much in evidence, with their signs and notice-boards at the doors and with their tables laid out at the disposition of the multitude."[104]

In prints and drawings, simple tables, stools, or benches sit in front of the tent, and the eating and drinking take place outside. Inevitably women are part of the scene, either as servers for male sutlers or as the

---

[103] See the Thirty Years' War sutler's area in ed. Hugh, *The Age of Expansion: Europe and the World, 1559–1660* (New York: 1968), pp. 156–57. It displays tavern-like placards attached to sutlers' tents. Also see Hyde Park sutlers' tents, ca. 1780, in Forty and Forty, *They Also Served*, p. 59. Turner uses the term "Mark-tenters," apparently for sutlers; for example, Turner, *Pallas Armata*, p. 207.

[104] A Struzzus, *Imago militiae auspiciis Ambrosii Spinolae* (Brussels: 1614) in Parker, *The Army of Flanders*, p. 177, n. 1.

sutlers themselves. Scenes also often portray men sitting with, holding, or jostling the women, demonstrating that the *vivandière*'s tent was a venue for contact between the sexes. Along with drinking, flirting, and fondling, came the occasional quarrels between soldiers warm with wine and, perhaps, contending over the attentions of the women present. One unusually explicit drawing of a sutler's tent in Flanders during the War of the Spanish Succession must be taken seriously, as it was sketched by Marcellus Laroon, who served in Marlborough's army at the time.[105] In the left foreground sits a large barrel of wine or beer. In the background, a few men play musical instruments as a couple dances in the right foreground. The attractive, lively stepping young woman has unbuttoned and opened her blouse down to the waist, revealing her breasts, as her partner, in spurs and sword, clutches a bottle while kicking up his heels. At the table two men drink, while another cavalryman embraces a second woman. It all comes off as a camp bacchanalia.

Whether or not the owner was a woman, the lure of female presence was an effective way to bring in clients. While Courage wanted to stand in the shadow of Tearaway to avoid problems, she still "played the part of the pretty cook or waitress the landlord keeps behind the bar to attract as many customers as possible."[106] Artists were very much taken with the theme of dalliance between soldiers and women around the sutler's tent.[107] The pretty *vivandière* became something of a fixture in artists' renditions of camp life.[108]

Involvement of sutlers and *vivandières* in the life of the campaign community went beyond purveying food and drink, particularly when plunder fueled the campaign economy. Sutlers fenced objects, turning plundered goods into cash, which was more convenient to carry and easier to spend. In fact, some sixteenth- and seventeenth-century merchants traveled with the army with the sole purpose of purchasing booty and the goods of dead soldiers.[109] Grimmelshausen's Courage boasts:

No article, whether gold, silver or jewelry, not to mention pewter, copper or cloth, whether clothing or anything else, whether legal booty, plunder or even

[105] Marcellus Laroon, A market tent in camp, ca. 1707, in Corelli Barnett, *The First Churchill: Marlborough, Soldier and Statesman* (New York: 1974), p. 145.
[106] Grimmelshausen, *The Life of Courage*, p. 108.
[107] Examples of dalliance around the sutlers' tents.
[108] See the painting of the typical pretty British female sutler, ca. 1700, in Forty and Forty, *They Also Served*, p. 61.
[109] Parker, *The Army of Flanders*, pp. 176–77.

stolen goods, was too expensive or too cheap for me to trade it. And if a man didn't know what to do with the things he had to sell, however he had acquired them, he was as safe with me as with the Jew, for we were both keener to protect thieves than to have the authorities punish them. As a result, the contents of my two carts were more like a general merchant's stock than just a victuallers, and I could supply anything—at a price—to any soldier, high or low.[110]

Ultimately, the sutler or *vivandière* would likely sell the goods to another more established dealer, often identified as a Jew, a term wielded with an anti-Semitic bite.[111] The role of sutlers in seizing and processing plunder and the weaker regulation of the campaign community during the first half of the early modern era probably means that they were more numerous than they later became.[112]

A *vivandière* on campaign could morph into a tavern-keeper during winter quarters or in garrison.[113] Keeping a small tavern or drink shop was a good venture for women in civilian society, thus the role fit camp women as well.[114] A series of letters from 1710 at the French military archives illuminates a few details of the life of one such enterprising woman. Castres, her husband who was a noncommissioned officer in the cavalry Regiment du Roi, petitioned authorities that since he was a soldier, his wife should not have to quarter soldiers at her home and business establishment in Guise.[115] The official inquiry reports: "This

[110] Grimmelshausen, *The Life of Courage*, p. 117.

[111] For example, see the comments in *The Life and Adventures of Mrs. Christian Davies*, pp. 62–63, 137, concerning selling to Jews. Also, see Courage's other statements about Jewish traders, e.g., her statement about dealing harder "than any old Jew." Grimmelshausen, *The Life of Courage*, p. 98. The use of "Jew" as a term of abuse and the implication that Jews swindled people out of valuable goods has the unmistakable ring of anti-Semitism.

[112] Here, I believe, Barton Hacker gets it wrong because he is too dependent on the visual record. He writes, "The increased frequency with which sutlers begin to appear in graphic works suggests how vital they were to the armies of the ancient regime." Hacker, "Women and Military Institutions," p. 656. While they were very frequently displayed in the graphic arts of the late seventeenth and eighteenth centuries, sutlers played a wider range of critical roles even earlier.

[113] It is interesting that one image of a tavern building has the wreath so typical of sutlers' tents hung above the door. Was this a sign for a tavern or for one approved by military authorities? This is entitled "Halte des soldats," and is the work of Louis Watteau. Gaëtane Maës, *Les Watteau de Lille* (Paris: Arthena, 1998), p. 50.

[114] See Hufton, *The Prospect Before Her*, pp. 170–71, and Wiesner, *Women and Gender in Early Modern Europe*, pp. 117–18 on the fact that tavern keeping was considered a suitable life for women. Also note that Egelen sstated that, in garrison, Prussian soldiers' wives often sold beer and worked as innkeepers. Engelen, *Soldatenfrauen in Preußen*, pp. 149–70.

[115] SHAT, AG, A12266, #87–90, February and March 1710.

woman is a kind of *vivandière* who works at that profession during the campaign season, and in the winter she returns to Guise, in a house ... [where] she now runs a cabaret." Mme. Castres obviously augmented the family income, perhaps pulling in more money than her husband did. He appealed both to the law and to his thirty years of service and his wounds to get a break, but to no avail. The authorities decided that there were so many troops in Guise, that Mme. Castres would have to quarter soldiers anyway.

Mother Ross reported that she also ran a tavern after she left the army: "As I had before kept a Publick-House, and was used to Sutleing in the Army, I could think on nothing better than that of my former, and accordingly, I took a House, put in a Stock of Beer, and by this and making Pies, I got a comfortable Support."[116] She later returned to the army and set up as a sutler in Hyde Park, where troops camped.[117]

While sutlers and *vivandières* provided valuable services and a site for entertainment and carousing, they were not always beloved. Sutlers snagged the soldier's money, for their alcohol provided one of the few comforts of camp. When the soldier in Erasmus's essay "A Soldier's Life" is asked to whom he will make restitution for all his theft, he answers, "That's made already ... to Whores, Sutlers, and Gamesters."[118] The oft-repeated charge that soldiers wasted their money on drink meant that much of their pay and plunder ended up in the hands of sutlers. Authorities in camp were supposed to protect soldiers from price gouging by setting prices. Turner stipulates that provost marshals were supposed to "take pains to learn what the Prices of things are in these Towns where the Mark-tenters buy their Wine, Beer, Tobaco, Vinegar, Oyl, Bread, Bacon, and other Provisions, that accordingly the General Auditor may know with the greater justice to impost the Prices." However, sutlers could conspire with provosts and auditors to cheat the troops: "But the truth is, the Buyers are too often abused, and the Prices set too high by collusion of the Provost-Marshal with the Sutlers, and the Sutlers bribing the Judg Marshal."[119] In Grimmelshausen's novel, Courage looks

---

[116] *The Life and Adventures of Mrs. Christian Davies*, p. 237.
[117] *The Life and Adventures of Mrs. Christian Davies*, p. 243. For illustrations of sutler's tents and emcampments at Hyde Park. See Forty and Forty, *They Also Served*, p. 59, for a view of sutler's tents in Hyde Park, about 1780.
[118] Erasmus, "A Soldier's Life," p. 63
[119] Turner, *Pallas Armata*, pp. 207–08. There could also be benefits to army regulation; for example, the Prussian king helped sutlers obtain beer and brandy. Duffy, *Army of Frederick the Great*, p. 137.

forward to "selling beer at double what I had paid for it and generally indulging in worse sharp practice than any old Jew."[120] She carefully ingratiates herself with the right people, being sure to, "grease quite a few palms to safeguard myself and my activities: the provost-sergeant was like a father to me, his old woman (his wife, I mean) like a mother; the colonel's wife was 'my lady' and the colonel 'my lord', and they all protected me and mine. ..."[121]

Serving as merchants, fences, and creditors, sutlers had many opportunities to gouge their soldier customers, who might well resent them. During the sixteenth and seventeenth centuries, troops that mutinied for lack of pay would sometimes attack sutlers who they believed had taken advantage of them. In the mid-seventeenth century work *The Life of Estevanillo Gonzales*, which may be a faked autobiography, the author comments: "The vivandiers being look'd upon as Thieves, that convey away all the money of the Army, the men had no more Pity on them than if they had been lineally descended from Nero."[122] Turner expressed concern over "debates and brawls betwixt Souldiers and Sutlers."[123] The beloved *vivandière* of eighteenth-century lore was, in reality, probably a much rarer figure.

PILLAGE AS FUNDAMENTAL TO THE CAMPAIGN ECONOMY

While hustling in improvised commerce and acting as *vivandières* offered some women commercial possibilities to garner necessities and make money within the campaign community, it may be impossible to establish how many women followed these paths. However, pillage was a nearly universal occupation involving the entire campaign community before 1650, and it seems reasonable to posit partnerships between men and women in this less-than-honorable profession. Pillage can be considered the ultimate family economy of the campaign community.

Here, the emphasis is primarily on the aggregate contract army. It was well known and much discussed that troops who were not paid turned to

---

[120] Grimmelshausen, *The Life of Courage*, p. 98.
[121] Grimmelshausen, *The Life of Courage*, p. 118.
[122] E. Gonzales, *The Life of Estevanillo Gonzales*, first published in 1646 and presented in English in *The Spanish Libertines*, J. S. Stevens, trans., (1707), p. 461, in Tallett, *War and Society in Early Modern Europe*, p. 115.
[123] Turner, *Pallas Armata*, p. 291.

pillage to find the means by which to survive. In an odd way, contemporaries even called upon the Bible to understand, even to justify, troops who plundered civilians. Luke 3:14 tells of preaching by John the Baptist: "And the soldiers likewise demanded of him, saying, And what shall we do? And he said unto them, Do violence to no man, neither accuse any falsely; and be content with your wages." This apparently innocuous passage attained a potent meaning in early modern Europe. In 1649, the military administrator, Charles Machault, complained to the French war minister that unless the troops who were Machault's responsibility received proper pay, they would turn to violence and theft. Machault appealed to the biblical passage cited above to defend his own intention not to enforce discipline in such a situation. Saint John the Baptist, he explained, "did not fly into a rage against the soldiers nor did he scold them [for their deeds], except when they did evil [after] they had been paid."[124] Turner refers to the same passage: "The *Baptist* insinuates, that Soudiers should be paid their wages, because he bids them *be contented with their wages, and do violence to no man.* But few or no Evangelick Precepts are obeyed, and this as little as any; Souldiers get not their wages, and violence is done to many men."[125] Rampages by unpaid troops were even a subject of discussion from the pulpit; in his "Whether Soldiers, too, Can be Saved," Luther referred to Luke 3:14 and commented that, "Thus he praised the profession of arms and, at the same time, forbade the abuse of it."[126]

After pillage reached its most outrageous extremes during the Thirty Years' War, the greater administrative effectiveness, enhanced military leadership, and heightened troop discipline that typified the state commission army certainly diminished this horrendous abuse; however, it never really disappeared. Even at the end of the period under discussion, French troops were forced to pillage because the revolutionary government proved incapable of supporting their greater numbers in the field. Also, a recent study of British soldiers in the Peninsular War showed that Wellington's men were irregularly fed and that, even with full rations, they were not given enough to maintain health in the strenuous environment of campaigning. In consequence, British troops enjoyed a dubious reputation as enthusiastic pillagers of edibles, although they did

---

[124] SHAT, AG, A1116, #482, 10 December 1649, Machault to Le Tellier.
[125] Turner, *Pallas Armata*, p. 198.
[126] Martin Luther, "Whether Soldiers, too, Can Be Saved," in *Luther's Works*, Robert C. Schultz and Helmut T. Lehmann, eds., vol. 46 (Philadelphia: 1967), p. 97.

not routinely commit the violent crimes that accompanied pillage during the Thirty Years' War.[127]

Women's Participation in Pillage

In reporting on the sack of Magdeburg in 1631, Peter Hagendorf penned a particularly revealing account. While he lay wounded, his wife went into the blazing city to search for bandages and bedding.

A cry then came from throughout the city as houses all fell on each other. Many soldiers and their wives who were searching to steal something died. God indeed protected [my wife]. After an hour and a half, she came out of the city accompanied by an old, holy woman, who helped her carry bedding. She also brought me a large tankard with four liters wine. In addition, she found two silver belts and clothes, which I was able to cash in for twelve Thaler in Halerstadt.[128]

This brief passage contains a great deal of enlightening information: women participated in pillage; they teamed with their male partners in searching for plunder; they pooled their take with the men; and they sought both necessities and riches.

Women from the campaign community took part in pillaging alongside their men or entirely on their own (see Plate 16). Courage was probably speaking within the realm of Grimmelshausen's experience when she boasted, "[N]o one could match me at foraging."[129] Christian Davies continually reports her unexcelled prowess in foraging and pillaging. She was happy, for example, to be with troops spearheading the advance of the army, for while it is "the most dangerous Post it is the most profitable, if there is any Plunder to be got, as there are but few to share it."[130] Sir James Turner, when praising women as helpmates to their soldier partners in the quotation that begins this chapter, also seems to credit women as capable pillagers, "especially they are useful in Camps and Leaguers, being permitted (which should not be refused them) to go some miles from the Camp to buy Victuals and other Necessaries."[131] In lauding women for their ability to "provide" meat and "buy" foodstuffs, he is probably

---

[127] Edward James Coss "All for the King's Schilling: An Analysis of the Campaign and Combat Experiences of the British Soldier of the Peninsular War, 1808–1814," Ph.D. dissertation, The Ohio State University, 2005.

[128] Hagendorf, *Ein Soeldnerleben im Dreissigjaehrigen Krieg*, pp. 138–39.

[129] Grimmelshausen, *The Life of Courage*, p. 59

[130] *The Life and Adventures of Mrs. Christian Davies*, pp. 174–75

[131] Turner, *Pallas Armata*, p. 277.

PLATE 16. Woodcut from Johannes Stumpf, *Schwytzer Chronica* published in 1554. This woodcut clearly portrays the participation of camp women in pillaging a village.

Bibliothèque de Genève.

reporting simply that they came back to camp with edibles, not necessarily that they got them by honest means.

Beyond such an artist's view as Plate 16, several paintings and engravings of quartering scenes show over-dressed soldiers' women inside village homes as men of the campaign community demand what they want and abuse peasants to ensure that they get it.[132] One painting illustrates the presence of women in a community of bandits.[133] Soldiers' women also appear in paintings showing the pillage of elegant homes of the wealthy and well born.[134] And often, women are portrayed as present during pillage, even if they do not participate.[135]

Wallhausen's particularly vivid tale of the fight between women over precedence on the wagon dovetails nicely with Hagendorf's diary entry quoted above. It should be remembered that the dispute between two women quickly escalated to a fight between the husband of one and the

[132] See paintings and engravings by and after David Vinckboons and plates of works after Peter Paul Rubens, Carousing Landsknechts, in Fishman, *Boerenverdriet*, Pls. 14–18 and 21–24.

[133] Pieter Jansz Quast (1606–47), Bandits, in Fishman, *Boerenverdriet*, Pl. 36.

[134] See two such paintings by Jacob Duck (ca.1600–67), in Fishman, *Boerenverdriet*, Pls. 28 and 35.

[135] See works by David Rijchaert (1612–61), J.M. Molenaer (1610–68), Pieter Molijn (1595–1661), and Joost Cornelisz Droochsloot (1586–1666) in Fishman, *Boerenverdriet*, Pls. 25, 26, 34, 37, and 38.

partner of the other. This clearly demonstrates that the two "teams" were busy at the business of pillage at the same time, and most probably shared the spoils.

The Hagendorf's wife sought first for things to care for her husband; such were the most pressing necessities. For most, however, foodstuffs were the most essential, and the most excusable, targets for plunder. A citizen of Freiburg complained of occupation by the Swedes and "the soldiers' abominable wives," who went into local gardens and cut produce as soon as it appeared; then they had the gall to sell what they did not consume in the Freiburg market.[136] Mother Ross talks of her exploits gathering fowl, pigs, and sheep, as well as beer and wine.[137] Being a sutler, she was feeding troops for profit. To provide herself with pillaged food, she had to be bold and fast. Once, while still masquerading as a man, she had to fight a corporal for a piglet, resolving the situation by bashing him over the head with the butt of her pistol.[138]

Foraging and pillaging provided more than sustenance; plunder could also produce money. The best find would be cash itself, but there were always individuals willing to convert valuable objects into money—at a stiff discount, to be sure. In Grimelshaussen's *Simplicisimus*, pillagers took pewter and silver vessels and plates, beating them flat to make them more portable.[139] All manners of items that were useless to survival in the field were stolen so that they could be converted into cash.[140] As already mentioned, sutlers and itinerant dealers bought pillagers' booty. Christian Davies stated that at the siege of Liege she pilfered a silver chalice and some plates, "which I afterwards sold to a Dutch Jew for a third part of their value."[141] Later she sold pillaged lace "to a Jew at five livres an ounce."[142]

---

[136] Thomas Mallinger, "Thomas Mallingers Tagbücher," *in Quellensammlung der badischen Landesgeschichte*, ed. F. J. Mone, 4 vols (Karlsruhe: 1848–67), vol. 2, p. 536, in Mortimer, *Eyewitness Accounts*, p. 36. See actions of British soldiers and their wives plundering gardens in Newport in 1779. Don N. Hagist, "The Women of the British Army in America."

[137] For accounts of her take at foraging, see *The Life and Adventures of Mrs. Christian Davies*, pp. 64 (hogs and piglets), 175 (fowl), 176 (sheep, beer), 206, and 211.

[138] *The Life and Adventures of Mrs. Christian Davies*, p. 64. Fight for plunder could extend into the camp: a painting by W. C. Duyster records soldiers viciously fighting over booty collected for distribution. Langer, *The Thirty Years' War*, Pl. 78.

[139] See the account of pillage in Grimmelshausen, *Simplicissimus*, pp. 22–27.

[140] After taking Pamier in 1628, pillaging troops were especially keen to seize furniture. Sandberg, "The Magazine of All Their Pillaging," pp. 83–86.

[141] *The Life and Adventures of Mrs. Christian Davies*, p. 62–63

[142] *The Life and Adventures of Mrs. Christian Davies*, p. 137.

Pillagers could also cart their plunder directly into towns for sale. When Swedish troops occupied Munich during the Thirty Years' War: "At this time much robbing and plundering took place, particularly in the countryside, and all kinds of things were brought in here. There was no scarcity of buyers, and in the mornings when the Swedes brought in a number of loaded wagons everything was sold out in a few hours, so then they went back out to get more booty. . . . "[143]

In fact, soldiers sold things for much less than they were worth. As Geoff Mortimer writes, "The principal beneficiaries of the plundering were often not the soldiers but the citizens of neighbouring towns, who bought up the stolen goods for a fraction of their value from looters mainly interested in cash, either as a more portable form of booty or as the price of the next meal."[144] Turning plunder into money paid for necessities, but plunder was also the promise of riches—" the stuff dreams are made of," or at least the dreams of early modern soldiers and their women.

Women continued to take part in pillage throughout the eighteenth and into the nineteenth centuries, although not at the levels that afflicted the sixteenth and seventeenth centuries. The duke of Wellington justified whipping women for plundering by insisting to Lady Salisbury: "It is known that in all armies the Women are at least as bad, if not worse, than the men, as Plunderers! And the exemption of the Ladies [from punishment] would have encouraged Plunder!"[145] And punished they were, as one soldier attested in his Scottish fashion: "sax and thirty lashes a piece on the bare doup."[146]

The Horrors of Pillage: Torture, Rape, and the Campaign Community

The campaign community inflicted great cruelty on those it pillaged, as the horrors went far beyond mere theft. In fact, the excesses that

---

[143] Johannes Hellgemayr, "Zeitgeschichtliche Aufzeichnungen des Bayerischen Hofkapell-altisten Johannes Hellgemayr aus den Jahren 1595–1633," *Oberbyerisches Archiv*, 100 (1975), p. 209, in Mortimer, *Eyewitness Accounts*, p. 82.

[144] Mortimer, *Eyewitness Accounts*, p. 82. One commentator stated that after the battle of Ponts-de-Cé in 1620, "I saw lots of other goods go for miserable prices." Sandberg, "The Magazine of All Their Pillaging," p. 85.

[145] Elizabeth Longford, *Wellington: The Years of the Sword* (New York: 1969), p. 201.

[146] Elizabeth Longford, *Wellington*, p. 201. A similar punishment was visited upon a British woman pillager in 1745. "Her tail was immediately turned up before the door of the house, where the robbery was committed, and the Drummer of the Regiment tickled her with 100 very good lashes." St. John Williams, *Judy O'Grady*, p. 15.

accompanied pillage constitute strong evidence for the separation and animosity between the campaign community and the civilians upon whom it preyed. Hagendorf also wrote of the sack of Magdeburg, "Beyond all measure was wrecked the most dreadful and awful havoc with the plunder, thievery, murder, and the violation of virgins and wives that was begun right away."[147]

Works of art leave chilling visions of troops on the rampage, and verbal descriptions of brutality validate the artists' portrayals of this hell. In his depiction of troops pillaging a large farmhouse during the Thirty Years' War, Jacques Callot indicts the excess of war for all time[148] (see Plate 2). Marauders ransack the farmhouse for anything of value, chasing down those who attempt to flee and slaughtering those who resist. In order to extract from them the hiding places of the family's wealth, soldiers torture the occupants; one helpless man hangs over a fire.[149] A similar fate ended the life of Krüger Möller, who marauders "caught [and] bound ... hand and foot and put him over the fire, where they roasted him for a long time until he was forced to disclose his remaining money." Then other greedy soldiers tortured him again by putting his face to the fire for "so long that his skin came off him like a butchered goose, and he died."[150]

In Plate 17, P. Vincent shows a catalog of tortures in his *The Lamentations of Germany* (1638), which includes what was called euphemistically "the Swedish draught," or which Vincent labels simply as "pisse poured down there [sic] throates."[151] This is apparently a twist on judicial water torture.[152] One contemporary left a chilling account: "The

---

[147] Hagendorf, *Ein Soeldnerleben im Dreissigjaehrigen Krieg*, p. 170.

[148] From Jacques Callot, Grand misères et les Malheurs de la Guerre, 1633, in Daniel, *The World of Jacques Callot*, p. 44, Hirth, Georg. *Kulturgeschichtliches Bilderbuch aus drie Jahrunderten*, 6 vols. (1882–90; reprint ed., New York: Arno Press, 1972), vol. 1, Pl. 358.

[149] With less artistry, and a more obvious political message, Romeyn de Hooghe displays similar barbarities on the part of the French in the Dutch Netherlands, 1672–74. Romeyn de Hooghe, "The Cruelties Committed by the French," in Hirth, *Picture book of the graphic arts*, vol. 5, Pls. 2680–90.

[150] Peter Thiele, *Peter Thiele's Aufzeichnungen von den Schicksalen der Stadt Beelitz im 30jährigen Kriege*, B. Elsler, ed. (Beelitz: 1931), p. 12, in Mortimer, *Eyewitness Accounts*, pp. 165–66.

[151] In his engravings publicizing and condemning the conduct of the French at the start of the Dutch War, Romain de Hooghe also pictures one man being forced to drink, "the Swedish draught" as a boy jumps on another's stomach forcing out the draught like a gyser. Georg Hirth, ed., *Picture Book of the Graphic Arts*, Pl. 2690.

[152] For an illustration of judicial water torture conducted much like the Swedish draught, see Pieter Breugel the Elder, *Justice* (1559) in Ruff, *Violence in Early Modern Europe*, p. 101, Fig. 7.

PLATE 17. Tortures committed by soldiers, in P. Vincent, *Lamentations of Germany* (1638).

The Huntington Library, Rare Books Department.

mouthes of some they have opened ..., and then poured downe their throats water, stinking puddle, filthy liquids, and pisse it selfe saying; 'This is a Swedish draught.'"[153] Others describe it as mixtures of manure and water.[154] In both his *Simplicissimus* and *The Life of Courage*, Gimmelshausen gives horrifying pictures of torture, rape, and murder as integral to pillage. "I will not waste time describing how the men of the captured town were all butchered by their conquerors, the women raped and the town itself plundered. Such events became so commonplace in the prolonged war that is now past that the world is only too familiar with them."[155] Women's bodies were also regarded as forms of plunder, rape being a common part of contemporary accounts.[156] Peter Thiele testified that the "shocking things that went on—rape and the like—are indescribable" as an imperial army passed by his town in 1637: "They behaved barbarically in Beeltz, despoiling old women, not a few of them 60 years old, to say nothing of the young ones."[157] Peter Hagendorf, a normally sympathetic character, reported how he took young women as pillage. When his regiment helped to take Lanshut, he "got a pretty lass as my plunder ... When we moved on I sent her back to Landshut again."[158] At Pforsheim, "I took a young girl out with me here too, but I let her go back in again because she had to carry linen out for me."[159]

---

[153] P. Vincent, *The Lamentations of Germany* (London: 1638), 4, 8, in Mortimer, *Eyewitness Accounts*, p. 168.

[154] See Geoff Mortimer, *Eyewitness Accounts of the Thirty Years' War 1618–48* (Basingstoke, Hampshire: 2002), pp. 165 and 168, for more decriptions of this disgusting and deadly torture.

[155] Grimmelshausen, *The Life of Courage*, p. 27. See the account of pillage in Grimmelshausen, *Simplicissimus*, pp. 22–27.

[156] On rape in early modern Europe, particularly on rape committed by troops, see: Miranda Chaytor: "Husband(ry): Narratives of Rape in the Seventeenth Century," *Gender and History* 7, no. 3 (November 1995), pp. 378–407; Rublack, "Wench and Maiden," pp. 1–21; John Theibault, "Landfrauen, Soldaten und Vergewaltigungen während des Dreißigjährigen Krieges," *Werkstatt Geschichte*, 19 (1998); and Georges Vigarello, *A History of Rape: Sexual Violence in France from the 16th to the 20th Century*, trans. Jean Birrell (Cambridge: 2001). Olwen Hufton writes, "In time of war, rape replaced seduction as armies went on the march." *The Prospect Before Her*, p. 316, which I find odd.

[157] Thiele, Peter Thiele's Aufzeichnungen von den Schicksalen der Stadt Beelitz, pp. 15 and 12, in Mortimer, *Eyewitness Accounts of the Thirty Years' War*, p. 165. For additional contemporaray accounts of rape linked with pillage during the Thirty Years' War, see Mortimer, *Eyewitness Accounts*, pp. 170–71.

[158] Hagendorf, *Ein Soeldnerleben im Dreissigjaehrigen Krieg*, p. 59, in Mortimer, *Eyewitness Accounts*, p. 35.

[159] Hagendorf, *Ein Soeldnerleben im Dreissigjaehrigen Krieg*, pp. 62–63, in Mortimer, *Eyewitness Accounts*, p. 35.

Hagendorf seems to excuse himself for this sexual plunder because he was not married at the time. In 1633, imperial troops also took women as plunder at Naumburg, although they pretended to marry them: "Their soldiers took more than 140 servant girls as wives, but when they had gone a few leagues from here they stripped the whores and chased them away."[160] Jacques Callot's print of a convent being sacked includes verses that read in part, "These enraged demons ... take from holy places the disconsolate virgins who they dare to carry off to be violated."[161]

Artwork from the period of the Thirty Years' War show many attacks on women, but it is not always easy to interpret the meaning of these portrayals. Collot, and Hooghe in his wake, show women forced into beds, as in Plate 2; these seem obviously to be rapes, but the artists refuse to be too graphic. Seventeenth-century artists may simply label something as rape without showing the sexual act, as in an illustration from *The Lamentations of Germany* in which a man is shown cutting the arms off a woman who is fully clothed and standing, but the legend is "A maide Ravisched and after quartered."[162] Artists also seem to employ codes for rape: distraught women stripped of their clothes or in a characteristic pose with a soldier brandishing his sword while grabbing the hair of a woman as she either tries to flee or begs for mercy. Often she is accompanied by a small child (see Plate 18).

Attacks on women bear a strong resemblance to portrayals of the slaughter of the innocents by noted artists, the likes of Raphael (1483–1520) and Pieter Bruegel the Elder (1525?–69).[163] It seems

---

[160] Zader, "Die Städte Naumburg und Zeiz während des dreissigjährigen Kriegs, aus Zade: Nauburgische undt Zeizishce Stiffts-Chronica," J. O. Opel, ed, *Neue Mittheilungen aus dem Gebiet historische-antiquarischer Forschungen*, 9.2 (1860), pp. 28–29, Mortimer, *Eyewitness Accounts*, p. 84.

[161] This engraving is widely available in a number of works; a particularly clear print can be found in Howard Daniel, *The World of Jacques Callot* (New York: Lear Publishers, 1948), p. 45.

[162] Vincent, *The Lamentations of Germany* (London: 1638), p. 15, in Donagan, "Atrocity, War Crimes, and Treason in the English Civil War," p. 1145. A 1514 woodcut by Urs Graf, himself a Swiss Reisläufer, shows a young women who has lost her arms and who has one wooden peg leg. Hale, *Artists and Warfare in the Renaissance*, p. 35, Pl. 48. In J. R. Hale, "The Soldier in Germanic Graphic Art of the Renaissance," *Journal of Interdisciplinary History* 17, no. 1 (Summer, 1986): 100, he describes her as a woman first raped and then disfigured.

[163] See for example Raphael, *Massacre of the Innocents*, ca. 1511, in Hale, *Artists and Warfare in the Renaissance*, p. 238, Pl. 299, and Breugel's *Massacre of the Innocents*, at http://www.eldritchpress.org/mm/mass2.html.

Mein Manheit zeig ich hier, Du schandhür sage ahn
Wo ist der schelm Der dieb, der hünd. dein Loser Man

PLATE 18. Christian Richter, attack on a woman, ca. mid-seventeenth century.
The text reads in part "My manhood I here reveal, you say rape but where is the
rogue, the thief."

Staatliche Graphishe Sammlung, Munich.

impossible that imitation can be a coincidence. Rather, it is another
example of artists interpreting their subject in light of traditional motifs,
as in the Flight to Egypt discussed in Chapter I. However, if reference to
the Holy Family implies a favorable attitude toward the campaign
community in the eighteenth century, references to the slaughter of the
innocents in the seventeenth century therefore charge the soldier with
inherent wickedness.

Camp women were integral to pillage, and rape was an extremely
common form of violence during pillage raids. Thus, the question seems

unavoidable: Did camp women oppose or countenance attacks on women from outside the campaign community? We should consider four possibilities in speculating how women of the early modern campaign community responded to the rape of civilian women. First, camp women did not witness rapes. This can be rejected out of hand. Women took part in pillage, and they must have witnessed or at least known about its worst extremes. The mass brutality that occurred when armies sacked cities provides strong evidence; women took part in the sack, and there is no way they could have been oblivious to the rapes going on around them. Second, they recognized what was happening and actively worked to defend their civilian sisters. If this were the case, there would be evidence; so, while some women may have adopted this course, it seems unlikely as a general phenomenon. Third, they knew what was going on, but given the likelihood of violence against women within the campaign community, they bit their tongues and said nothing. Fourth, camp women realized what was happening and tolerated it since those attacked were "others," and women within the campaign community shared the identity and values of that community to the point of seeing outsiders as enemies.

Individual women's responses must have varied, following one or the other of the last two alternatives. However, I would suspect that most camp women acted in accord with the fourth option, seeing the women who were attacked as remote and hostile others. Men committed or observed and tolerated barbaric acts against other men; why would it not be reasonable, then, to expect camp women to have tolerated the rape of women from outside their community?[164] We already know that acts of deadly violence were committed by women upon women. For example, during the English Civil Wars, the good wives of Lyme captured an Irish woman from a royalist regiment, robbed her, stripped her, and stuffed her into a barrel studded on the inside with nails. They then rolled her into the sea, where she drowned. Such evidence demonstrates that women were capable of acts of brutality and might well be capable of realizing that rapes were occurring and simply looking the other way.

French government records supply a large amount of evidence of brutal treatment inflicted on town and country women by troops who were not inhibited by the camp women who accompanied them. A lurid

---

[164] See Tara McKelvey, ed., *One of the Guys: Women as Aggressors and Torturers*, (Emeryville, CA: 2007), for modern feminist disillusioned reactions to the violence committed by women in modern war.

case involved the larger town of Sancoins, in the Bourbonnais. In 1650, some 3,000 troops approached Sancoins and demanded entry. The townsmen denied them, but the soldiers convinced a few traitors to let them in at one gate. The troops then "lived as they pleased, raping, pillaging, and robbing." They "compelled the inhabitants to put together a sum of four thousand livres" and stole horses. They reserved a particular brutal treatment for the "women from whom they took away nursing children and locked these infants in rooms for twenty-four hours in order to force the women to become the soldiers' concubines or to buy their babies back with money rather than to see them die miserably."[165] That a body of 3,000 troops would march without a considerable number of campaign women is incomprehensible, and it seems equally incomprehensible that these women did not realize what was happening, including the abuse of babies in order to rob and rape their mothers.

David Rijckaert III painted a very disturbing portrayal of pillage from the mid-seventeenth century (see Plate 19). The most interesting figures in this image of force and deadly violence are the women. In the right foreground, women of the village plead with the commander for mercy. Behind them, another woman is seized by two men and apparently forced onto a horse to be taken away as plunder, thus to be raped. While violence reigns around her, a well-dressed women stands off at the left foreground. She and a soldier affectionately entwine their arms about each other as she daintily holds a glass of wine. Her expression seems unmoved by what is going on. She apparently is with the soldiers, although it is somewhat ambiguous. Rijckaert painted another similar canvas that included a young woman sitting on a soldier's knee while he raises a glass of wine as violent pillage and an assault on a woman take place around them.[166] Rijckaert's paintings sear the mind, but, to be sure, they prove nothing except that he, too, believed that women could tolerate attacks on other women. He was not alone as an artist in believing this to be so.[167]

---

[165] SHAT, AG, A1122, #401, 21 November 1650.

[166] David Rijchaert, Plundering, in Fishman, *Boerenverdriet*, pl. 26. It is hard to tell if the women with the soldiers are well-dressed women of the town or soldiers' women, but it seems more likely that they are the latter. Deadly violence goes on around them, with a dead man and grieving woman in the right foreground. It is not very clear, in the background, it appears that a man with weapon raised has seized a woman by the hair. See also Pieter Wouwerman, Raid on a Village, in Fishman, *Boerenverdriet*, Pl. 40.

[167] One engraving by Jaques Callot gives us another vision of women who seem to turn a blind eye. In his series on the "Bohemians," a band of Gypsies accompanied by soldiers, he shows what seems at first to be a quiet scene of rest with women and children, but in the

PLATE 19. David Rijckaert III, *Plundering*, mid-seventeenth century.
Koninklijk Museum voor Schone Kunsten, Antwerp. Lukas, Art in Flanders.

Despite the occasional rhetoric of outrage, military law was often ambivalent and usually ineffective concerning rape. "But what are we to say of the license to rape the wives or the daughters of the Enemy?" questioned Hugo Grotius (1583–1645) in his classic *De Jure Belli ac Pacis*. He ultimately condemned rape himself but had to concede, "It is allowed by some and forbidden by others."[168] Many articles of war prohibited it, as in Gustavus Adolphus's 1621 articles, which dictated, "He that forces any Woman to abuse her; and the matter be proved, he shall dye for it."[169] Yet Swedes were infamous for violence during the Thirty Years' War.

background mayhem is afoot, with what seems a raid on the farm by the same band. This appears to include the classic rape pose of a man pursing a woman with sword in hand as he holds her by the hair. Daniel, *Callot's Etchings, 338 Prints*, Pl. 151.

[168] H. Grotius, *Le droit de la guerre et de la paix* (Basle, 1746, 1st Latin edition 1625), vol. 2, p. 263, in Vigarello, *A History of Rape*, p. 15.

[169] Article 88 of Gustavus Adolphus's 1621 Articles of War available at http://www.icrc.org/Web/eng/siteengo.nsf/html/57JN8D. Maximilian of Bavaria sent the following order to Gustavus Adolphus's great adversary Johan Tserclaes, count Tilly, instructing him to punish rape:

Now, it seems strange and unexpected to me that the execution prescribed against such a clearly defined crime to this date has not taken place, and that my express command has not been more closely observed. Because of this, then, it is my earnest wish and opinion that you properly observe my command and allow the proceedings with fitting

When rape occurred during the sack of a besieged city, it was regarded as legitimate if regrettable. Contemporaries even appealed to biblical authority to sanction the harsh treatment meted out to cities that refused to surrender and then fell to assault. Deuteronomy 20:10–20 legitimated killing all men and taking women when a city resisted the Jews:

12. And if it will make no peace with thee, but will make war against thee, then thou shalt besiege it:
13. And when the LORD thy God hath delivered it into thine hands, thou shalt smite every male thereof with the edge of the sword:
14. But the women, and the little ones, and the cattle, and all that is in the city, *even* all the spoil thereof, shalt thou take unto thyself.[170]

Shakespeare expressed contemporary opinion through the dialogue he wrote for Henry V before the still-resisting walls of Harfleur, as the king announced his final terms to the town fathers. Should they not yield and thus require the English to take the town by storm, "What is't to me, when you yourselves are cause, if your pure maidens fall into the hand of hot and forcing violation?"[171] Soldiers expected to be allowed to rape; in fact, troops commanded by Bénédict-Louis de Pontis turned their weapons on him when he prohibited them from pillage and rape at the Flanders convent of Tourlement in 1635.[172]

It is important to bear in mind the brutal excesses committed by the campaign community when pillaging, because resolution to curtail these abuses and to impose discipline was the motivation for new standards and practices within European armies. Therefore, the most essential role of women in support of early modern armies—their part in the family economy of pillage—explained both their earlier extensive presence in the campaign community and their later exclusion from it.

punishment and execution, not only this time, but also henceforth, for the command and whole business is hardly useful if you will not execute it.

Bayerisches Hauptstaatsarchiv Muenchen (HStAM) Dreissigjaehriger Krieg Akten 83, fol. 39, in Theibault, "Landfrauen, Soldaten und Vergewaltigungen," pp. 34–35. It should be remembered that Tilly's troops were those that sacked Magdeburg.
[170] Parker regards these bible verses as one of the foundations of the law of war throughout the early modern period. Geoffrey Parker, "Early Modern Europe," in *The Laws of War: Constraints on Warfare in the Western World*, Michael Howard, George J. Andreopoulos, and Mark R. Shulman, eds. (New Haven, CT: 1994), p. 41.
[171] William Shakespeare, *Henry V*, act 3, sc. 3. Wellington wrote in 1820: "I believe that it has been understood that the defenders of a fortress stormed have no claim to quarter." Wellington in Parker, "Early Modern Europe," p. 48.
[172] Vigarello, *A History of Rape*, p. 15.

MORE HARD WORK: HEFTING, CARRYING, DIGGING

Returning to the more palatable subject of work *within* military camps, we should note that plebian women went from job to job. The picaresque figure Courage ran the gamut from officer's wife to prostitute, sutler, and fence. Later, Mother Ross began as a cross-dresser who played the part of a male soldier and, once discovered as a woman, spent years as cook, sutler, and soldier's wife. Very few of the tasks taken on by camp women were easy; most were physically demanding.[173]

Even the simple act of partnering with a soldier obligated a camp woman to heft heavy packs and tote a surprising quantity of goods. Several sources from the seventeenth century make this point. Kirchoff (1602) gave them a rough compliment: "The women or prostitutes of the common foot-soldier are not unlike the Spanish mule burdened as they are with knapsacks, cloaks, shawls, pots, kettles, pans, brooms, small bags, roosters and all kinds of trash, with their skirts trussed up to their knees, with mud up to the shoetops, many of them barefoot, of course."[174] Writing later, the Scottish mercenary Turner uses much the same analogy in describing men and women at the siege of Breda (1624–25): "The married Souldiers fared better, look'd more vigorously, and were able to do more duty than the Batchellors; and all the spite was done the poor women, was to be called their husbands mules, by those who would have been glad to have had such mules themselves"[175] (see Plates 6 and 20). It would seem that in some armies, women performed the function of servants, or boys.

Examining the contents of the bundles they balanced on their heads or the packs they carried on their backs tells us even more about the labors of these hardy women. An anonymous, handwritten German manuscript of 1612 detailed the load carried by women on the march:

How very helpful the German women in Hungary were to the soldiers in carrying necessities and in their care of sickness. Seldom is one found who does not carry at least 50 or 60 pounds. Since the soldier carries provisions or other materials, he loads straw and wood on her, to say nothing of the fact that many of them carry one, two, or three children on their back. Normally, however, aside from

---

[173] Speaking of the garrison community of eighteenth-century Prussia, Engelen listed the following common occupations of soldiers' wives: washing, nursing, cooking, work in the textile industry in Brandenberg-Prussia, nursing, hosting and "attending" soldiers, hawking wares and cooked foodstuffs, inn-keeping, managing bordellos, prostitution, and begging. Engelen, *Soldatenfrauen in Preußen*, pp. 149–70.

[174] Kirchhoff in Haberling, "Army Prostitution and Its Control," pp. 33–34.

[175] Turner, *Pallas Armata*, p. 277.

PLATE 20. Daniel Hopfer, *Soldier and His Wife*, ca. 1530. Note the man carries only his arms on the march, while the woman carries a heavy load. She also has a heavy purse. This is a copy of an earlier print in which the two are identified as a sutler or cook and his wife.[176]

> *The Illustrated Bartsch*, vol. 17 [Formerly Volume 8 (part 4)], ed.
> Walter L. Strauss (New York: Abaris Books, 1981), Pl. 62
> (487), p. 139. Used with permission from Abaris Books.

the clothing they are wearing, they carry for the man one pair of breeches, one pair of stockings, one pair of shoes. And for themselves the same number of shoes and stockings, one jacket, two *Hemmeter*, one pan, one pot, one or two spoons,

---

[176] *Der Sudler und sein Sudlerin*, ca. 1635, Walter L. Strauss, ed., *The German Single-Leaf Woodcut, 1550–1600*, vol. 3, p. 1158.

one sheet, one overcoat, one tent, and three poles. They receive no wood for cooking in their billets, and so they pick it up on the way. And to add to their fatigue, they normally lead a small dog on a rope or even carry him in bad weather.[177]

According to Wallhausen, when a captain tried to eliminate impediments to his company's rapid march by leaving the women of the unit behind at a river crossing, his soldiers rebelled, yelling "Ho, what the devil, I must have my whore back; she has my shirts, collars, shoes, and stockings."[178]

In his *Kriegsbuch*, Fronsperger has "whores" describe their varied and demanding tasks, from household work to heavy lifting:

> We, whores and rogues in the wars
> Care for and wait on our masters
> With the best of our skills.
> We are whores direct from Flanders;
> And while we change one foot-soldier for another
> We are useful in the army nevertheless.
> We cook, we sweep, and him who is ill
> We nurse until he is well again.
> We whores and rogues, we are a pack;
> And even if we are often badly beaten;
> We do it all for the soldier's sake;
> It is pleasant for him to be lifted up by us.
> When cleaning or digging is to be done,
> Is wood to be carried we are the ones,
> And if we don't do it, beatings are ours. [179]

Women performed even more strenuous work when necessary. Wilwort of Schaumburg reports that Charles the Bold of Burgundy (1467–77) detailed the 4,000 "common women" accompanying his army to cart earth for entrenchments at the siege of Neuss (1474–75).[180] Wallhausen provides another reference to particularly hard physical siege work: "The prostitutes and the boys [of the camp] also helped in binding fascines, filling ditches, digging pits and mounting cannon in difficult places."[181]

---

[177] Text in Hans Delbruck, *History of the Art of War*, vol. 4, *The Dawn of Modern Warfare*, trans Walter J. Renfroe, Jr (Lincoln, NE: 1990), pp. 65–66. Also in Haberling, "Army Prostitution and Its Control," p. 33.

[178] Wallhausen, *Defensio Patriae* (1621), in Haberling, "Army Prostitution and Its Control," pp. 42–43.

[179] Fronsperger in Haberling, "Army Prostitution and Its Control," p. 32.

[180] Wilwort of Shaumburg in Haberling, "Army Prostitution and Its Control," p. 27.

[181] Wallhausen in Haberling, "Army Prostitution and Its Control," p. 36. It is interesting that armies commandeered women in civil communities near their encampments to wield spades for them. Kaspar Preis testified that his wife was forced to dig

Plebian women were no strangers to toil in the civilian world, so their labors in camp were not by definition masculine in themselves; however, combined with other dimensions of military life and values, camp women did, indeed, inhabit a gendered border zone. This overlap of masculinity with femininity within the campaign community was not only expected and tolerated, it was enforced. Camp authorities inflicted physical punishment on prostitutes, "whores," and wives who did not do their share. Contrast this with the fact that men would be ridiculed for doing women's work—"Ho, Ho the Diaper-Washer"—and it seems very clear that the gender overlap worked only in one direction. *Women often had to be mannish, while men dare not ever be womanish.*

* * *

Thus, the duties that fell to camp women covered a great range of tasks, many of them normally the province of men. The range was greatest and the contributions most essential before 1650, when women were more numerous in the campaign community. Then, women were porters who carried burdens for their male companions. Metaphorically, those men were themselves carried by their women, because soldiers were supported to a significant degree by what their women could bring in. They were partners in the family economy of makeshifts that required entre-preneurship and pillage. The poem accompanying a sixteenth-century woodcut reflects the several responsibilities of one Landsknecht's woman:

> Do well with me, my pretty lass
> And stay with me in the Landsknechts
> You'll wash my shirts
> Carry my sacks and flasks
> And if some booty should be mine
> You shall keep it safe and fine
> So when we put paid of this crew
> We'll sell the booty when we are through. [182]

fortifications, "Although she had never thrown a shovelful of earth out of a ditch in her life it made no difference." Kaspar Preis, "Stausenbacher Chronik des Kaspar Preis, 1637–67," *Fuldaer Geschichtsblätter*, 1 (1902), p. 133, in Mortimer, *Eyewitness Accounts*, pp. 172–73.

[182] Max Geisburg and Walter Strauss, eds., *The German Single-Leaf Woodcut*, vol. 3 pp. 1158–1661 in Rublack, "Wench and Maiden," p. 17.

IV

Warrior Women: Cultural Phenomena, Intrepid Soldiers, and Stalwart Defenders

On 28 May 1696, Major Rochepierre faced a situation that was new to him. He knew how to deal with soldiers who were deserters and, thus, by definition, men. But now he had discovered a female deserter, and he required guidance to deal with such an anomaly. From the fortress of St. Omer, he appealed to the war ministry:

All the ordinances against deserters make no mention of women, I believe that your intention is not that the said Marie Magdelaine Mouron suffer any other punishment than prison for having deserted from the company of Desbrière in the Regiment du Biez, in which she had enrolled as a soldier disguised as a man.[1]

The individual concerned belonged to a rare group: women who adopted male dress and male identity to serve in the ranks of European armies. Few in number, these female soldiers nonetheless captured the popular imagination of their time. Their importance was more cultural than military, but there is no denying their presence, as Major Rochepierre discovered.

Women soldiers have received a fair amount of attention for several reasons that range from simple curiosity about their unusual lives to sophisticated concern with the malleability of gender. Stories of such women also have been of use to those who would argue for the inclusion of women in combat today, and consequently, a number of books have treated individual women combatants. Yet despite its undeniable appeal, the phenomenon of the cross-dressing woman soldier is of limited

---

[1] SHAT, AG, MR 1785, #53–55, 28 May 1696, *procès verbal* and accompanying documents concerning Marie Magdelaine Mouron.

significance to the history of warfare; certainly, the lives and works of those women already described should be of greater concern. While we will never know the actual numbers of women soldiers in the early modern campaign community, they cannot have been very numerous, whereas there were legions of women who retained their female identities as they followed armies into the field.

If the woman soldier fascinates twenty-first century–readers, she also caught the fancy of early modern Europeans, and, in fact, she became far more common as a legend of popular culture than she was as a truth of the campaign community. The unusual, intriguing, and potentially titillating stories of women soldiers drew a wide audience for popular literature, plays, songs, and art. This can be viewed as another aspect of the fascination with the world turned upside down and the gendered "battle for the pants." The sword was always a symbol of male power, and in the person of the female soldier, it literally passed to a woman's hands.

The romanticized view of woman soldiers provided by popular culture differed very much from the actual lives of those women who chose to dress as men and bear arms. In the majority of cases, poverty compelled their transformation, and once within the ranks, they endured not only the hard life of a soldier but also the fear of discovery and expulsion. There is no question that woman soldiers existed and that some of them boasted courageous combat records, but their stories were usually a long way from the pursuit of love and glory presented in the songs of the day.

There is a paradox, however. Civilian women who did not abandon their feminine identities when they fought to defend their city walls were far more prevalent as women-at-arms than were transvestite women soldiers. Resident women were ordinary, not extraordinary, participants in the defense of towns, either working alongside men to maintain walls and dig trenches or, in many cases, taking up arms themselves to repel the enemy. Such women did not pretend to be anything but what they were. Because siege warfare was the most common form of combat from the Renaissance to the French Revolution, women had plenty of opportunity to display their fortitude as they resisted besieging armies to protect home, family, and religion.

The French Revolution brought important changes in the nature of wars and the character of armies, and for a time it seemed like women would openly join men in the field to combat the enemies of the new France. It was an interesting experiment in political thought and language, but it was only tentative and temporary in the field. Ultimately the politically extreme Jacobins proved to be immensely conservative about defining the proper roles for women, and serving in the army fell outside that definition. Women would continue to don men's clothing to fight surreptitiously, but their service would follow the patterns of the old regime, little changed by the new patriotic character of the army under the Republic or the Empire.

THE WOMAN SOLDIER IN POPULAR CULTURE

Celebration of the cross-dressing woman soldier in popular culture lasted for about two centuries, picking up in the early or mid-seventeenth century and dying out in the first half of the nineteenth century. Chapters II and III emphasized the period of the aggregate contract army, when the contribution of women in the campaign community was essential to the very existence of the army; the actual heyday of the woman soldier came later, however. Particularly after 1650, tales of these women became a staple of songs, literature, and stage performances. Popular culture recognized and reflected the fact that women served as soldiers; however, it also filtered and elaborated this reality to titillate the public, to highlight issues of gender in society, and to stimulate military values.[2] The existence of real, embellished, and fictional accounts of women in the ranks helped to spread the idea that such gender transformation was possible, and, as such, probably encouraged some women to make the decision to adopt this course.

Examples of Amazons and Heroic Noblewomen

The allure of woman soldiers within popular culture relates to two other phenomena: an enduring European fascination with the mythology of women warriors, particularly Amazons, and the prominence of elite heroic women active from the 1630s through the 1650s. Both of these phenomena seem to have percolated down through all strata of European society.

Amazons captured the seventeenth-century European imagination, particularly, it would seem, the imaginations of notable women of power

---

[2] For interesting discussions of the phenomenon of the woman soldier in popular culture, albeit mainly in the nineteenth-century, see two works by David M. Hopkin: *Soldier and Peasant in French Popular Culture 1766–1870* (Woodbridge, Suffolk: 2003), and "Female Soldiers and the Battle of the Sexes in France: The Mobilization of a Folk Motif," *History Workshop Journal*, 56 (2003): 79–104.

and birth.[3] Interiors of elegant homes were decorated with paintings of Amazons and other ancient heroines. Between 1637 and 1642, the flamboyant Marie de Cossé Brissac, maréchale de La Meilleraye, embellished her study with a series of portraits of deadly heroines, including three Amazon queens. She was not alone in this interest; no less a personage than the queen regent of France, Anne of Austria, intended to create such a gallery for herself. Literature echoed this attention on valorous women of the past. Jacques Du Bosc's *La Femme héroïque* appeared in 1645, followed two years later with the far more successful *La Galerie des femmes fortes* by Pierre Le Moyne.

At the same time, a number of extraordinary women turned myth into reality during the turmoil of the Thirty Years' War, the Fronde, and the English Civil War. For example, in Lorraine during the late 1630s and early 1640s, the magnificent Alberte-Barbe d'Ernecourt, Comtesse de Saint-Baslement (1606–60), defended her lands against raiders while her husband was away fighting with Charles IV of Lorraine.[4] She donned appropriate men's attire, summoned her tenants, and led them in combat, although she was always the lady of her estates. Barbe was celebrated with two equestrian portraits of her dressed and armed to fight and a biography, suitably entitled *L'Amazone chrestienne*.[5] Her exploits were echoed by those of Catherine Meurdrac de La Guette (1613–ca. 1680) during the rebellion of the Fronde, when she too defended her lands in the absence of her husband. Catherine's memoirs appeared posthumously in 1681. At the height of the Fronde, the rebels who challenged the authority of monarchy included other flamboyant grand noblewomen, such as Anne-Marie-Louise d'Orleans, duchess de Montpensier, who played the part of frondeuses at the head of rebel forces.

Songs

Popular culture displayed a related but distinct interest in contemporary cross-dressing warrior women who passed for male soldiers in the ranks.

---

[3] For a discussion of Amazons, heroic women, and European culture, see Joan DeJean, "Violent Women and Violence against Women: Representing the 'Strong' Woman and Early Modern France," *Signs: Journal of Women in Culture and Society* 29, no. 1 (Autumn 2003): 117–47. See as well, Simon Shepherd. *Amazons and Warrior Women: Varieties of Feminism in Seventeenth-Century Drama* (New York: 1981).

[4] Micheline Cuénin, *La derniére des Amazones, Madame de Saint-Baslemont* (Nancy: 1992).

[5] Jean-Marie de Vernon, *L'Amazone chrestienne; ou, les avantures de Madame Saint-Baslemon* (Paris: 1678).

Songs about women soldiers caught the ears of a wide spectrum of listeners because the consumers need not be literate. By nature, songs are easily acquired and highly portable, but they also simplify. The appeal of songs about women in uniform derived from the novelty of their theme and from their way of turning a hard existence into a romantic fantasy.

Dianne Dugaw provides the best scholarly discussion to date of this phenomenon in her *Warrior Women and Popular Balladry, 1650–1850*. She centers on English-language songs, of which she has collected 120. Dugaw's transvestite heroines "flourished from the Renaissance to the Victorian Age ... in plays, poems, life histories, and songs that were known to a wide range of people, especially people of the lower classes."[6] In these ballads, young women abandon homes, often overcoming parental resistance, in a quest for love and glory. While some go to pursue or accompany a lover or husband, others leave in search of adventure, but even those who seek adventure generally discover romance as well. Dugaw terms the songs "success stories" with a predictable plot whereby the "masquerading heroine—a model of bravery, beauty, and pluck—proves herself deserving in romance, able in war, and rewarded in both."[7]

The heroine of *Polly Oliver* declares, "I'll list for a soldier and follow my love."[8] Such maidens march off with gusto, as in *The Valiant Commander, with his Resolute Lady* from the 1640s:

> She took a Musquet then,
>   and a sword by her side
> In disguise like a man
>   her valour so she try'd
> And with her true-love she,
>   march'd forth courageously,
> And made away with speed,
>   quite through the Enemy[9]

They do not shirk from deadly combat, as in *The Drum Major*:

> Just in the midst of battle where many one did fall
> She fought with such courage she excell'd them all,
> She fought with such courage on every degree,
> Though never a one took her a woman to be.[10]

[6] Dianne Dugaw, *Warrior Women and Popular Balladry* (Chicago: 1996), p. xi.
[7] Dugaw, *Warrior Women and Popular Balladry*, p. 1.
[8] Dugaw, *Warrior Women and Popular Balladry*, p. 123.
[9] Dugaw, *Warrior Women and Popular Balladry*, p. 46.
[10] Dugaw, *Warrior Women and Popular Balladry*, p. 123.

Love is usually the reward of such gallant service, as in the case of
Susan's Adventures on a British Man of War:

> At length to England they returned and quickly married were,
> The bells did ring and they did sing and banish every care,
> They often think upon the day when she received a scar,
> When Susan followed her true love on board a man of war.[11]

At present, we lack a thorough study of songs from the European
continental but do have some contemporary lyrics in praise of the
woman soldier. A Dutch ballad about a French female soldier and her
lover has much the same theme as typified the English ditties:

> Her valour was acclaimed by all
> And the Council did agree
> That these two might be
> By the marriage vow united
> And to remain thus undivided
> And so in the hangman's stead
> The priest was called
> And the two were wed.[12]

Literature: The European Genre of Women Soldier's Memoirs

Books and pamphlets presented the lives of women soldiers to the literate
population. In contrast to song, literature allowed for a broader and deeper
range of exposition. The authority of the printed page gave these accounts
more weight, which could be misleading to the naïve because much of the
content in the biographies, memoirs, and correspondence of women soldiers were less likely to be fancy than fact. The fiction could be intended
merely to boost sales, or it could have more sophisticated purposes.

The "true" story of a woman soldier's life became a seventeenth- and
eighteenth-century literary genre. Sylvie Steinberg, a historian who has
written perceptively on the subject, concludes, "Such adventures form a
veritable motif in the most popular of literature."[13] She points out how

---

[11] Dugaw, *Warrior Women and Popular Balladry*, p. 140.

[12] Rudolf M. Dekker and Lotte C. van de Pol, *The Tradition of Female Transvestism in
Early Modern Europe*, trans. Judy Marcure and Lotte Van de Pol (Basingstoke,
Hampshire: 1989), p. 89.

[13] Sylvie Steinberg, *La confusion des sexes: Le tranvestissement de la Renaissance à la
Révoltution* (Paris: 2001), p. 80. Although the woman soldier's story is primarily a
seventeenth- and eighteenth-centrury form, there are earlier bits and pieces, such as the
"pleasant story" of Long Meg of Westminster of 1582. On Long Meg, see Olwen

events from one woman's life had the disturbing habit of popping up in the tales of another. One of the earliest examples of the genre, a short version of the life story of Catalina de Erauso (1592–1642), first saw light about 1625, although the longer version read today did not come out until the nineteenth century[14] (see Plate 23). Catalina swaggered through the Spanish colonies in South America until she was discovered as a woman; she then returned to Spain where she enjoyed some fame in her own lifetime. Later she voyaged to Mexico where she died. It is very difficult to believe all the details of her autobiography; one has to suspend doubt to believe that someone could have engaged in so many fights and duels yet escaped with limb and life.

French accounts of woman soldiers include a number of volumes that first reached the public during the late seventeenth century. The story of Christine de Meyrac appeared as *L'héroine mousquetaire* in 1679 and later saw print in other French editions, along with Dutch and English translations. This volume claims to document her exploits from 1675 to 1676 during the Dutch War, but it is a novelized and embellished version of her life.[15] The publication of two volumes that depicted the lives of different women who both went by the name chevalier Baltazar confuses things: *L'Héroïne travestie ou Mémoires de la vie de Mademoiselle Delfosses ou le Chavalier Baltazar* (Paris: 1695) and *Histoire de la dragonne contenant les actions militaire et les aventures de Geneviève Prémoy, sous le nom de chevalier Baltazar*

Hufton, *The Prospect Before Her: A History of Women in Western Europe*, vol. 1 *1500–1800* (New York: Vintage Books, 1998), p. 53, and Chapter II of this volume.

[14] Joaquim María de Ferrer, *Historia de la monja alférez, doña Catalina de Erauso* (1625); this was republished in Paris in 1829. Mary Elizabeth Perry, *Gender and Disorder in Early Modern Seville* (Princeton, NJ: Princeton University Press, 1990), p. 131 and fn. 55. An English translation of this work is Catalina de Erauso, *Memoir of a Basque Lieutenant Nun Transvestite in the New World*, trans. Michele Stepto and Gabriel Stepto(Bostong: 1996). Recent commentaries on Erauso include Sherry Velasco, *The Lieutenant Nun: Transgenderism, Lesbian Desire, and Catalina de Erauso* (Austin, TX: 2001) and Nerea Aresti, "The Gendered Identities of the 'Lieutenant Nun': Rethinking the Story of a Female Warrior in Early Modern Spain," Gender and History 19, no. 3 (November 2007):401–18.

[15] Jean Préchac, *L'héroine mousquetaire* (Paris: 1679). More versions are mentioned in Dekker and van de Pol, *The Tradition of Female Transvestism*, p. 114 and in Rudolf M. Dekker and Lotte C. van de Pol, "Republican Heroines: Cross-Dressing Women in the French Revolutionary Armies," trans. Judy Marcure, *History of European Ideas* 10, no. 3 (1989), p. 360. The titlepage ofthe Dutch edition of the book is reproduced in Dekker and van de Pol, *Tradition of Female Transvestism*, between pp. 48 and 49, Pl. 6. On *L'héroine mousquetaire*, see Joseph Harris, *Hidden Agendas: Cross Dressing in 17th-Century France* (Tübingen: 2005), pp. 197–99.

(Paris: 1703).[16] Both of these would see later editions as well. The first assumed the form of a series of letters, a device meant to add credibility. In the second, Geneviève Prémoy performs her military duties with such bravado that she receives the order of St. Louis from Louis XIV, but there is no record of the king actually conferring this order on her or any other woman. It is tempting to see the tales of Christine de Meyrac and Geneviève Prémoy as repackaged forms of the flamboyant and warlike *frondeuses*, now transformed into loyal servants of the king.

Invention and plagiarism in French tales may have reached its worst in *La fille capitaine* by Louis, chevalier de Mailly. In 1711, Parisian authorities arrested him for having lifted much from other memoirs and mixed them with "several very indecent stories."[17] The texts of such novels often involved love, rejection, disguise, confusion, and complicated twists that played on the cross-dressing disguise, such as the heroine being accused of getting a girl pregnant.

The woman who transforms herself into a male warrior was even enshrined in the fairy tale *Belle-Belle or the Chevalier Fortuné* by Marie-Catherine Le Jumel de Barneville, baronne d'Aulnoy, whose *Contes Nouveaux ou Les Fées à la mode* (1698) contained this charming fable.[18] This woman of the French aristocracy may well have known of the stories of Christine de Meyrac and the Chevalier Baltazar before she wrote her piece. Belle-Belle's tale follows the pattern of song: the youngest daughter of an impoverished noble, she saves the family fortunes by donning men's clothing to defend the king. In the course of events wins at many manly challenges, from hunting to slaying a dragon, and, when discovered as a women, is rewarded with the hand of the king in marriage.

Dutch accounts featured female sailors as well as soldiers. The extensive story of a woman who lived as Hendrik van de Berg and fought in the 1660s and 1670s appeared in 1706 as *Het Wonderlik Leven En de Oorlogsdaaden, Van de Kloekmoedige Land en Zee Heldin* and came out as a later edition in 1720.[19] A generation later, a Dutch publisher released an account

---

[16] A plate portending to be the Chevalier Balthazar is reproduced in Dekker and van de Pol, *Tradition of Female Transvestism*, between pp. 48 and 49, Pl. 7.

[17] September 15, 1711 report by the lieutenant-general of police, René d'Argensen, in Steinberg, *La confusion des sexes*, p. 80.

[18] Marie-Catherine d'Aulnoy, *Belle-Belle, or The Chevalier Fortuné* in Jack Zipes, ed. and trans., *Beauty and the Beast: And Other Classic French Fairy Tales* (New York, NY: 1997), pp. 383–430.

[19] *Het Wonderlik Leven En de Oorlogsdaaden, Van de Kloekmoedige Land en Zee Heldin. Waarachtige geschiedenis*, 2 vols. (Maastricht: 1982), 1st ed. Amsterdam: 1706, reprinted 1720. This title translates as *The Stout-Hearted Heroine of the Land and the*

of the formidable and very real Maria van Antwerpen, *Bredasche heldinne, of merkwaardige levansgevallen van Marie van Antwerpen* (The Hague: 1751).[20] Maria's exploits were especially scandalous, because she married two women. As so often happened, a fictional biography of another woman published in 1759 appropriated parts of Maria's story.[21]

Nadezhda Durova published her autobiography, *The Cavalry Maiden: Journals of a Russian Officer in the Napoleonic Wars*, in 1836.[22] Her journals seem legitimate, although she revised and published them only in the 1830s, when she needed to make money to eke out an existence. She certainly was known as a soldier in her day.

The genre depicting women soldier's lives crossed the Atlantic. Deborah Sampson served in the ranks of the Continental Army during the War of Independence as Robert Shurtleff, and Herman Mann told her story in *The Female Review, or Memoirs of an American Young Lady*, published in 1797.[23] Another American account details the life of a female marine at sea during the War of 1812, *The Adventures of Louisa Baker* or *The Female Marine*. It enjoyed such popularity that it was reprinted nineteen times in three years and called for sequels, which earned the author more money. The author, it turns out, was a man, Nathaniel Wright, and the stories were entirely fictitious.[24]

British Literature: Christian Davies and Hannah Snell

Two popular biographies of British woman soldiers have attracted particular scholarly attention.[25] They deserve a closer look here, because

Sea. The title page of the book is reproduced as Plate 16 in Dekker and van de Pol, *Tradition of Female Transvestism*, between pp. 48 and 49.

[20] F. L. Kersteman, *De Bredasche heldinne, of merkwaardige levansgevallen van Marie van Antwerpen* (The Hague: 1751).

[21] Steinberg, *La confusion des sexes*, p. 80.

[22] Nadezhda Durova, *The Cavalry Maiden: Journals of a Russian Officer in the Napoleonic Wars*, trans. Mary Fleming Zinn (Bloomington, IN: 1989).

[23] For an exhaustive modern history of Deborah Sampson see Alfred Young, *Masquerade: The Life and Times of Deborah Sampson, Continental Soldier* (New York: 2005).

[24] Lucy Brewer, *The Adventures of Louisa Baker* (New York: Luther Wales, 1815). This has recently been republished in an edited edition as *The Female Marine and Related Works: Narratives of Cross-Dressing and Urban Vice in America's Early Republic*, ed. Daniel A Cohen (University of Massachusetts Press, 1997). See the discussion of the imaginary Lucy Brewer, aka Louisa Baker, in David Cordingly, *Heroines & Harlots: Women at Sea in the Great Age of Sail* (London: 2002), pp. 54–61.

[25] The women in question, Christian Davies and Hannah Snell, receive attention in Fraser Easton, "Gender's Two Bodies: Women Warriors, Female Husbands and Plebeian Life," *Past and Present*, no. 180 (2003): 131–74, and Scarlet Bowen, "The Real Soul of a Man

they tell us much about women in European armies on campaign and because they exemplify the use made of women's stories to spur the martial values of contemporary society.

The lengthy English biography, *The Life and Adventures of Mrs. Christian Davies, Commonly Called Mother Ross* (London: 1740) presents itself as "taken from her own mouth," covering her military experiences in a life claimed to span from 1667 to 1739. Scholars have debated back and forth if Christian Davies actually existed, and her story was once attributed to Daniel Defoe, although this view is now discredited.[26]

Recent scholarship establishes that she was quite real and lived to receive a pension of "Five Pence a Day for her future Support and Maintenance" owing to "divers Wounds she receiv'd in follg. the said Regt." during "the late Warr in Flanders" while "disguis'd in the habit of a man," according to the records of the Royal Hospital at Chelsea.[27] *The Life and Adventures of Mrs. Christian Davies* lacks much of the romantic nonsense of the French volumes and speaks with some authority about camp life; however, it is padded with historical reports on the War of the Spanish Succession across Europe, facts Davies probably would not have known, certainly not first-hand.[28] Whatever its truth or authorship, *The Life and Adventures of Mrs. Christian Davies* became a primary staple of the literature on women soldiers; after its first appearance in 1740, it saw another full edition in 1741 and abridged editions in 1742 and 1744.[29] Her story would then be briefly told in a series of later volumes.[30]

in her Breast: Popular Oppression and British Nationalism in Memoirs of Female Soldiers, 1740–1750," *Eighteenth-Century Life* 28, no. 3 (Fall 2004): 20–45. Snell is also the subject of Matthew Stephens, *Hannah Snell: The Secret Life of a Female Marine, 1723–1792* (London: 1997).

[26] Bowen, "The Real Soul of a Man in her Breast," p. 34. Some scholars still attribute the volume to Defoe; see the article on Davies in Pennington, ed., *Amazons to Fighter Pilots*, vol. 1, p. 86. We lack a real portrait of Christian Davies. The frontispiece of her biography simply has a vague image of a mounted dragoon, an image reproduced in Dekker and van de Pol, *Tradition of Female Transvestism*, between pp. 48 and 49, Pl. 19.

[27] Letter from the Secretary of War to the Commissioners of Chelsea Hospital, 19 July 1717, PRO WO 4/20, fol. 182, in Easton, "Gender's Two Bodies," p. 144. Fraser also quotes two other documents that substantiate her pension.

[28] *The Life and Adventures of Mrs. Christian Davies, Commonly Called Mother Ross* (London: 1740).

[29] Bowen, "The Real Soul of a Man in her Breast," p. 43, fn 4.

[30] These works include: James Caulfield, *Portraits, Memoirs and Characters of Remarkable Persons from the Revolution of 1688 to the End of the Reign of George III Collected from the Most Authentic Accounts Extant*, 4 vols. (London: 1819); *The Soldier's Companion or Martial Recorder, consisting of biography, anecdotes, poetry*

The accounts of the service of Hannah Snell (1723–92), *The Female Soldier: Or the Surprizing Life and Adventures of Hannah Snell* may lie closer to reality. On 25 May 1750 she returned from her adventures at sea and in India, where she had fought as a marine, and soon thereafter, she drew her final pay and revealed her true identity to her comrades.[31] After making an appeal to the Duke of Cumberland for support, a notice of her adventures and her actions appeared in *The Whitehall Evening Post* on 23 June. The enterprising publisher Robert Walker, sensing the possibility of profit, signed a declaration and agreement with her on 27 June that gained him exclusive rights to her biography. The next day he advertised the upcoming publication of her story, and on 3 July it appeared in a shortened, forty-two page form. He then issued a longer serialized account beginning 14 July. Her story also appeared in the pages of the *Gentleman's Magazine* and the *Scots Magazine*.[32] As demonstrated in a study by one of her descendents, Mathew Stevens, there is absolutely no doubt that Hannah Snell served as a marine, and there is evidence that she was eventually given support through the old soldiers' home at Chelsea.[33] Yet even here, the unvarnished truth was not good enough for the editor, who added fanciful material at the start of the story and shifted the dates of major events for the sake of drama.[34]

Both Davies and Snell left home in search of lost husbands, but they did not follow the romantic course of the songs. Davies hoped to find her

and miscellaneous information peculiarly interesting to those connected with the military profession (London: 1824); G.R. Gleig, *Chelsea Hospital and its Traditions,* (London: 1839); Thomas Carter, *Curiosities of War and Military Studies* (London: 1860); Ellen Clayton, *Female Warriors: Memorials of Female Valour and Heroism, From the Mythological Ages to the Present Era,* 2 vols. (London: 1879); and Menie Muriel Dowie, *Women Adventurers: The Adventure Series,* vol. 15 (London: 1893). For a listing and discussion of these works, see Julie Wheelwright, "'Amazons and military maids:' An examination of female military heroines in British literature and the changing construction of gender," *Women's Studies International Forum* 10, no. 5, pp. 489–502.

[31] For an account of her actions upon her return, see Stephens, *Hannah Snell,* p. 37–43.

[32] Bowen, "The Real Soul of a Man in her Breast," p. 43, n 4.

[33] The Chelsea Hospital Board Minutes for 9 June 1785 show that she requested and was granted an increase in her pension. PRO, WO 250/463 and 250/477, in Easton, "Gender's Two Bodies," p. 145.

[34] Matthew Stephens, *Hannah Snell: The Secret Live a Female Marine, 1723–1793* (London: 1997). Bowen in her 2004 article seems unaware of this examination into the reality of Hannah Snell. When the life of Deborah Sampson appeared as a book in 1797, the author, Hermann Mann similarly embellished her story to appeal to readers. He conferred with Deborah in writing the account, but did warp the tale. Young, *Masquerade.*

HANNAH SNELL *Born at* Worcester *1723.*

Inlisted herself by the name of James Gray in General Guise's Regiment then at Carlisle 1745 where she Received 500 Lashes, Deserted from thence and went to Portsmouth where she Inlisted in Colonel Fraser's Regiment of Marines, went in Admiral Boscawen's Squadron to the East Indies, at the Siege of Pondicherry where she Received 12 Shot one in her Groin Eleven in her Legs 1750 came to England without the least discovery of her Sex, and on her Petitioning His Royal Highness the Duke of CUMBERLAND, He was pleas'd to order her a Pension of 30 a Year.

PLATE 21. Hannah Snell in a mezzotint print by John Faber, 1750, after a painting by Richard Phelps.

Trustees of the British Museum, used with permission.

beloved husband, who was Shanghaied to fight in The Netherlands during the Nine Years' War. She donned her husband's clothes, signed up for the army in 1693, and served out the last years of that war. She then returned home, and once again enlisted at the start of the War of the Spanish Succession. Davies was discovered to be a woman when treated for wounds in 1706, after which she stayed with the regiment as cook and sutler. Along the way she found her husband in the embrace of another woman; they reconciled as friends, and he died in battle.

The Female Soldier claims that Snell was abandoned by her good-for-nothing husband when she was pregnant. After the death of her baby in 1745, she signed on as a soldier to track down the culprit and wreak her revenge on him. However, parish records show that her child was born in 1746 and died in 1747; so the first part of her story has to be a fabrication. Yet ship records establish that in late 1747 she did, indeed, sign on to sail to India as a marine. *The Female Soldier* reports that, while serving, she learned that her husband had been executed for stabbing a man. After her return to England, military records state that, in recognition of her service she was admitted as an out pensioner at the Royal Hospital at Chelsea.[35]

Beyond their commercial success as entertainment, Davies's and Snell's memoirs work on deeper levels. Scarlet Bowen argues that the depiction of these women in the ranks should be regarded as constituting the kind of female masculinity proposed by Judith Halberstam.[36] Bowen takes this back into the literary world of the eighteenth century in a way similar to Halberstam's reliance upon modern literature and film. Although Halberstam concentrates on current butch lesbians, Bowen finds Halberstam's arguments applicable to Davies and Snell, although they are portrayed as heterosexual. Yet to consider the cross-dressing woman soldier as an early modern equivalent of the twentieth-century butch lesbian is an ahistorical distortion.[37] Early modern women soldiers were usually escaping conditions into which they were born or into which they had been cornered by life; their appearance hid their fundamental identity. In contrast, the butch lesbian is embracing and announcing her true identity.

There is a second aspect of Bowen's argument that is more convincing. She asserts that, "far from reifying male masculinity or serving simply as a 'proxy' for the heroism of male soldiers, the female heroine possesses her

---

[35] Stephens, *Hannah Snell*, pp. 44–45.

[36] Bowen, "The Real Soul of a Man in her Breast," p. 26; Judith Halberstam, *Female Masculinity* (Durham: 1998).

[37] Martha Vicinus writes, "The predecessor to the modern 'butch' cannot be traced back to those women soldiers who posed as 'female soldiers.'" " 'They Wonder to Which Sex I Belong': The Historical Roots of Modern Lesbian Identity," in Henry Abelove, Michèle Aina Barale, and David M. Halperin, eds., *The Lesbian and Gay Studies Reader* (New York, 1993), p. 436.

own brand of female masculinity that she uses in order to cajole other male characters in the memoirs into being 'real men.' "[38] In a similar vein, Julie Wheelwright concludes that during the eighteenth century, "female soldiers ... were hailed as heroines, albeit exceptions."[39] Nineteenth century notions of proper femininity would treat Davies and Snell as "freaks of nature," but that was a later age. For early modern Europe, intrepid female heroines who exemplified masculine virtues were accepted, and they were ready and able to show men what men ought to do.

For Bowen, the memoirs of Davies and Snell were intended to inspire patriotic fervor and argue in favor of the unpopular war of 1739–48. Publishers were consciously pursuing political programs, and these tales were intended to shame men into military service. "Embodying populist support for war, both Davies and Snell are members of plebeian families that willingly sprang into military service in order to defend the nation."[40] *The Life and Adventures of Mrs. Christian Davies* appeared the very year that British audiences first heard the patriotic air, "Rule Britannia!":

> The Muses, still with freedom found,
> Shall to thy happy coast repair:
> Blest isle! with matchless beauty crowned,
> And manly hearts to guard the fair.
> Rule, Britannia! Britannia, rule the waves:
> Britons never will be slaves.[41]

We will see a similar theme of shaming men to "guard the fair" used by women who appeared as female soldiers on the stage.

Davies and Snell provided the British with their most powerful examples of women soldiers, but the literary genre presented other cases.[42]

---

[38] Bowen, "The Real Soul of a Man in her Breast," p. 28.

[39] Wheelwright, " 'Amazons and military maids:' An examination of female military heroines in British literature and the changing construction of gender," p. 490.

[40] Bowen, "The Real Soul of a Man in her Breast," p. 32. For Bowen, "As a figure at once masculine and feminine, heroic and mock-heroic, the plebeian female soldier embodies and refashions notions of Britishness during a period of history when its identity was most in dispute." p. 22.

[41] Poem by James Thompson, 1740, put to music by Thomas Augustine Arne, ca. 1740

[42] The military experiences of an Italian woman, Cattarina Vizzani, first appeared on the Continent during the mid-1740s and were then published in an English translation on the heels of Hannah Snell's story in 1751. Giovanni Bianchi, *Breve Storia della vita di Catteriina Vizzani, romana, che per ott'anni vesti abito da uomo in quality di servidore, la quale dop vari casi essendo in fine stata uccisa, su trovata pulcella mella sezzione del su cadavero* (Venezia: S. Occhi, 1744). *Hist and Physic Dissertations on the Case of Catherine Vizzani, containing the adventures of a young woman who for eight years*

English sailors got their due as well, for example in Mary Lacy, *The History of the Female Shipwright* (London: 1773), which, like Snell's story, checks out at several points.[43]

Brief popular pamphlets, called chapbooks, also spoke of women soldiers. These consisted of one printed sheet, printed on both sides and folded in quarto or octavo to produce a small uncut booklet. One of the most enduring tales told in this pamphlet literature was that of Long Meg of Westminster, discussed in Chapter II. Two other chapbook tales, *The Surprizing Life and Adventures of Maria Knowles* (1798) and *The Life and Extraordinary Adventures of Susanna Cope, the British Female Soldier* (printed repeatedly from 1798 to 1819), followed very much the romantic formula of popular songs. Young Susanna, "fell in love with a handsome young soldier belonging to the Guards, and being disappointed by her father, eloped from his house, came to London, disguised in men's apparel, and entered into the same regiment with her lover."[44]

Plays and Stage Performances

Women masquerading as male soldiers appeared on many stages across Europe. A play portraying the notable adventures of Catalina de Erauso, *La monja alférez, comedia famosa* by Juan Pérez de Montalván, was first performed in Madrid in 1626, shortly after she came to public attention.[45] It stressed her taste for women, gambling, and fighting.

Diego and José de Figueroa y Cordoba's *Dama capitán* was produced in the 1660s.[46] A number of French plays from the reign of Louis XIV featured cross-dressing women with the heroine masquerading as a

---

passed in the habit of a man With some curious and anatomical remarks on the nature and existence of the hymen To which are added certain needful remarks by the English editor (London: 1751). It also appeared in another English edition in 1755. The title illustration and page is reproduced as plate 10 in Dekker and van de Pol, *Tradition of Female Transvestism*, between pp. 48 and 49.

[43] Mary Lacy, *The History of the Female Shipwright* (London: M. Lewis, 1773).

[44] *The Life and Extraordinary Adventures of Susanna Cope, the British Female Soldier* in Dugaw, *Warrior Women and Popular Balladry*, pp. 130, 185–87.

[45] Nerea Aresti, "The Gendered Identities of the 'Lieutenant Nun': Rethinking the Story of a Female Warrior in Early Modern Spain," trans. Rosemary Williams, *Gender and History* 19, no. 3 (November 2007): 406. At roughly the same time Ana Caro Mallén y Soto wrote *Comedia famosa de valor, agravio y mujer* in which the heroine dresses as a man to outwit, humble, and reform Don Juan.

[46] Paul Patrick Rogers, "Spanish Influence on the Literature of France," *Hispania* 9, no. 4 (October, 1926): 226.

soldier. These include Antoine-Jacob Montfleury's *La fille capitaine* (1672), which was borrowed from Figueroa's play. The era also saw *La fille savante* by Anne-Mauduit de Fatouville, *La fille de bon sens* by Jean Palaprat, and *Les folies amoureuses* by Jean-François Regnard.[47] Isabelle, the heroine of *La fille savante*, disdains the weakness and foolishness of femininity as she explains her cross-dressing to her father: "Father please realize that the softness and the idleness of women have given me such an aversion to my sex, that being unable it to change, I try, at least, to disguise it by my clothes and my actions."[48] Such a view mirrors the observations made by Madame de Sévigné, the noted woman of letters, who commented on masculine glory and feminine weakness in 1683: "Since one constantly tells men that they are only worthy of esteem to the extent that they love glory, they devote all their thoughts to it; and this shapes all French bravery. As women are allowed to be weak, they take advantage of this privilege without scruple."[49] In this literature, the civilian, upper-class femininity that is criticized did not include any of the toughness typical of camp women, demonstrating that the overlap between femininity and masculinity varied greatly by social position and circumstance.

The English stage also saw its share of women soldiers. One count found that out of the 300 plays given their initial performance in London from 1660 to 1700, about ninety featured women who dressed in male attire, and many of these appeared as soldiers.[50] George Farquhar's *The Recruiting Officer* (1706) features a heroine, Silvia, who is an athletic young woman who boasts, "I can gallop all the morning after the hunting horn, and all the evening after a fiddle." She also expresses her frustration with femininity, finding "a petticoat a mighty simple thing" and becoming "heartily tir'd of my sex." Her friend Melinda comments, "You begin to fancy yourself in breeches in good earnest."[51] In a tortured plot, Silvia

---

[47] Jan Clarke, "Female Cross-Dressing on the Paris Stage, 1673–1715," *Forum for Modern Language Studies* 35, no. 3 (1999): 238–50, lists twenty-nine plays from this period, all but one of which were presented at the Guénégaud, the Comédie-Française, and the Comédie-Italienne. See as well Paul Patrick Rogers, "Spanish Influence on the Literature of France," *Hispania* 9, no. 4 (October, 1926): 226, on *La fille capitaine*.

[48] *La fille savante* in Clarke, "Female Cross-Dressing on the Paris Stage," p. 243.

[49] Madame de Sévigné, *Lettres de madame de Sévigné*, 7:394, letter of 23 October 1683.

[50] From Pat Rogers, "The Breeches Part," in Paul-Gabriel Boucé, ed., *Sexuality in Eighteenth-Century Britain* (Manchester: 1982), p. 249, in Julie Wheelwright, *Amazons and Military Maidens: Women Who Dressed as Men in Pursuit of Life, Liberty and Happiness* (London: 1994), p. 7.

[51] George Farquhar, *The Recruiting Officer* (London: 1997), pp. 17–18.

masquerades as a man to enlist in the company of Captain Plume, who has caught her fancy; Silvia is eventually discovered but wins Plume as her prize. Interestingly, at one point Plume's friend, Worthy, challenges a foolish man of the country named Bullock, "Hast thou no more sense, fellow, than to believe that the captain can [en]list women?" to which Bullock replies "I know not whether they list them or what they do with them, but I'm sure they carry as many women as men with them out of the country."[52]

Such amusing comedies delighted audiences with their exotic themes of inverted gender, including the inherent sexual double entendres and occasional homosexual innuendos. But they also demonstrated a frustration with the limited possibilities of femininity and expressed women's possession of masculine traits. Often the heroine is quite happy to adopt masculine tastes for drinking and gambling, and to draw her sword in earnest.

Public performances carried similar messages of female power through masculine skills. English popular entertainment included public fights with women as active participants. The *London Journal* of June 1722 reported a boxing match "when two of the feminine gender appeared for the first time on the theater of War at Hockley in the Hole, and maintained the battle with great valour for a long time, to the no small satisfaction of the spectators."[53] *The Weekly Dispatch* of London reported that in October 1813, boxers Peggy Carey and Mary Flaharty went at each other mightily until the latter was floored and "taken away senseless" in a cart.[54] Women also dueled with swords and quarter staves. These women were not soldiers, but their representation of the woman in combat was an expression of the military ideal of courage. In the late 1720s, James and Elizabeth Stokes of London took on challengers, such as the Irish combatants Robert Barker and Mary Welsh for the entertainment of paying crowds. The Stokes boasted of "our ability of body, dextrous hands, and courageous hearts."[55] Prizes were to be awarded for the best cuts and blows.

With more elevated purpose, Peg Woffington performed *The Female Volunteer, or an Attempt to Make our Men Stand* on the London stage during the Scottish rebellion of 1745–46 (see Plate 22). This actress made

[52] Farquhar, *The Recruiting Officer*, p. 39.
[53] Dugaw, *Warrior Women and Popular Balladry*, p. 125.
[54] *The Weekly Dispatch* in Wheelwright, *Amazons and Military Maidens*, p. 14.
[55] Advertisement for the 17 July 1727 performance in Dugaw, *Warrior Women and Popular Balladry*, pp. 125–26.

THE
FEMALE VOLUNTEER:
OR,
an Attempt to make our Men STAND.

An EPILOGUE *intended to be spoken by Mrs.* Woffington *in the Habit of a Volunteer upon reading the* Gazette *containing an Account of the late Action at* FALKIRK.

PLAGUE of all Cowards, fay I—why blefs my Eyes—
No, no, it can't be true—The Gazette lies.
Our Men retreat! before a Scrub Banditti!
Who fearce could fright the Buff-Coats of the City!—
Well, if 'tis fo, and that our *Men* can't *ftand,*
'Tis Time we Women take the *Thing* in *Hand.*
Thus in my Country's Caufe I now appear,
A bold, fmart, *Kevenhuller'd* Volunteer;
And really, mark fome Heroes in the Nation,
You'll think this no unnat'ral Transformation:
For if in Valour real *Manhood* lies,
All Cowards are but Women in Difguife.
They cry, thefe Rebels are fo ftout and tall!
Ah lud! *I'd totter the proudeft of them all.*
Try but my *Metal,* place me in the Van,
And poft me, if I don't—*bring down my Man.*
Had we an Army of fuch valorous Wenches,
What Man, d'ye think, would dare attack our *Frenches?*
O! how th' Artillery of our *Eyes* would maul 'em.
But, our *mask'd Batteries,* lud! now they would *gall 'em!*
No Rebels 'gainft fuch Force dare take the Field;
For, d--mme, but we'd die ere we'd yield.
Jefting apart—We Women have ftrong Reafon,
To ftop the Progrefs of this Popifh Treafon:

For fure when Female Liberty's at Stake,
All Women ought to *buftle* for its Sake:
Should thefe audacious Sons of *Rome* prevail,
Vows,--CONVENTS,--and that heathen Thing--the VEIL,
Muft come in Fafhion. Oh! fuch Inftitutions
Would fuit but odly with our—CONSTITUTIONS.
What gay Coquet would brook a Nun's Profeffion?
And I've fome *private* REASONS 'gainft Confeffion,
Befides, our good Men of the Church, they fay,
(Who now, thank Heav'n, may *love* as well as *pray,*)
Muft then be only wed to cloifter'd Houfes,
Slap then we're nick'd of 20,000 Spoufes;
Faith, and no bad ones, as I'm told : then judge ye,
Is't fit we lofe our BENEFIT of CLERGY?

In Freedom's Caufe, ye Patriot-Fair, *arife,*
Exert the facred Influence of your Eyes;
On valiant Merit deign alone to fmile,
And vindicate the Glory of our Ifle;
To ao bafe Coward proftitute your Charms,
Difband the Lover who deferts his Arms:
So fhall you fire each Hero to his Duty,
And *Britifh* Rights be fav'd by *Britifh* Beauty.

LONDON: Printed for M. MOORE, in *Pater-nofter-Row,* 1746. Price SIX PENCE.

PLATE 22. Handbill for Peg Woffington performing "The Female Volunteer,"
1746, reproduced in Augustin Daly, *Woffington: A Tribute to the Actress and the Woman.* With photogravure illustrations, 2nd ed. (Troy, NY: 1891).
University of Illinois at Urbana-Champaign Library.

a reputation playing men in uniform to appreciative audiences; her first such role was *The Female Officer* in 1740.[56] As the female volunteer, she light-heartedly, but directly, shamed the men in the audience to fight for king and country. Considered alongside Davies's and Snell's memoirs, her performance was another mid-eighteenth-century appeal to burgeoning national feeling in Britain. Noting initial defeat at the hands of Scottish rebels, she chidingly played the card of her own manliness: "if 'tis so, and that our Men can't stand, 'Tis Time we Women take the Thing in Hand." But ultimately she counseled women to put their feminine charms to noble service, rewarding only the brave warrior:

> In Freedom's Cause, ye Patriot-Fair, arise,
> Exert the sacred influence of your Eyes,
> On valiant Merit deign alone to smile,
> And vindicate the Glory of our Isle;
> To no base Coward prostitute you Charms,
> Disband the Lover who deserts his Arms;
> So shall you fire each Hero to his Duty,
> And British Rights be sav'd by British Beauty.[57]

At Sadlers Wells circa 1790, Mrs. Wrighten performed another song, *The Female Captain*, written by her husband. This ditty cut much in the same direction as the Peg Woffington's act. It reminded the men " 'Tis your king and your country now calls for you aid," and threatened them that should they fail the call, she would step forward "the breaches to assume."[58]

Woffington and Wrighten both issued a gendered challenge to the men of the audience to fulfill their manly duties or be shunned, or even replaced, by women.[59] Incidentally, their appeals to duty also assume higher-minded rationales for service than those that typified mercenaries in the sixteenth and seventeenth centuries. Another English stage song at

---

[56] Wheelwright, *Amazons and Military Maidens*, p. 115.

[57] Handbill for Peg Woffington as the Female Volunteer from Augustin Daly, *Woffington: A Tribute to the Actress and the Woman* (Troy, NY: Nims and Knight, 1891), between pp. 112 and 113.

[58] Dugaw, *Warrior Women and Popular Balladry*, p. 52. The text of the song is in *Roundelay, or the New Syren* (London: W. Lane, n.d.), p. 14.

[59] It should be noted that the founder of the first Women's Battalion of Death, Maria Bochkareva, argued explicitly: "What was important was to shame the men." Bochkareva in Melissa K. Stockdale, " 'My Death for the Motherland Is Happiness': Women, Patriotism, and Soldiering in Russia's Great War, 1914–1917," *American Historical Review* 109, no. 1 (February 2004): 91–92. Also on Russian women soldiers during the First World War and the Revolution, see Laurie S. Stoff, *They Fought for the Motherland: Russia's Women Soldiers in World War I And the Revolution* (Lawrence, KS: 2006).

the end of the 1700s, also sung by a woman in military attire and also entitled the *Female Volunteer*, suggested that women might actually follow the martial careers of men:

> When our gallant lads are obliged to roam
> Why should women idly stay at home.[60]

Hannah Snell herself took to the footlights, performing even before Walker published his printed accounts. On 29 June she marched on stage at the New Wells theater for the first of sixty appearances that stretched on until 6 September. The New Wells offered harlequinades, variety shows appealing to a popular audience. *The Whitehall and General Evening Post* reported the success of her first performance, "Last Night there were the greatest Number of reputable Persons ever known at the New Wells, Goodman's Fields, to see and hear the famous Hannah Snell sing two songs. She appeared in her Marine Habit, and met with universal Applause, as she behaved with great Decency and good manners."[61] However, Hannah was no success at singing, and by 19 July, she had augmented the content of her show by demonstrating "the manual exercises of a soldier in her new regimentals."[62] Walker's quick reaction to Snell and her ability to immediately exploit her experience in print and on stage provides a powerful demonstration of the fascination that greeted the phenomenon of the woman soldier.[63]

Hannah Snell was not the only woman to perform the manual of arms on stage. During 1802 and 1803, Deborah Sampson, the American

---

[60] Dugaw, *Warrior Women and Popular Balladry*, p. 52. The text of the song is in *The Songsters Multum in Parvo*, 6 vols. (London, John Fairburn, n.d.), III, pp. 113.

[61] *The Whitehall and General Evening Post*, 30 June, in Stephens, *Hannah Snell*, p. 41.

[62] See contemporary engraving, "Hannah Snell in Her Regimentals as She performs the Manual Exercise of a Soldier at Goodman's Fields Wells 1750" reproduced in Stephens, *Hannah Snell*, p. 42.

[63] Snell was not alone in exploiting her notoriety as a woman warrior as a source of financial gain. An Amsterdam woman of the seventeenth century put herself on display in her tavern, where she posted the following notice to bring in customers:

> Her Aagt de Tamboer dwells
> That which she does, she does it well
> Twice as tar with Tromp she sailed
> But still is sound of limb and hale
> She swims as well as fish or whale
> Lately, she saved a drowning lass
> The cost to see her: a mug or glass!

Dekker and van de Pol, *The Tradition of Female Tranvestism*, p. 83. "Tamboer" is Dutch for drummer.

woman soldier, went on a lecture tour in which she was "equipped in complete uniform" and went "through the Manual Exercise," as advertised in a Boston handbill.[64] In a more light-hearted vein, Sadlers Wells featured a review in 1803, *The British Amazons*, that closed with "female volunteers" performing military drills.[65]

Popular Culture as Condemning Lesbian Conduct

Tales of plucky young maidens out to win love and glory, or the stories of stout-hearted women in arms, were amusing, with their entertainment value multiplied by a taste for the unusual, even the bizarre. As the title page of the biography of Catherine Vezzani, a female soldier, proclaims: "What odd fantastic Things, we Women do!"[66] The age was clearly fascinated by women who crossed over into a man's world with a male identity; this was tolerated, and even praised, as strength, toughness, and courage, but popular sensitivities did not accept the dominant woman as a rule nor did they approve of overt female homosexuality.

Songs could turn from praising the courage of spirited maidens to condemning the perversion of damnable women who disobeyed the laws of nature. In 1632 Barbara Adriaens dressed as a man and served as a municipal militiaman as Willem Adriaens. She was discovered before long, when another woman said that she had slept with Barbara when she still dressed as a woman. She was then arrested. A song described her as:

> In appearance and in dress
> An indignity to her sex.[67]

Another unnamed woman who dressed as a man was condemned in similar fashion:

> Let Sir Bawd in prison spin
> I have no pity for her, no;
> Who doth with such sport begin
> Begins in sport and ends in woe.[68]

---

[64] See Young, *Masquerade*, p. 204, for the handbill. He discusses her tour at length, pp. 197–224.
[65] Dugaw, *Warrior Women and Popular Balladry*, p. 52, n. 35.
[66] See the title page reproduced as Pl. 10 in Dekker and van de Pol, *The Tradition of Female Tranvestism*, between pp. 48 and 49.
[67] Dekker and van de Pol, *The Tradition of Female Tranvestism*, p. 89.
[68] Dekker and van de Pol, *The Tradition of Female Tranvestism*, p. 87. See as well the story and of Cornelia Gerrits and Elisabeth Boleyn and the song concerning it, pp. 86–87.

From such evidence, Dekker and van de Pol conclude that, "These songs corroborate the notion that it was precisely among the common folk that the greatest disapproval of these women existed."[69]

Popular Culture and the Presence of Women in the Campaign Community

The impact of popular culture's fascination with the woman soldier can only be conjectured, given the anecdotal nature of the evidence. Popular culture must have spread the word of this alternative course for women throughout the lower classes. It is important to remember that, when the court questioned Catharina Linck in 1721 as to why she had decided to adopt male dress and identity, she answered that "other women had done this."[70] The fact that women followed this path means that they recognized it as a possibility, and the avenues for this knowledge must have included the media of popular culture. Women in despair of finding an acceptable life within the confines of the usual societal norms probably found hope, or at a bit of escapism, in stories of love and glory in uniform. Julie Wheelwright argues that, real or fictional, the persona of woman soldier shone as a beckoning example of liberation for plebeian women from the eighteenth to the twentieth centuries.[71] To the extent that popular culture encouraged women to change their identities and their lives by enlisting, it influenced real world behavior.

Yet the mannish woman soldier as presented in popular culture may also have given a sharper edge to the battle between the sexes discussed

---

[69] Dekker and van de Pol, *The Tradition of Female Tranvestism*, p. 87.

[70] We know quite a bit about Catherina Linck because her trial record was discovered, published, and then translated. She is sometimes identified as Catherina Lincken, but Linck is the more common spelling in the trial record. Brigitte Eriksson, trans. and ed., "A lesbian execution in Germany, 1721: The trial records," in Salbatore J. Licata and Robert P. Petersen, *The Gay Past: A Collection of Historical Essays* (New York: 1985), p. 33. This work states: "Of course she knew that God had forbidden women to wear men's clothing, but this applied to married women only, not to maidens."

[71] Wheelwright, *Amazons and Military Maids*, pp. 9, 13–14, and 21–22. Emma Edmonds, who served in the Union Army during the U.S. Civil War, reported that she was inspired to do so by the novel, *Fanny Campbell or the Female Pirate Captain*. p. 14. Edmonds reported that "When I read where 'Fanny' cut off her brown curls, and donned the blue jacket, and stepped into the freedom and glorious independence of masculinity, I threw up my old straw hat and shouted, as I have since heard McClellan's soldiers do when he rode past the troops on a march–only one small throat could not make so much noise." *Winfield Courier*, January 24, 1884, at http://www.ausbcomp.com/~bbott/wortman/CivilWar_Female.htm.

in Chapter II. The tough and strong traits of the camp woman already overlapped with the masculinity of her male companions, but the fictionalized female soldier took it to a more extreme level. Because the metaphor was a "battle for the pants," it is no small thing that the woman soldier was ready for battle and wore pants. Oddly enough, if the woman warrior enshrined in popular culture exacerbated gender frictions within the campaign community, these would not have affected the actual woman soldier, because she would have disappeared in her masculine persona; it would have been the skirt-wearing women of the campaign community who paid the price for increased gender tensions.

BEING A FEMALE SOLDIER

Even if it yields some glimpses, popular culture cannot completely reveal the lives of actual women in the ranks. The fact that authors embellished stories to please their audiences marginalizes the use of such tales in reconstructing the experience of women under arms. Fortunately, there are other places to go. Women soldiers left traces and trails in documents not meant for a popular audience and, consequently, free from the same temptations to distort. These include interrogations and court proceedings of those arrested for various infractions and requests for gratifications or pensions from women who had served in uniform.

Just as the women soldier became a theme in popular culture primarily from the mid-seventeenth century, the reality of the women soldier seems to have hit full stride after 1650. This is not to say that cross-dressing women were not found in the ranks before then. Catalina Erauso was a harbinger of the phenomenon in the early 1600s.

To date, our best collections of materials on women in the ranks during the seventeenth and eighteenth centuries concern the Dutch Netherlands and France. The most important studies have not been the work of scholars focused on the history of military institutions, but historians concerned with the phenomenon of cross-dressing and gender. For their *The Tradition of Female Transvestism in Early Modern Europe*, Rudolf M. Dekker and Lotte C. van de Pol collected 119 cases of women living as men in The Netherlands in the period 1550–1839; nearly all of these date from the seventeenth and eighteenth centuries. Of the ninety-three individuals with known professions, eighty-three were soldiers or sailors at some point.[72] Sylvie Steinberg in her *La confusion des sexes:*

---

[72] Dekker and van de Pol, *The Tradition of Female Transvestism*, p. 9.

Le travestissement de la Renaissance à la Révoluion discusses the cases of forty-eight women who enlisted as soldiers in France before the French Revolution, and about fifty who served in the armies of the Republic.[73] These historians also consider some cases from outside The Netherlands and France. Dekker's and van de Pol's "far-from-exhaustive" search of the literature discovered "fifty authentic cases of female transvestism" during the same centuries in England. This count would have to include Christian Davies, Hannah Snell, and the renown Phoebe Hessel, who claimed to have fought and been wounded at the Battle of Fontenoy.

Because Dekker, van de Pol, and Steinberg deal with the phenomenon of cross-dressing *per se*, they examine other rationale for this behavior. Some women donned men's clothing in order to travel more easily or more securely; some did so out of personal taste or whim. Others cross-dressed for sexual reasons, such as lesbians who wished to have access to women. In addition, prostitutes assumed male attire simply as a prop to draw a special clientele. Other prostitutes chose to dress as soldiers in order to ply their trade in military encampments and barracks that forbade entrance to unauthorized women.[74] Specifically in an attempt to hamper prostitution, Charles I announced a ban on women adopting male attire.[75] This explains why military authorities were so careful to inquire about the sexual activities of women who masqueraded as men. In any case, the known examples of women who cross-dressed to serve as soldiers and sailors outnumber those who adopted a long-term masculine identity for other reasons.

Although we can document perhaps a few hundred women who became soldiers and sailors from 1500 to 1815, when we consider this

---

[73] Steinberg, *La confusion des sexes*, pp. 76. In her paper, "The Heroic Imaginary: Women Soldiers in the Republican and Imperial Wars," delivered at the 2006 meeting of the Society for French Historical Studies, Barbara Day-Hickman tallies various authors' counts of women who served in the Revolutionary armies figures on the instances found in several works. She gives fifty as the figure for Steinberg. On France, see as well Joseph Harris, *Hidden Agendas: Cross Dessing in 17th-Century France* (Tubingen: 2005).

[74] For example, see Steinberg, *La confusion des sexes*, pp. 4 and 86–87. During World War I, there were stories that prostitutes bought nurses uniforms on the black market to ply their trade among the troops. Wheelwright, *Amazons and Military Maidens*, p. 75.

[75] "Let no woman presume to Counterfeit Her Sex by wearing man's apparel under pain of the Severest punishment which Law and our displeasure shall inflict," from Antonia Fraser, *The Weaker Vessel: Woman's Lot in Seventeenth-Century England* (New York, 1984), p. 196. This was directed against the "prostitute Impudency of some women" who donned men's clothing and "thus conversed in our Army."

number in relation to the hundreds and hundreds of thousands of men who joined the ranks of European armies or sailed in merchant and naval fleets, the presence of such cross-dressing women was extremely limited. The numbers who stood in the ranks of any particular European army at any particular time was most probably miniscule. For example, Peter H. Wilson's research into the Stuttgart archives for the seventeenth and eighteenth centuries discovered only a single woman soldier, Anna Maria Christmännin, who served from 1716 to1718.[76] Don N. Hagist as well concludes that "we cannot fully document any cases of women serving as British regulars in the American War."[77] Historians who argue for a sizeable participation by women in the ranks are *assuming* that there were great numbers of women who went unnoticed, and that is a big assumption.

Thus, it is an exaggeration to conclude, as does Alfred Young concerning his case of the American Deborah Sampson, that "in the larger Atlantic world of the eighteenth century, Sampson would not have raised many eyebrows."[78] It is precisely because the existence of woman soldiers was rare, even in Europe, that it caught the public interest. Stories of cross-dressing soldiers definitely "raised many eyebrows" or they would not have been told. Also, Arlette Farge misleads her readers when she asserts, "To march off to war as men did, to rebel by passing as men: cross-dressing was one of the traditional forms of popular protest."[79] To call cross-dressing as a male soldier a "tradition" implies that it was reasonably common, which it was not. Yes, it occurred, and, yes, people

---

[76] Peter H. Wilson, "German Women and War, 1500–1800," *War in History*, vol. 3, no. 2 (1996), p. 152.

[77] Don N. Hagist, "The Women of the British Army in America." a series of four brief articles published in *The Brigade Dispatch*, 1993–95. This is a reenactors' publication put out by The Brigade of the American Revolution. The Hagist piece can also befound on the web at at http://www.revwar75.com/library/hagist/britwomen.htm

[78] Young, *Masquerade*, p. 8.

[79] Arlette Farge, "Protesters Plain to See," in Arlette Farge and Natalie Davis, eds., *A History of Women in the West*, vol. 3 (Cambridge, MA: 1993), p. 499. This statement mixes cross-dressing as a solder with cross-dressing *per se*, so Farge may be justified regarding the latter, but as it stands, the statement is misleading. See as well what I see as a similar slippage in the argument presented by Dianne Dugaw in her "Balladry's Female Warriors: Women, Warfare, and Disguise in the Eighteenth Century," *Eighteenth-Century Life* 9.2 (1985), p. 3.

In fact, there is a real tendency to slip from the idea of cross-dressing in ritual and celebration to that of serious, long-term changes in identity. Before making sweeping generalizations about women soldiers, we need to remind ourselves that assumptions cannot be used to prove assumptions.

knew about it, but while it was a known route, there is no real evidence that it was a road taken by more than a tiny minority.[80]

Marie Magdelaine Mouron and her Sisters-in-Arms

Since human interest draws us to the subject, we can best capture the phenomenon by organizing the story around the personal history of one woman, Marie Magdelaine Mouron. She enlisted in the army of Louis XIV and served in three regiments in about six years, until arrested for desertion in May 1696. The record of her interrogation is a short but rich account intended only for the military administrators in charge of her fate.[81] So much of her story parallels the histories of other women in military service that it provides a good representative case.

Marie testified that she was born in Desvres, a small town in Picardy. She never stipulated her age; however, the circumstances of her flight suggest that she was in her mid or late teens. Sylvie Steinberg has found that most French women who adopted men's clothing did so when they were young, between sixteen and twenty years of age.[82] Popular songs about female soldiers usually portray them as choosing to enter service to follow a lover or husband; however, this was not the case for most women who chose the military life in reality. They usually enlisted to escape either bad family situations or economic misery in a world that offered poor women few alternatives.[83] One young woman who dressed as a man to work in a tavern explained that her "chief Motive was, that Boys could shift better for themselves than Girls."[84] After the death of her mother, Marie's father

[80] For another example claiming extensive participation of women in combat, Linda Grant De Pauw, declared "During the American War for Independence tens of thousands of women were involved in active combat." Linda Grant De Pauw, "Women in Combat - The Revolutionary War Experience," *Armed Forces and Society* 7, no. 2 (Winter 1981), p. 209. Janice E. McKenney, takes strong and convincing exception to this conclusion in " 'Women in Combat': Comment," *Armed Forces in Society*, vol. 8, no. 4 (Summer 1982) 686–92.

[81] SHAT, AG, MR 1785, #53–55, 28 May 1696, *procès verbal* and accompanying documents concerning Marie Magdelaine Mouron. I earlier described her life briefly in "The Strange Case of the Maiden Soldier of Picardy," *MHQ, The Quarterly Journal of Military History* (Spring, 1990): 54–56. My wife, the author Andrea Lynn, and I have done further research on her case since then.

[82] Steinberg, *La confusion des sexes*, p. 62. See the table of ages she supplies, based on the known ages of 57 women, p. 315, fn 24.

[83] See the discussions of economic and family necessities in Steinberg, *La confusion des sexes*, pp. 59–60 and 256–57, and Dekker and Van de Pol, *Tradition of Female Transvestism*, pp. 25–27 and 32–35, and Easton, "Gender's Two Bodies," pp. 134, 138, and 142.

[84] *Daily Advertiser*, 8 September 1762, in Easton, "Gender's Two Bodies," p. 138.

married a woman who Marie could not abide. Here her life is similar to that of the much better-known Dutch woman, Maria van Antwerpen, also the subject of court documents. Maria, who lost her mother at age eleven and her impoverished father at twelve, was left in the care of an aunt who "mistreated" her, Maria reported that she "did not have the life of a dog, much less that of a child."[85] Although the record does not detail Marie's economic condition, her family was certainly not well off.

Marie grew up in Desvres where her father worked as a butcher. There she became used to soldiers because Desvres was defended by a small fort. Later the family moved to Trépied, where her father served under arms as a *garde sel*, a paramilitary soldier who protected stores of salt and fought smugglers for the salt-tax farmers.[86]

Marie thus mirrors the situation of many other French women soldiers, who tended to come from those provinces that were heavily garrisoned. The frontier provinces of Picardy, Champagne, Lorraine, Franche-Comté, and Burgundy were the most heavily represented among the women soldiers with identifiable geographical origins.[87] Not surprisingly, women of adventurous spirit who grew up around the army were most likely to take this option." Maria van Antwerpen as well came from the garrison town of Breda, and the biography of Christian Davies states that she too was "accustomed to Soldiers, when a Girl, and delighted with seeing them exercise."[88]

It also is probable that Marie had heard the stories and songs about women soldiers. Such an alternative may have been common knowledge. An example of this is in the story of another Marie, Marie van der Guise, who while begging met sympathetic peasants who gave her men's clothing and suggested she enlist as a soldier.[89]

Unwilling to go on living as she was, Marie Magdelaine Mouron bought men's clothes at the nearby town of Montreuil and "there engaged herself as a soldier under the name of Picard" in the Royal Walloon Regiment. Her first enlistment must have been about 1690, when Louis's armies were growing to unprecedented size, and recruiters were none too picky.

[85] Dekker and van de Pol, *Tradition of Female Transvestism*, p. 11.

[86] The *gardes sel* constituted a kind of private army in service to the tax farmers; it numbered nearly 20,000 in 1768. Roland Mousnier, *The Institutions of France under the Absolute Monarchy, 1598–1789*, 2 vols. (Chicago: 1979–84), 2:457–58.

[87] Steinberg, *La confusion des sexes*, p. 76. The same pattern of provincial origins typified the Revolutionary era.

[88] *The Life and Adventures of Mrs. Christian Davies*, p. 29.

[89] Dekker and van de Pol, *Tradition of Female Transvestism*, pp. 32–33.

Her regiment marched from the channel coast to Sisteron, where she was dismissed for some unnamed reason. Why she might have had to leave is uncertain, but perhaps she was discovered to be a woman. A woman found in the ranks would not suffer a penalty beyond discharge, as long as she was innocent of any other infraction.

This raises the intriguing question of how Marie and her sisters-in-arms protected themselves from discovery. They had to cope with matters of physical appearance and bodily functions. Women volunteers lacked facial hair and had higher-toned voices, so they had to sell themselves as adolescents not yet grown to full manhood. As a consequence, women tended to claim to be younger than they actually were. Maria van Antwerpen stated her age as sixteen on her first enrollment, when she was actually twenty-eight, and she reported that in male garb that she resembled a handsome boy.[90] Recruits received only minimal physical inspections, designed mainly to verify that they were healthy with sound limbs, and men did not disrobe frequently; therefore, a clever individual might avoid discovery.

The fact that Marie became a dragoon tells us that she was probably a large girl, since the dragoons tried to secure taller recruits. Steinberg establishes that French women soldiers whose height is known were quite tall for their time, usually standing higher than average men.[91] Some historians surmise that the cases of actual female soldiers multiplied after 1650 because weapons became lighter then, and thus more manageable for women, but the fact that these women were generally larger than average men undermines this thesis.[92] Women who served as men had to pass for men, and are often described as masculine in appearance, being large and stout. Catalina de Erauso was said to be "tall and powerfully built, and with a masculine air"[93] (see Plate 23). Maria van Antwerpen described herself as "exceptionally stout."[94]

[90] Dekker and van de Pol, *The Tradition of Female Transvestism*, pp. 15–17.

[91] Steinberg, *La confusion des sexes*, p. 143.

[92] See, for example, Holly A. Mayer, *Belonging to the Army: Camp Followers and Community during the American Revolution* (Columbia, SC: 1996), p. 20, for a guess that the replacement of the larger matchlock by the lighter flintlock facilitated the female soldier.

[93] Description of her by Pedro del Valle, whom she met in Rome, Erauso, *Memoir of a Basque Lieutenant Nun*, p. xxxiii–iv. A near contemporary also described the American Deborah Sampson as "tall, muscular and very erect and considered one of the very best specimens of womanhood." She was not thin. Young, *Masquerade*, p. 43.

[94] Dekker and van de Pol, *The Tradition of Female Transvestism*, p. 16. Geertuid ter Brugge also served as a dragoon at the same time, and a contemporary engraving shows

PLATE 23. Engraving of Catalina de Erauso based on 1630 portrait, from *Historia de la monja Alférez doña Catalina de Erauso* (Paris: 1829).
Courtesy Amsterdam University Library.

The only information Marie provided regarding how she hid her sex was that she wore military clothing and performed a soldier's duties. But this was probably a more effective disguise than it would be today. Sylvie Steinberg makes the point that wearing men's clothing concealed women behind such strong symbols of manhood that it was hard for observers to

her as a husky woman. Dekker and Van de Pol call this plate the only "authentic print of a Dutch female soldier." Dekker and van de Pol, *The Tradition of Female Transvestism*, between p. 48 and p. 49.

see through them.[95] She also contends that such surface appearance could be reinforced by comporting oneself like a man.[96] Obviously this disguise would involve doing a man's job, and soldiering was the ultimate male occupation.

If Marie mentioned no other subterfuge, other women did. Catalina de Erauso told the writer Pedro del Valle that she had "no more breasts than a girl" and that "she had used some sort of remedy to make them disappear ... [I]t was a poultice given her by an Italian—it hurt a great deal, but the effect was very much to her liking."[97] Christian Davies claimed that her breasts were "not large enough to betray my Sex," and, in addition, she wore a quilted waist-coat.[98] Deborah Sampson was said to have small breasts and to have bound them with a bandage.[99]

A woman who did not take precautions might risk rapid discovery. The August 1761 *Annual Register* noted: "As a sergeant was lately exercising some of the soldiers on board one of the transports at Portsmouth, he observed one of them, who went by the name of Paul Daniel, had a more prominent chest than ordinary. After the firings were over, he sent for the person to the cabin, when telling his suspicions, that he was a woman, and insisting upon searching him, after some evasions, the soldier confessed her sex."[100] During the same year, Maruerite Goubler, was discovered to be a woman when her comrades danced with her on Mardi Gras; the bouncing steps betrayed her breasts.[101]

The modesty and embarrassment of both the women soldiers themselves and those to whom they told their stories leave us largely in the dark concerning the way in which women were able to keep the physical necessities of urination and menstruation from exposing their true sex. The German, Catharina Linck, served as a soldier in three different units during the War of the Spanish Succession, continued to dress as a man after the war, and eventually married a woman. She reported employing "a leather-covered horn through which she urinated and [which she kept]

[95] Steinberg, *La confusion des sexes*, pp. 159–63. Young, *Masquerade*, p. 102, makes the same case, arguing that the uniform was "gendered male."

[96] Steinberg, *La confusion des sexes*, p. 147, speaks extensively of male "comportment."

[97] Erauso, *Memoir of a Basque Lieutenant Nun*, p. xxxiii–iv.

[98] *The Life and Adventures of Mrs. Christian Davies*, p. 28. *The Adventures of Louisa Baker* tells of a woman who hid her identity as she served as a sailor on the U.S.S. Constitution by wearing "a close waist-coat or bandage about my breasts, effectually concealed my sex from all on board." Cordingly, *Heroines & Harlots*, pp. 54–55.

[99] Young, *Masquerade*, p. 104

[100] John Laffin, *Women in Battle* (London: 1967), pp. 29–30.

[101] Steinberg, *La confusion des sexes*, p. 140.

fastened against her nude body."[102] This device was apparently only partially successful, as her wife commented: "Other men can piss quite a ways, but you always piss on your shoes."[103] A Dutch song of the era about a female sailor for the East India Company contains the line, "She pissed through a horn pipe."[104] Such an instrument was made of wood and animal horn.

One form of the story of Christian Davies explained that she used another device for urination:

And here it may be necessary to gratify the Curiosity of many, who, as we understand, have been greatly puzzled to conceive how a Woman could so long perform a certain natural Operation, without being discovered; since Soldiers are obliged to perform it, not only standing, but often publickly, and even at the Head of the Regiment. This indeed seems to have been a difficult Task; and yet it was very easy to her by Means of a Silver Tube painted over, and fastened about her with leather Straps.[105]

This account says that she found the "Urinary Instrument" when it was left behind by a cross-dressing woman captain who had visited her home, but had to leave in a great rush. Julie Wheelwright interprets this as a dildo, but it may have been a copy of the device used by Ottoman eunuchs who had undergone a radical removal of testes and penis.[106]

The Davies story also implies that women in uniform learned from other such women. According to the historian Linda Grant De Pauw, "Some individuals made a living recruiting women for the army or navy, and they almost certainly had a wealth of useful information. Anna Spiesen was recruited by a woman who took care of everything."[107]

Alfred Young suggests another behavior that may have helped disguise a woman. Since all soldiers had to drop their trousers to defecate, a woman could have masked urination as defecation. Also, if a camp used outhouses, as did some in the American Revolutionary War, privacy

---

[102] Eriksson, "A lesbian execution in Germany," p. 33.

[103] Eriksson, "A lesbian execution in Germany," p. 35.

[104] Dekker and van de Pol, *The Tradition of Female Transvestism*, p. 16

[105] *The Life and Adventures of Mrs. Christian Davies, the British Amazon, Commonly Called Mother Ross* (London: 1741), pp. 1–2. This is the edition published by Richard Montagu. The woman captain, Captain Bodeaux, is discussed on pp. 6–7.

[106] Alexander Moore, *Cultural Anthropology: the Field Study of Human Beings*, 2nd ed. (Rowman & Littlefield Publishers: 1998), p. 398. Noted military historian, John F. Guilmartin, has told me that this practice extended to eunachs with the army.

[107] Linda Grant De Pauw, *Battle Cries and Lullabies: Women in War from Prehistory to the Present*, (Norman, OK: 1998), p. 107.

could have been guaranteed.[108] I have to wonder how effective such subterfuges would have been in the long run, however.

Because of the delicacy of the matter, we have almost no information about menstruation. Modern historians have played down this problem by arguing that women in extreme physical stress or women with poor diets cease menstruation, but such a dismissal does not accord with the conditions of military life.[109] Even if the exertions of the campaign did impose a pause on a woman's cycles, that would not account for the time spent in winter quarters when soldiers' activities were much less strenuous to allow them to rest and return to full health.

The difficulty of hiding menstruation would have been compounded by the close proximity of women to their male comrades. At no time would this pose more problems than at night, when soldiers in quarters often slept two or three to a bed. Jeanne Bensac, a particularly praiseworthy woman soldier, reported that as often as possible she got an officer to assign her a room by herself, "And when she was lodged with the soldiers of her company, she never slept at night for fear of being recognized."[110] The interrogation of nineteen-year-old Marie Bertrand, who was discovered about 1758, revealed how she avoided contact with men: "She took the precaution every month of picking a quarrel with her sergeant or her corporal, in order to be put in the guard house so she could better hide her sex."[111]

Women must have found some dependable way of hiding the signs of menstruation, and perhaps this was by using some form of tampon. The authors of *The Curse: A Cultural History of Menstruation* state that Roman women used tampons made of soft wool and that women in Japan and Indonesia employed other absorbent materials.[112] Patricia Crawford argues that seventeenth-century English doctors showed "no unwillingness to advise married women to insert objects into the vagina, although women were told to remember to attach a string for their removal."[113] Maria van Antwerpen testified that she provided herself

[108] Young, *Masquerade*, pp. 104–06.
[109] Most of 119 female cadets entering West Point in 1976 had stopped menstruating by the end of "beast barracks," the physically exhausting introduction to life at the Academy. Young, *Masquerade*, p. 107.
[110] A. G., series A1, ms 1768, pièce 484, in Steinberg, *La confusion des sexes*, p. 139.
[111] A. G., Ya 507, dossier Bertrand, pièce 2, in Steinberg, *La confusion des sexes*, p. 138.
[112] Janice Delaney, Mary Jane Lupton, and Emily Toth, *The Curse: A Cultural History of Menstruation* (Urbana, IL: 1988), p. 138.
[113] Patricia Crawford, "Attitudes to Menstruation in Seventeenth-Century England," in *Past and Present* 91 (May 1981), p. 55.

"with a certain precaution about which chastity forbids me to tell."[114]
Could she have been referring to some kind of improvised tampon? If
women counseled one other about how to get along as men in the
campaign community, could the use of such means be one of the secrets
they shared? There is also the technique of using rags, but one wonders
how a female soldier could have protected her uniform from stain in the
long run simply by using a rag.

An important way in which women such as Marie Magdelaine
Mouron blended into the ranks was by seeming to share the interests and
bravado of their male comrades. This would include the apparent pursuit
of women and the serious business of proving one's courage by dueling.
A modern reader might suppose that a cross-dressing woman who
courted another woman was clearly lesbian. Certainly there were cases of
lesbian or transsexual woman soldiers; however, many more were not, or
at least they certainly acted as if they were heterosexual. Davies and Snell
both married three times, and Snell had two children. The Dutch female
dragoon Geertruid ter Brugge also married and had children after her
service, as did Deborah Sampson. Romantic mythology certainly mis-
represents the motives of most female soldiers, but some actually did
serve primarily to be with their husbands or male relatives.

Catalina de Erauso was a lesbian and quite open about her "taste ...
for pretty faces."[115] Catharina Linck, who served for a time as a soldier,
testified that she had many sexual encounters with women and eventually married one. She also said that at the touch of a woman "she became
so full of passion that she did not know what to do."[116] Maria van
Antwerpen married women twice, first as a soldier in 1747 and then
again in 1762, after she left the service.[117] She was arrested, tried, and
condemned for "gross and excessive fraud in changing her name and
quality" and "mocking the holy and human laws concerning marriage."
We possess both her trial records and her autobiography. Maria denied
having sexual relations with her wives, but stated before the court that
she was "by nature and character, a man, but in appearance a
woman."[118] Dekker and van de Pol conclude that she was probably
transsexual.

---

[114] Maria in Dekker and van de Pol, *Tradition of Female Transvestism*, p. 16.
[115] Erauso, *Memoir of a Basque Lieutenant Nun*, p. xxxvii. See Velasco, *The Lieutenant
Nun: Transgenderism, Lesbian Desire, and Catalina de Erauso.*
[116] Eriksson, "A lesbian execution in Germany," p. 31.
[117] Dekker and van de Pol, *The Tradition of Female Transvestism*, pp. 3–4.
[118] Dekker and van de Pol, *The Tradition of Female Transvestism*, p. 26.

Yet attention to other women seems most often to have been a ruse used by heterosexual women.[119] After serving for over two years, Hannah Snell, who went by the name of James Gray, became suspected for her lack of beard: "to enquire why she did not shave her Beard; her Answer was, that she was too young. Upon which they used to damn her, calling her Miss Molly Gray... During this long Voyage, they often used, as I have just said, on account of her smooth Face, to burlesque her, by swearing she was a Woman." In response to these taunts she gambled over the favors of a prostitute with her comrades and lost, much to her relief.[120] Nadezhda Durova explains that she paid attention to women as part of her disguise, as a matter of curiosity, and as a way of enjoying the casual social company of another women.[121] A soldier who did not flirt with the ladies would seem odd. Artwork of the time show soldiers dallying with pretty girls as a matter of course; it was a major theme in the works of the Watteaus.

It might be argued that stories of pursuing maids that were reported in the memoirs of women soldiers were simply embellishments to amuse or titillate the reader. Such seems to have been the case in *The Female Review*, in which the author, Herman Mann, describes an attractive young woman falling for Robert Shurtleff, Deborah Sampson's assumed identity.[122] However, considering the probability of older soldiers chiding the cross-dresser to act like a man, the need to feign interest in women sounds very plausible to me.

Marie Magdelaine Mouron mentioned nothing of any attentions to other women, but she did duel. As mentioned in Chapter I, dueling could be a rite of initiation for French troops; therefore, it might have been a way that a female could establish her place as a soldier and as a "man." After leaving her first regiment in Sisteron, Marie drifted down the river,

---

[119] See the intelligent discussion of this phenomenon in Wheelright, *Amazons and Military Maidens*, chap. 3, "Becoming One of the Boys." Snell, Davies, Susanna Cope, and, later, Deborah Sampson all showed attention to women although they were heterosexual.

[120] Hannah Snell, *The Female Soldier* (London: 1750), pp. 27–28. The very heterosexual story of Christian Davies describes her several marriages to men, but it also explains that as a soldier, she courted a burgher's daughter while "In my Frolicks" but that the affair did not "go beyond a platonick love." *The Life and Adventures of Mrs. Christian Davies*, pp. 37–38. Henri de Campion wrote of a cross-dressing woman officer, Captain Hendrich, who married a woman "in order to better fool the world," and he insisted on her chastity. Henri de Campion, *Mémoires* (Paris: 1990), p. 128, in Steinberg, *La confusion des sexes*, p. 43.

[121] Durova, *The Cavalry Maiden*, pp. 83.

[122] Young, *Masquerade*, pp. 152–55.

reaching Avignon where she enlisted as a dragoon in the regiment de Morsan and took part in the siege of Roses in Catalonia. She then pulled back to the garrison of Collioure in 1693 where she fought a duel and was so badly wounded that she had to appeal to the regimental surgeon and, as a consequence, reveal herself as a woman.

Marie was hardly unique in dueling. Women soldiers may have fought duels because they heartily accepted the violent mores of the campaign community or because they did so to heighten their disguise. Catalina de Erauso is supposed to have fought a number of duels that claimed several victims, including her brother, whom she killed in a deadly mistake.[123] Christian Davies, while attired as a soldier, also claimed to have fought a sergeant over his abuse of a girl she pitied.[124]

As in Marie's case, wounds or illness were common routes to discovery. Jeanne Bensac was forced to admit her sex when she became ill and was sent to the military hospital at Antibes in 1704. Virginie Guesquière was injured by a bayonet thrust near Lisbon in 1812, and while she was somehow able to keep her secret when this wound was first treated, her subsequent illness at the hospital exposed her true sex.[125] Some women were discovered to be women only in death, when their bodies, stripped of clothing, were found on the battlefield.[126]

Pregnancy could also compel women to admit their sex to military authorities, although such women must have already revealed themselves or been discovered by male comrades in the close quarters of military life. At age 20, Catherine Ferrière became pregnant by a fellow soldier in 1745, and was forced to leave her regiment.[127] The father made efforts to

---

[123] Erauso, *Memoir of a Basque Lieutenant Nun.* See p. 22–25 for the fight in which she killed her brother.

[124] *The Life and Adventures of Mrs. Christian Davies*, pp. 37–44.

[125] Journal de l'Empire, 31 October 1812, in Steinberg, *La confusion des sexes*, p. 141.

[126] A plate published in 1659 shows the discovery of a woman dead on the battlefield of Varambone in 1589. She was recognized as a woman when the corpses were stripped of their clothing. Dekker and van de Pol, *The Tradition of Female Transvestism*, illustration between pp. 48 and 49, Pl 2. Consider, as well, the case mentioned in Chapter III, of the women who died before the walls of Leucate. The Bishop of Albi in Frank Tallett, *War and Society in Early Modern Europe, 1495–1715* (London: 1992), p. 133. Henri de Campion wrote of a cross-dressing woman officer, Captain Hendrich, found dead at the battle of Turin in 1640. Henri de Campion, *Mémoires* (Paris: 1990), p. 128, in Steinberg, *La confusion des sexes*, p. 43. The body of a seventeen-year-old woman, who had "served well for a year" in a Swiss regiment was discovered on the field during the fighting before Gibraltar in 1782. A. G., series A1, ms 3722, p. 196, in Steinberg, *La confusion des sexes*, p. 132.

[127] Seriu, "Faire un soldat," pp. 365–76.

support the woman and child. Another French woman soldier became pregnant by a comrade after eighteen months of service, and when the truth was known, she successfully requested to stay with the regiment as a *vivandière* and married a grenadier who was not the father of her child.[128]

In order to stay in the ranks, women disguised their appearance as best they could; however, there must have been flaws in the masquerade for many. Even at the start of her military career, Nadezhda Durova notes in her journal that she was repeatedly recognized as a woman, particularly by other women. A woman in her colonel's household scolded her for not joining her troop fast enough: "And why are you still standing here alone, young lady?"[129] Moreover, after a certain age, a cross-dresser looked like a weathered woman rather than like an adolescent boy without whiskers. An observer described Catalina de Erauso's face as "not ugly, but very worn with years. Her appearance is basically that of a eunuch, rather than a woman."[130] Some women served long enough that they could hardly have resembled teenage boys.

There is no question that some women were recognized as women by their male comrades. This explains Marie Magdelaine Mouron's desertion, as we shall see, and the doubts of Hannah Snell's companions compelled her to gamble for the prostitute to prove them wrong.

Recognition and retention are matters upon which we can only speculate. It is entirely possible that some women were suspected or identified as women, and their comrades simply did not care, particularly if the woman had proved herself as a comrade and a soldier.[131] During the wars of the French Revolution, some women soldiers were recognized as female were allowed to continue serving.[132] Yet the actual

---

[128] *Mémoires du chevalier de Mautort*, p. 39, in Seriu, "Faire un soldat," p. 365.

[129] Durova, *The Cavalry Maiden*, p. 25.

[130] Erauso, *Memoir of a Basque Lieutenant Nun*, p. xxxiv.

[131] Linda Grant De Pauw, wrote to Alfred Young, "we should allow for women serving undetected and even serving detected and no one giving a damn." Young, *Masquerade*, p. 8, fn 5.

[132] For examples, see *Recueil des actions heroiques et civiques des Républicains français, présentée à la Convention Nationale au nome de son comité d'instruction publique*, par Léonard Bourdon, député par le département du Loiret (Paris: an II), vol. 1, pp. 23–24, in Steinberg, *La confusion des sexes*, p. 255; Rudolf Dekker and Lotte C. van de Pol, "Republican Heroines: Cross-Dressing Women in the French Revolutionary Armies," trans. Judy Marcure, *History of European Ideas* 10, no. 3 (1989), p. 353. We know that some women soldiers were recognized as female during the American Civil War, but their comrades allowed them to continue in uniform. DeAnne Blanton and Lauren M. Cook, *They Fought Like Demons: Women Soldiers in the American Civil War* (Baton Rouge: 2002), and Elizabeth D. Leonard, *All the Daring of the Soldier: Women of the Civil War*

number of women who served in early modern armies with the knowledge of their comrades will never be known.

Marie only faced punishment when she was recognized as a woman the second time, and then she was tried not for cross-dressing, but because of other serious infractions. While there were laws against cross-dressing, penalties were light unless some other offense was committed.[133] A Saxon court condemned Catharina Linck to be hanged and burned in 1721, not as a transvestite or even as an admitted lesbian, but for repeatedly penetrating other women with a false penis she fashioned out of stuffed leather.[134] Punishments for female cross-dressing and homosexuality were less severe when no device was used for penetration.[135] In fact, during her on-again off-again military career, Linck was discovered to be a woman in men's clothing when she deserted and was recaptured. Although initially sentenced to hang for desertion, she was released when discovered to be a woman.[136]

Authorities were particularly indulgent toward women who cross-dressed to serve in the army when these individuals were otherwise innocent. Women discovered in the ranks might even receive a bit of money from their officers to help them at their discharge. French women soldiers were known to petition the royal government for financial support, gratuities, and pensions, demonstrating that as long as they served well and behaved in a "moral" manner, they were not penalized, although they could not stay in the ranks. Christian Davies and Hannah Snell, it will be remembered, also received military pensions.

Marie testified that when first discovered to be a woman as a result of her duel at Collioure in 1693, she was taken under the protection of the army commander, the duke de Noailles. He detailed the wife of an artillery officer

---

Armies (New York: 1999), pp. 126–27. For an account of a cross-dressing American woman soldier, immediately after the Civil War, see Phillip Thomas Tucker, *Cathy Williams: From Slave to Female Buffalo Soldier* (Mechanicsburg, PA: 2002).

[133] See the comments by Easton, "Gender's Two Bodies," p. 135. Fraser supplies examples in which even women who dressed as men and married women were not sentenced to death during the eighteenth century. Mary Hamilton was condemned to six months imprisonment and a public whipping. pp. 153–57.

[134] Eriksson, "A lesbian execution in Germany," p. 37. Her lesbian partner was only condemned to three years in prison to be followed by exile. Linck fashioned a penis and testicles of stuffed leather which she bound to herself with a leather thong. Her wife complained that it made her sore. Eriksson, "A Lesbian Execution in Germany," pp. 31 and 33.

[135] Perry, *Gender and Disorder in Early Modern Seville*, p. 125. In 1624 another woman who had used a false penis was hanged.

[136] Eriksson, "A Lesbian Execution in Germany," pp. 30 and 33.

to nurse Marie back to health, and then sent her to what was probably a church-run school where girls were taught a useful trade, possibly needle-work.[137] The protection of de Noailles implies that she had a good repu-tation as a soldier, otherwise he would have refused her pleas for forgiveness.

Marie's interrogation does not detail her actions after leaving the army in 1693, but somehow she returned to the north, where she enlisted in the infantry regiment de Biez at St. Omer in early March 1696. But her com-rades in that regiment identified her as a woman; unfortunately, while she could reenlist in the army, she could not regain her youth. As a consequence, she deserted that regiment after only two months in the hope of finding a more congenial unit. She did not want to return to civilian life. This is in line with Julie Wheelwright's conclusion in her study of cross-dressing women soldiers: "Many women dreaded the return to domesticity as much as the loss of their newly acquired and mightily enjoyed male power."[138]

After slipping away, Marie walked to the nearby fortress of Aire and tried to join the regiment de Sanzay, but the officer there noticed she still wore parts of her old uniform and ordered her arrested as a deserter. This officer also recognized her as a woman and had her "visited," that is, physically examined, by a matron.[139] This inspection revealed that she was a woman and a virgin, and she claimed to have never engaged in sexual relations. Marie's virginity and her testimony that she had not slept with men freed her from suspicion of being a prostitute with the army.[140] As Julie Wheelwright comments, "Since any woman attached to the military was suspected of working as a prostitute, the emphasis on the female soldier's sexual innocence is vital."[141] However, while inno-cent of prostitution, Marie was guilty of other sins.

Marie Magdelaine Mouron had to be tried for desertion and theft. She had enlisted in a regiment du Biez and had accepted an enlistment

---

[137] It was common to teach poor girls and women a needle trade or some textile craft to give some hope of an income or to reform them. See for example Olwen Hufton, *The Prospect Before Her: A History of Women in Western Europe, vol. 1, 1500–1800* (New York: Vintage Books, 1998), pp. 331 and 394–95.

[138] Wheelwright, *Amazons and Military Maidens*, p. 84.

[139] Tests of virginity were important to the age. For an engraving of a young woman for virginity, see the anonymous eighteenth-century French engraving in Hilary Evans, *Harlots, Whores & Hookers: A History of Prostitution* (New York: Taplinger Publishing Company, 1979), p. 98.

[140] It is to be noted that Catalina de Erauso also insisted she was a virgin and was inspected and proven to be so. In her case she was also a novice nun, so without her virginity was would have been even more jeopardized. Perry, *Gender and Disorder in Early Modern Seville*, p. 135.

[141] Wheelwright, *Amazons and Military Maidens*, p. 77.

bounty. Two months later she deserted, itself a serious crime, and then subsequently presented herself as a potential recruit eligibile for another bounty. This made her a *rouleur*, one who "rolled" from regiment to regiment to collect multiple bounties of the king's money. This was a serious matter, and so she faced punishment.

Her fate is uncertain, although notations on her file suggest that she was condemned to prison. This is a sad ending to her story, for she seems to have been a good soldier with a preference for the military life ultimately denied her.

BESIEGED WOMEN

For all the fascination they inspire, the number of cross-dressing women in the ranks cannot compare with the extensive participation in siege warfare by women who maintained their female identity. It has already been explained that camp women with attacking armies lent a hand in the spadework required by siege warfare. At the same time, besieged towns were defended by women. A few elite women exercised command; many non-noble women fought on the walls, and a greater number built and repaired defensive works. Compelling incentives inspired them in command, combat, and construction. Their homes and families were under assault, and should the attackers break into the town, their possessions would be destroyed or stolen, their lives and those of their loved ones put at risk, and perhaps their own bodies taken as plunder.

Earlier in this chapter I mentioned the European fascination with Amazons; in addition to this, the Old Testament provided compelling images of women who employed deadly violence in the name of a divine cause. Unlike ancient mythology or literary fancy, these stories had the power of biblical authority. The Kennite women, Jael, slayed the Canaanite general, Sisera, after he had been defeated by the Israelites. When Sisera came to her tent, she offered him milk, suggested he rest, and, when he slept, hammered a tent spike through his temple. She was then praised as a heroine by Deborah, the judge. The story is contained in Judges 4 and 5. Her story was told and illustrated in Le Moyne's *La Galerie des femmes fortes*.[142]

---

[142] See the discussion of Jael as a heroine during the seventeenth century in Joan DeJean, "Violent Women and Violence against Women: Representing the 'Strong' Woman and Early Modern France," *Signs: Journal of Women in Culture and Society* 29, no. 1 (Autumn 2003): 120–31. This article also presents two contemporary images of Jael, p. 127, Fig. 4, and p. 130, Fig. 6.

The story of Judith gave Europe a still more relevant and immediate image of the sword-bearing woman.[143] Not only was she praised from the pulpit, but artists such as Botticelli, Donatello, Caravaggio, and Rembrandt celebrated her beauty, resolve, and deadly blade. In an age of sieges, Judith shown like a beacon. When the Assyrians attacked her town of Bethulia, all hope seemed lost, and the men of the town were ready to capitulate. However, the widow Judith entered the Assyrian camp, where she captivated the enemy general, Holofernes. When he was "overcome with wine" she "took down his sword," cried out "Give me strength this day, O Lord God of Israel!", and "struck his neck twice with all her might, and severed his head from his body."[144] She saved Bethulia, and enjoyed great renown and respect for the rest of her long life.

As Brian Sandberg points out, proper feminine women were expected to protect family, home, and religion, all suitable and sacred women's concerns.[145] During the French Wars of Religion, the example of Judith carried particular weight. Defense of religion was linked to siege warfare, as at Bethulia, when Huguenots fought off attacks by Catholic armies, and the citizens of Catholic towns resisted Protestant conquest. At times, elite women commanded the defense of threatened towns. In 1590, Françoise de Cézelly held the town of Leucate against a Spanish siege when her husband, the fortress governor, was captured. Her bravery, level head, and skill in fighting won her praise from Henri IV, who awarded her the post of governor.

The English Civil Wars, also with religious overtones, supply several examples of land-owning women who defended their homes and estates.[146] Lady Blanche Arundell, whose husband was off fighting for the king led the defense of her estate, Wardour, which held out for six days in May 1643 before capitulating. Mary Bankes and Charlotte Stanley, countess of Derby, also won renown for their actions in defense of their estates.

Although men usually performed the bloody business of combat on the walls and in the trenches, in numerous cases, armed women fought

[143] See the discussion of Judith in Ulinka Rublack, "Wench and Maiden: Women, War and the Pictorial Function of the Feminine in German Cities in the Early Modern Period," trans. Pamela Selwyn, *History Workshop Journal*, 44 (January 1997).

[144] Judith 13:2–8.

[145] Brian Sandberg, " 'Generous Amazons Came to the Breach': Besieged Women, Agency and Subjectivity during the French Wars of Religion," *Gender & History*, vol. 16, no. 3 (November 2004): 654–688.

[146] Alison Plowden, *Women All on Fire: The Women of the English Civil War* (Stroud, Gloucestershire: 1998).

beside them. Kenau Simons Hasselaar (1526–88) has become a Dutch national heroine for her contribution to the defense of Haarlem against an attacking Catholic Spanish army in 1572–73. She not only bore arms, but organized a battalion of 300 women and equipped them at her expense; they fought several actions wearing female attire but with light armor.[147] During the 1578 siege of Sommières, when attackers breached the walls, "a group of women of 'the lowest condition' dressed as men, wearing hats with paper plumes, ... bravely defended a section of wall assigned to them by the militia captain, beating back a Catholic assault as well as any battle-hardened soldiers."[148] A pamphlet published during the siege of Protestant Montpellier in 1622 described the actions of "a great number" of women who fought there:

[O]ne named Mourete ... performed an act of an Amazon, for having encountered a man armed with cuirass and helmet, she killed him with a sword that she had and withdrew from the fight only when two wounds in the head and the thigh forced her to retire. Another girl killed an enemy soldier with her own dagger. It is thus that the zeal of religion and the desire to preserve free conscience ... makes women bravely scorn death.[149]

During a more strictly political battle, the three-month-long siege of Braunschweig in 1615, a contemporary chronicle reported that, "an unmarried female person known as Gesske Magdeburg thirty-four years old" and "armed with a sword/mace and musket" defended the walls. This woman, whose actual name was Gesche Meiburg, "behaved valiantly, wounded a number of warriors, and put out their lights." She was such an

---

[147] David E. Jones, *Women Warriors: A History* (Washington: 2000), p. 186. See Els Kloek, *Kenau. De heldhaftige zakenvrouw uit Haarlem (1526–1588)* (Hilversum: 2001), for a recent biography of Kenau.

[148] Michael Wolfe, 'Writing the City Under Attack During the French Wars of Religion,' in *Situazioni d'Assedio / Cities Under Siege / Etats de Siege*, edited by Lucia Carle and Antoinette Fauve-Chamoux (Montalcino: Clio-Polis, 2002), p. 201, in Sandberg, "Generous Amazons," pp. 675–76. See Sandberg's treatment of "Combattants," pp. 674–77, with a number of examples. Jeanne Maillotte won renown defending Lille against the Protestant Hurlus who attached Lille in 1582. Steinberg, *La confusion des sexes*, p. 75.

[149] 'Memoire ou journal du siege de Montpellier'. BNF, Mss. fr. 23339, f° 184–187. Baumel, *Montpellier au cours des XVIe et XVIIe siècles. Les guerres de religion*, pp. 189–190, in Sandberg, "Generous Amazons," pp. 669–70. Another pamphlet published in 1621 in La Rochelle proclaimed that "during our past wars, France has seen its towns furiously assaulted and courageously defended by the means of women who, with arms in their hands, have made great efforts and performed magnificent exploits." *L'Exercise militaire faite a present par les femmes de La Rochelle. Avec ordonnances à ce subject* (Paris: 1621), in Sandberg, "Generous Amazons," p. 669.

effective warrior that she "remained uninjured."[150] At least four prints memorialized her exploits (see Plate 24). One print bore the poem:

> Brought honour to Braunschweig's women
> Some of them ran to the city walls
> And indefatigably among the foe
> Threw stones
> And fired balls
> Defended themselves with all their might
> With all their weapons well chose
> With water hot
> And burning pitch
> Blackened many a man's nose...
> Tis that which many days from now
> Will be said of Braunschweig's women.[151]

This poem may exaggerate, because the chronicle does not speak of other women, but it does make the point that women who defended their towns in a display of masculine virtue were not objects of rebuke but of great praise.

Women contributed most commonly and generously as laborers to build and repair the defenses of their towns. With normal life and commerce halted by siege, town residents provided a willing pool of workers to the outnumbered garrisons. Men, women, and even children did what they could. A diarist reported that during the siege of Turin in 1706, "the orphans of the Spedale della Carità, who had no other guide than their innocence, marched in small squads to lend a hand in counter-mining. Some of the boys were crushed to death beneath the debris, from where their little bodies were retrieved with some difficulty, and carried shoulder-high to burial within the same precincts they had left such a short time before."[152]

Women were commonly organized as work crews in sieges. As Brian Sandberg informs us, when an enemy army approached to attack Montauban in 1621, officers in charge of preparing its defenses "made the women who were there at the time work, running around the town, searching for barricades and barrels to complete the [fortifications] ... in

---

[150] Chronicle in Rublack, "Wench and Maiden," p. 6.
[151] Rublack, "Wench and Maiden," p. 7 and p. 10, Pl. 3. For other accounts of women fighting from the walls, see Rublack, p. 7.
[152] Diary entry in R. Deputazione, *Sovra gli Studi di Storia Patria* (1907–10), *Le campagne di Guerra in Piemonte (1703–1708) e l'assedio di Torino* (1706), 10 vols. (Turin), vol. 7, p. 244, in Christopher Duffy, *The Fortress in the Age of Vauban and Frederick the Great, 1660–1789* (London: 1985), p. 53.

Corpore sum Virgo, fateor: sed Pectore Vir sum
Ille videre virûm, quos recit ipsa, Viri.
Brunsuigin vitam dedit hanc mihi Patria: vitam
Pro Patria multis eripui ipsa viris,
Vita euanescet mea Fama, heroica Fama,
Quam mihi Mars peperit, non euitura manet

PLATE 24. A contemporary print of Gesche Meiburg, the Judith of Braunschweig, with the weapons detailed in the chronicle. Note that the rendering of the helmet, with its peculiar feathers, suggests a rooster sitting on her shoulder, as in Plates 7 and 12. The rooster here probably reminds us that Gesche bested men.

Hertzog August Bibliothek, Wolfenbuettel.

less than two hours the [work] ... was completed, all lined with barricades along with the bastion."[153] Also, when the French royal army besieged the rebel Huguenot town of La Rochelle, 1627–28, authorities in the town organized women into twenty-one companies, subdivided into squads. Squads rotated their labor to provide 250 women at all times to work on the fortifications. "Some carried baskets full of earth on the ramparts of the town, others dug, and made very hollow ditches at the foot of the walls."[154]

During the English Civil Wars, women did their parts. They pitched in to build ramparts around London in 1642:

> Raised rampiers with their own soft hands
> To put the enemy to stands;
> From Ladies down to oyster-wenches
> Labour'd like pioneers in trenches,
> Fell to their pick-axes and tools,
> And help'd the men to dig like moles.[155]

Reporting on the contribution of women to the successful defense of Gloucester against royalist forces in 1643, the town clerk praised "the cheerful readiness of yong and old of both sexes ... to labour in the further fortification of our citie. Nay, our maids and others wrought daily without the works in the little mead, in fetching in turfe in the very faces of our enemies."[156] They also participated at Bristol, Hull, Lyme, and elsewhere. Such labors could cost more than sweat; the noble leading the defense of Mas-d'Azil in 1625 testified that "the men and women worked with great courage" to repair its defenses, during which effort a woman "lost her leg to a cannon shot."[157]

Such heroics were not limited to the sixteenth and seventeenth centuries. Much later, the Maid of Saragossa, Agustina Zaragoza y

---

[153] 'Tableau du siege de Montaulban'. BNF, Mss. fr. 18756, f° 1, in Sandberg, "Generous Amazons," p. 672.

[154] *L'Exercise militaire faite a present par les femmes de La Rochelle. Avec les ordonnances à ce subject. Ensemble les fortifications qu'elles ont faictes, & tout ce qui s'est passé en ladite ville, jusques à present* (Paris: Matthieu LeBlanc, 1621), in Sandberg, "Generous Amazons," p. 672.

[155] Plowden, *Women All on Fire*, p. 64.

[156] Plowden, *Women All on Fire*, p. 64.

[157] Jacques de Saint-Blancard, *Journal du siège du Mas-d'Azil en 1625 écrit par J. de Saint-Blancard, défenseur de la place, contré le maréchal de Thémines*, edited by C. Barrière-Flavy (Foix: Veuve Pomiès, 1894), pp. 16–17, in Sandberg, "Generous Amazons," p. 673. Another woman working lost both arms to a cannonball at a siege during the English Civl Wars. Plowden, *Women All on Fire*, p. 66.

Doménech, inspired the defense of her city in 1808.[158] There, this twenty-two-year-old bore a musket, and at one point fired a cannon into the attacking French after the gunners fell. She was rewarded with a decoration and the rank of officer in the Spanish artillery. Goya drew a tribute to her, and Lord Byron celebrated her heroism in *Childe Harold's Pilgrimage*. She was not the sole female defender; according to another English poet, Robert Southey, her efforts inspired the women of Saragosa to form "themselves into companies, some to relieve the wounded, some to carry water, arms and provisions, to those who defended the gates."[159]

The woman who masqueraded as a man to serve in the ranks was an anomaly, real but rare. Women who fought bravely and publicly as women in siege warfare were anything but rare.

REVOLUTION IN POLITICS, REGRESSION IN WOMEN'S OPPORTUNITIES

During its first few years, the French Revolution transformed military institutions by ushering in the popular conscript army, which superseded the state commission army. Moreover, the Revolution intensified inter-state conflicts by replacing the limited wars of kings with the intense wars of peoples. It also seemed to promise a third transformation by openly incorporating women into combat.

On the morrow of the fall of the Bastille, a street pamphlet fictitiously declared the formation of "Bellona's Amazons," named after the Roman goddess of war.[160] "News" of the female battalion was followed shortly by a broadsheet, *The French Amazons*. In August of 1790 a mock ordinance claimed that there would be a female militia commanded by "the archduchess Bellona." This last included a song.

The popular broadsheet was followed by a political petition. With the monarchs' attempted flight in 1791, revolutionary French feminists advocated arming women as part of the national defense. Olymphe de

---

[158] For a short description of the Maid of Saragosa, see the article Aràgon, Agustina by John Lawrence Tone in Reina Pennington, ed., *Amazons to Fighter Pilots: A Biographical Dictionary of Military Women*, 2 vols. (Westport, CT: 2003), vol. 1, pp. 21–22. Agustina changed her name to Aràgon after the death of her soldier husband at the siege of Saragosa.

[159] Southey in Laffin, *Women in Battle*, p. 38.

[160] On the advocacy of female units in Parisian street culture in 1789, see Hopkin, "Female Soldiers," p. 82. Some historians have misread the games of street hawkers as meaning there were real female units, e.g., Alfred Tranchant and Jules Ladimir, Les *Femmes militaires de la France* (Paris: 1866), p. 348. Hopkin, "Female Soldiers," p. 84.

Gouges, who authored the Declaration of the Rights of Women in response to the Declaration of the Rights of Man, appeared before the Assembly to advocate establishing a National Guard for women, just as the French had formed National Guard units for men.[161] The next year she followed this request with a demand to create a regiment of "Amazons," whose first duty would be to guard the Queen, who it was feared would try to escape again.[162]

In March 1792, Pauline Léon demanded that the Legislative Assembly distribute "pikes, pistols, sabers, and even muskets for those women who had the strength to serve" and allow women to go to the Champs de Mars to drill with their weapons.[163] She was applauded for her patriotism, and the president of the session expressed his hope that men who had yet to volunteer would be shamed by her dedication. However, no real action was taken. Within days, another feminist, Théroigne de Méricourt, forcefully addressed women in the working-class area of faubourg Saint-Antoine: "Let us arm ourselves, we have the right to do so by nature and by law. Let us show men that we are not inferior, either in virtue or in courage."[164]

When war broke out in April 1792, many women were ready to answer the call to arms. In response to setbacks at the front, the Legislative Assembly declared "La patrie est en danger"—the country is in danger—on 11 July 1792. On 25 July, Claire Lacombe addressed the Assembly to argue that single women should be mobilized. Women from the neighborhood of the Hotel de Ville took offense that she would not also call up mothers: "You cannot better confide the defense of the homeland than to mothers, spouses, and sisters who burn with the desire to defend the value of what they hold most dear by exterminating the monsters who seek to destroy the Constitution."[165] But once again

---

[161] Mary Woolstonecraft (1759–97) defended the Revolution to an English audience in her *Vindication of the Rights of Man* (1790), and she soon followed this with her *Vindication of the Rights of Woman* (1792).

[162] Steinberg, *La confusion des sexes*, pp. 247–48.

[163] Cited by Paule-Marie Duhet, *Les femmes et la Révolution*, pp. 115–16, in Steinberg, *La confusion des sexes*, pp. 248–49.

[164] Cited by Elisabeth Roudinesco, *Théroigne de Méricourt. Une femme mélancolique soud la Révolution* (Paris: 1989), pp. 109–10, in Steinberg, *La confusion des sexes*, pp. 249.

[165] Cited by Paule-Marie Duhet, *Les femmes et la Révolution*, p. 117, in Steinberg, *La confusion des sexes*, p. 251. It should be noted that patriotic British women made similar appeals during the Napoleonic Wars. In 1803 the women of Neath petitioned Henry Addington to be allowed "to defend ourselves as well as the weaker women and children amongst us. There are in this town about 200 women who have been used to

the Assembly issued no call for women's units; instead it treated such demands by steadfast women as ways of shaming men into enlisting, just as was done in Britain at mid-century.

Patriotic fervor in 1793 gave birth to more songs: *Departure of the French Amazons for the Frontier,* followed by a song by the self-appointed master of Parisian street singers, Leveau, called *The Republican Heroines,* and yet another by his rival, Poirier, entitled *The Parisian Girls' Departure for the Army.*[166] It may be that these songs were meant to poke fun at aggressive political women, but the idea of female service was still there.[167] Reine Chapuy, who masqueraded as a man and joined the cavalry, testified that she was moved by the Bellona examples.[168]

A petition by Manette Dupont in early 1793, which may or may not be authentic, carried the appeal again. Dominique Godineau questions whether it was an actual petition to the National Convention, but concludes that it contained the aspirations of a real woman. It put forward a detailed and elaborate scheme to organize five battalions, totaling 10,000 "female citizens." Like a broadsheet it included a song by Poirier:

> Long live the sanculottes,
> And you will wear them;
> Abandon your hearths
> Dressed as lads,
> Let us march
> We wear pants
> That's the way women are now[169].

The petition expressed a wish, but one that would not be granted.

Appeals and petitions by women had little effect on the Parisian government, which mobilized no women's battalions to fight in the

---

hard labour all the days of their lives such as working in coal-pits, on the high roads, tilling the ground, etc. If you would grant us arms, that is light pikes ... we do assure that we could in a short time learn our exercise." Philip Ziegler, *Addington: A Life of Henry Addington, First Viscount Sidmough* (London: 1965), p. 114, in Wheelwright, *Amazons and Military Maidens,* pp. 8–9.

[166] Hopkin, "Female Soldiers," p. 82.

[167] Hopkin, "Female Soldiers," p. 85, reluctantly concludes that they were probably intended as mockery.

[168] Hopkin, "Female Soldiers," p. 86.

[169] Dominique Godineau, *The women of Paris and their French Revolution,* trans. Katherine Streip (Berkeley: 1998), pp. 243–44. See as well the discussion of Dupont's petition in Hopkin, "Female Soldiers," p. 86.

revolutionary armies.[170] Local patriotic women were able to form about 150 military or paramilitary "legions of Amazons," which grew out of provincial women's political clubs, but none took part in actual armed combat.[171] A female National Guard unit at Pérouges, echoed the popular broadsides in its title, the "Guard of Bellona."[172]

Lacking their own actual battalions, some women marched off as individuals, determined to fight without hiding their sex, Théophile and Félicité Fernig, aged 13 and 16, enlisted in their father's regiment. They won praise from officials and enjoyed considerable celebrity as examples of patriotic service. In March 1793, Rose Barreau joined her husband's battalion, where her brother also served. Rose, known in the regiment as Liberté, won fame in July during combat against the Spanish. She saw her brother killed in this fight, and then her husband fell wounded at her side. However, "Republican virtue triumphed over love as it triumphed over nature," and she pressed the attack, firing all of her cartridges and then taking more from a dead Spaniard. Once the battle was won, she returned to her stricken husband, had him taken to the hospital, and

---

[170] The following works deal with the participation of women in military forces during the period of the French Revolution, 1789–99:

Raoul Brice, *La Femme et les armées de la Révolution et de l'Empire (1792–1815)* (Paris: 1913).

Rudolf M. Dekker and Lotte C. van de Pol, "Republican Heroines: Cross-Dressing Women in the French Revolutionary Armies," trans. Judy Marcure, *History of European Ideas* 10, no. 3 (1989), pp. 353–63.

Dominique Godineau, "De la guerrière à la citoyenne. Porter les armes pendant la Révolution française et la Révolution française", *Clio*, 2004, 20 : 43–69.

Linda Grant De Pauw, *Battle Cries and Lullabies: Women in War from Prehistory to the Present* (Norman, OK: University of Oklahoma Press, 1998).

Jean-Clément Martin, "Travetissements, impostures la communauté historienne: À propos des femmes soldats de la Révolution et de l'Empire," *Politix: Revue des sciences sociales du politique*, 74 (impostures), 19, no. 74 (2006), pp. 31–48.

Sylvie Steinberg, *La confusion des sexes: Le travestissement de la Renaissance à la Révolution* (Paris: 2001).

Marc de Villiers, *Histoire des clubs de femmes et des Légions d'Amazones* (Paris: 1910).

See as well the unpublished paper by Barbara Day-Hickman, Barbara Ann Day-Hickman, "The Heroic Imaginary: Women Soldiers in the Republican and Imperial Wars," 2006 meeting of the Society for French Historical Studies, University of Illinois at Urbana-Champaign.

[171] On these legions, see Maïté Albistur and Daniel Armogathe, *Histoire du féminisme français du Moyen ge à nos jours* (Paris: 1977), p. 233, and Villiers, *Histoire des clubs de femmes et des Légions d'Amazones*, chap. 5.

[172] Hopkin, "Female Soldiers," p. 85.

nursed him back to health. At this point she had to reveal her sex, but was allowed to continue with the regiment even though she was pregnant. She left the army only in September and was soon praised as a revolutionary heroine in the *Recueil des actions heroiques et civiques des Républicains français* in December 1793.[173]

Scholars put forward different estimates for the number of women known to have borne arms in the revolutionary armies, either openly as women or dressed as men, but even the highest estimates fall short of ninety.[174] Of those women who fought, Jean-Clément Martin counts at least sixteen who experienced combat and eighteen who suffered wounds.[175]

We must consider French women fighting against the Revolution, as well as those who fought to defend it. Among these notable counter-revolutionaries, Renée Bordereau stands out. Better known as the Brave Angevin, she joined the Vendée rebellion as a relentless fighter, never disguising her identity as a woman.[176]

If no flood of woman soldiers transformed warfare, there was another strong influx of soldier wives into the campaign community. In the name of granting the private soldier his full rights, the revolutionary government released enlisted men from any requirement to seek officers' permission to marry. This well-intentioned policy injected crowds of wives into the campaign community once again. In a sense, the increased rights accorded to the citizen soldiers of the popular conscript army paralleled the leverage enjoyed by mercenaries of the aggregate contract army. Both were empowered to shape the conditions of camp life, although this policy proved a brief experiment for the revolutionary soldier.

---

[173] *Recueil des actions heroiques et civiques des Républicains français, présentée à la Convention Nationale au nome de son comité d'instruction publique, par Léonard Bourdon, député par le département du Loiret* (Paris: an II), vol. 1, pp. 23–24, in Steinberg, *La confusion des sexes*, p. 255. See as well Rudolf Dekker and Lotte C. van de Pol, "Republican Heroines: Cross-Dressing Women in the French Revolutionary Armies," trans. Judy Marcure, *History of European Ideas* 10, no. 3 (1989), p. 353. See as well the account of Rose Bouillon in Godineau, *The women of Paris*, pp. 244–45.

[174] Jean-Paul Bertaud give thirty women as his count, Dominque Godineau tallies forty-four, Sylvie Steinberg estimates fifty, and Raoul Brice comes in highest at 88. See Barbara Day-Hickman, "The Heroic Imaginary," for a summary of the counts given by different authors.

[175] Jean-Clément n, "Travetissements, impostures la communauté historienne: À propos des femmes soldats de la Révolution et de l'Empire," *Politix: Revue des sciences sociales du politique*, 74 (impostures), 19, no. 74 (2006), p. 33.

[176] An illustration of Bordereau on horseback, from her memoires, is reproduced Dekker and van de Pol, *Tradition of Female Transvestism*, between pp. 48 and 49, Pl. 22.

The experiments with openly female soldiers and soldiers' wives at the front soon faltered, as the Parisian legislators turned away from this kind of progress. *La patrie* may have been idealized as feminine, but *le gouvernement* was very definitely masculine. From the front, Representative Jean-Baptiste Delacroix alerted his colleagues to the growing problem in a letter of 22 March 1793: "The National Convention has permitted soldiers to marry without the consent of their chiefs; this law has brought an inconvenience which is urgent to reform. It is necessary to set the number of women who ought to follow the army; they are in such great numbers that they encumber the troops on the march, consume much, and occupy a great number of wagons meant only for the transportation of the army's baggage and provisions."[177] A month later Lazare Carnot, famed as "The Organizer of Victory," fumed against "the flock of women and prostitutes."[178] These appeals read much like criticisms penned in the sixteenth and early seventeenth centuries.

The National Convention responded by voting on 30 April 1793 to expel all "useless" women from camps and garrisons.[179] Soldiers might marry but could not keep their wives with them. Legislation limited the number of women, allowing only four per battalion as washerwomen and *vivandières*. In addition, the legislation decreed: "Women who presently serve in the armies will be excluded from military service."[180] The woman soldier was to be sent home along with soldiers' wives.

When the National Convention declared the *levée en masse* in August, it left no doubt what the masculine and feminine roles would be in national defense. In accord with the teachings of Jean-Jacques Rousseau, men would wield the sword, while women would ply the needle. Such an appeal to proper gendered work disappointed many women. The 1789 call for "Bellona's Amazons" had included the assertion: "And we also know how to fight and win; we know how to handle other arms than needle and thread."[181]

---

[177] Etienne Charavay, ed., *Correspondence générale de Carnot*, 4 vols., Paris : 1892–1907), vol. 2, pp. 116–17, fn. 3

[178] Letter from Carnot and Duquesnoy to the National Convention, 16 April 1793 in Charavay, *Correspondence de Carnot*, vol. 2, pp. 116–17.

[179] On this decision, see John A. Lynn, *Bayonets of the Republic: Motivation and Tactics in the Army of Revolutionary France, 1791–94* (Urbana, IL: 1984, reprt. Boulder, CO: 1996).

[180] Article XI in Steinberg, *La confusion des sexes*, p. 254.

[181] Hopkin, "Female Soldiers," p. 82.

Feminism suffered at the hands of the earnest men of the Revolution. Male politicians who saw themselves as guardians of the public welfare sent Queen Marie Antoinette to the guillotine on 16 October 1793 for representing the old sins of autocratic monarchy and for transgressing against the new virtues of proper womanhood. These same stalwarts reversed military reforms that benefited women and sent Olympe de Gouges to the scaffold two weeks after the queen. The Napoleonic Code would later enshrine a fiercely patriarchal ideal of society.

The revolution did not transform the presence of women in the campaign community. In this respect, the army of the new revolutionary France resembled the army of the old monarchy.

* * *

Having surveyed the range of women's relationships and participation within the campaign community, this study concludes by returning to the question of numbers posed in the introduction. However, it is clear that the least important aspect of women's presence with armies was the one most celebrated in popular culture: the transvestite woman-in-arms. To explain the decline in the presence of women, we must place the more mundane women at center stage. The answers are to be found in the intersection between their daily lives and the evolution of armies and states.

Conclusion: Proposing Answers and Suggesting Hypotheses

Driven by their need to survive, aggregate contract armies were predatory; their hunt for pillage defined the conduct of war and determined the pattern of life within the campaign community during the sixteenth and early seventeenth centuries. Robert Monro's account of the sack of Frankfurt-am-Oder in 1631 linked the lust for booty with a near complete collapse of discipline, control, and combat effectiveness: "All men that were carelesse of their dueties, were too carefull in making of booty, that I never did see Officers lesse obeyed, and respected than here for a time ... and well I know, some Regiments had not one man with their Colours were lost the whole night, till they were restored the next day, such disorder was amongst us, all occasioned through covetousnesse, the roote of all evill and dishonesty."[1] The draw of plunder was that powerful. As do many military writers of his time, Monro attacks pillage as an abuse, but it was also a necessary form of compensation among troops at a time when states were habitually unable to pay and supply their soldiers. Pillage meant survival for the individual and for the army.

This study has documented how women abounded within the campaign community before the mid-seventeenth century but, after that point, constituted a smaller percentage of the camp population. This major change resulted from complex causes; no single factor totally explains the decline in women's participation, but the most compelling reason lies in the economy of makeshifts driven by pillage, examined in

[1] R. Monro, *Monro, his Expedition with the Worthy Scots* Regiment Called Mac-Keys, William S. Brockington, Jr., ed. (Westport, CT: 1999), p. 160.

Chapter III. It is not enough to ascribe the culling of women to an act of the royal will. Even so formidable a monarch as Louis XIV could not have winnowed women from the baggage train of his armies simply by drafting an edict. Before the legions of women could be reduced, the circumstances that made them so valuable had to be altered. The reforms and innovations that created the state commission army and the absolutist state could diminish the presence of women. Shifting away from primary reliance on mercenary troops, improving provision of supply and pay, and asserting state authority over troops and officers were major advances in military institutions. Of course, they took time to become established but were ultimately effective in fielding more disciplined, more powerful, and ultimately much larger armed forces.

The abundant presence of women underwrote the survival of armies before 1650, and a decrease in their numbers reflected the new efficiency of forces after that date. These fundamental conclusions position the subjects examined here within much broader discussions of early modern European history, including hypotheses concerning absolutist government and the Military Revolution. The declining presence of women with armies also raises questions related to the power, independence, and status of women in European society.

EXPLAINING WOMEN'S CENTRALITY WITHIN THE CAMPAIGN COMMUNITY BEFORE 1650

To trace the declining numbers of women with the campaign community is to gauge their decreased centrality within field armies, as the aggregate contract army gave way to the state commission form. The question of declining numbers posed in the introduction of this volume is not simply about a head count, it is about importance. What, then, explains the need for so many women in the campaign community during the sixteenth and early seventeenth centuries? This phenomenon cannot be ascribed to the usual gender-defined tasks assigned to camp women, nor to non-gender-specific heavy labor imposed on them by necessity. Of greatest importance was the essential participation of women in the pillage-driven economy of the campaign community. Of lesser, but still considerable, significance was the lure of women's presence as part of the libertine lifestyle that attracted men to the military life.

No one can dispute that women performed certain gender-defined jobs in camps throughout the period from 1500 to 1815. Civilian and military societies thought laundering, sewing, and nursing to be proper work for women and, more importantly, unsuitable for soldiers. The need for women to perform in these support roles explains why even the austere government of revolutionary France had to allow four women per battalion with their troops. However, the fact that the French could make do with four per battalion, or that British units could ship out with six women per hundred soldiers, indicates that a modest crew of women, at this point all wives, sufficed for basic support services.

Of course women's duties extended beyond gender-defined chores; the broader range of physical tasks they performed must be considered. When women were present in abundance, they were assigned a portion of the hard labor of maintaining and cleaning the camp. Descriptions of women's duties often involved digging, so women were no strangers to the shovel and pick. In siege warfare women might be organized to use those tools in the attacking army's trenches, just as their sisters within besieged towns labored with these tools to shore up defenses. Traditional notions of gender had nothing to do with this kind of spade work combined with courage and assertiveness; however, the campaign community assumed that its women had to possess certain masculine traits. Yet these labors did not explain women's large numbers; rather, their large numbers explain why they were available for such work. As the presence of women in camps diminished, much of the hard labor they once performed could be transferred to soldiers, and the demanding chore of digging siege lines could be imposed on local peasants, who were regularly conscripted by the thousands for such temporary duty.[2]

Women's contribution to the economy of the campaign community far surpassed the importance of gender-defined support functions and hard camp labor. The all-too-common inability of the state to maintain its troops before 1650 compelled them to fend for themselves. This led soldiers and soldiers' women to turn to expedients in an economy of makeshifts; they improvised and hustled to find something extra. Faced with the need to survive, many soldiers created small enterprises, and in such *ad hoc* businesses, having a female partner improved the chances of turning a profit. Women became entrepreneurs on their own, including being sutlers or *vivandières*, to supplement the incomes of their male partners.

However, the primary source of extra income for the great majority of the campaign community was pillage, not more regular commerce.

---

[2] For example, at Mons in 1691, 20,000 commandeered peasants labored to dig the lines of circumvallation. Charles Sévin, marquis de Quincy, *Histoire militaire de Louis le Grand roi de France* (7 vols., Paris, 1726), vol. ii, p. 347.

Members of the campaign community stole and extorted food, goods, and money, using violent means, if necessary, even when this contradicted military ordinances. Troops who were irregularly paid, if paid at all, sought sustenance and compensation by plundering.

The plunder-driven campaign economy of the aggregate contract army was not just an affair of marauding soldiers; it also encompassed the crowds of noncombatants who accompanied armies in the field, women prominent among them. Throngs of women in the train of armies meant there were many more mouths to feed when the state could not even pay and feed the *soldiers* on its muster rolls. In fact, women imposed even greater burdens than did men because their presence was unofficial, and the state did not generally accept responsibility for their maintenance. Thus, the presence of so many women within the campaign community magnified pillage beyond what it would have been if only fighting troops had required sustenance. This escalated the demand side of the camp economy. On the supply side, women were active pillagers assisting men or operating independently.

Conclusions about women and pillage must consider that servants, or boys, were also noncombatant pillagers, and they could be quite numerous as well[3] (see Plate 25). At times the boys outnumbered the women present, although the ratio between boys and camp women must have varied. Should Walhausen be correct that a German regiment arrived with more women and children than soldiers, camp women must have greatly outnumbered the boys in such units. Also, the description of women as being like mules means that they probably took on the carrying and care-taking duties of servants.[4] Yet there is also clear evidence for large numbers of boys within certain campaign

---

[3] Contemporary illustrations show boys engaged in plundering. See Plate 19, and for another example, the late sixteenth-century print by Johann Sadeler, *Plundering Soldiers*, shows a boy engaged in pillaging with the solders. Andrew Cunningham and Ole Peter Grell, *The Four Horsemen of the Apocalypse: Religion, War, Famine and Death in Reformation Europe* (Cambridge: 2000), p.108, Pl. 3.6.

[4] It is worth noting that when Peter Hagendorf described the pillage of Magdeburg, he spoke of soldiers and their women, not of the boys. Peter Hagendorf, *Ein Soeldnerleben im Dreissigjaehrigen Krieg*, ed. Jan Peters (Berlin: 1993), pp.138–39. It is a small thing perhaps, but the woodblock artist who portrayed pillage in the *Schwytzer Chronica* (1554) put sixteen live figures in his scene—there is one dead man in the background, probably an unfortunate peasant. Nine of these are adult men—Riesläufers with beards; six are camp women; and one is nondescript, but probably another women. It is clear that none are boys. Also consider the servant work laid out for women in "May Marriages," work that the would seem to have women in lieu of servants.

PLATE 25. Virgil Solis, *A Boy and a Woman of the Baggage Train*, mid-sixteenth century. The boy seems to be carrying the armor and sword of his master. Note also the dead rooster hanging from the boy's belt; this is a characteristic image of pillage.

The Illustrated Bartsch, vol. 19, part 1 (formerly vol. 9, part 2), ed. Walter L. Strauss (New York: Abaris Books, 1987), Pl. 251 (274), p. 119. Used with permission from Abaris Books.

communities.[5] It is so difficult to get reliable counts of women that the ratio of women to boys from army to army and era to era may never be known with certainty.

One role within the pillage economy that seems to have been a woman's prerogative was the custody and management of booty and funds. Here again, the evidence is not plentiful or solid enough to allow for hard conclusions, but positing women's participation in this way parallels their civilian roles. Also, I have come across no mention of boys as pillage managers. Boys, it should be remembered, were young and, according to Turner, regarded as "the very Vermine of an Army."[6] Had they been reliable men of size and force, they would have been in the ranks, not serving those who were. But camp women were, on the whole, adults meant to share the lives as well as the beds of their partners. Women marched in the baggage train where they were probably responsible for plunder and money. Several references identify "whores" and wives as carrying soldiers' valuables.

Economic relationships between men and women in a plunder-driven environment go furthest to explain the need for "whores" and wives in the field, and consequently their large numbers. Women were probably as susceptible as men to dreams of riches through plunder. Pillaging, born of need, inspired greed. Fool's gold it may have been, but it still glittered brightly enough to draw men—and women—into the community.

Women were essential to another attraction of military life: the lure of sex, either in more conjugal forms or as part of a libertine lifestyle.[7] Of course,

[5] Consider the counts of servants for the Black Bands in Maurizio Arfaioli, *The Black Bands of Giovanni* (Pisa: 2005), p. 65, and the number of servants with Spanish troops in Geoffrey Parker, *The Army of Flanders and the Spanish Road* (Cambridge: 1972), Appendix I, pp. 288–89. Also see Turner's estimate of the number of boys. Sir J. Turner, *Pallas Armata: Military Essayes of the Ancient Grecian, Roman and Modern Art of War* (New York, 1968—facsimile reproduction of the London edition of 1683), p. 275.

[6] Turner, *Pallas Armata*, p. 275. The punishment of women by throwing them to the boys indicates their image as "vermine." Johann Jakob Christolffel von Grimmelshausen, *Simplicissimus*, trans. Mike Mitchell (Sawtry, Cambs: 2005), p. 172, refers to them as "fiends."

[7] To be sure, there must have been homosexual soldiers who were attracted by the availability of camp boys. John R. Hale, *War and Society in Renaissance Europe, 1450–1620* (Baltimore: 1985), p. 188, tells how a Neapolitan soldier, when he was in garrison, set up a children's brothel for homosexuals. Sabina Loriga, *Soldats—Un laboratoire disciplinaire: l'armée piémontaise au XVIIIe siècle* (Paris: 2007), pp. 50–51, discusses reports of a homosexual soldier molesting town boys. However, homosexual soldiers attracted to camp boys seem have been a small minority, and the campaign community was probably not tolerant of their desires. Rudolf M. Dekker and Lotte C. van de Pol, *The Tradition of Female Transvestism in Early Modern Europe*, trans. Judy Marcure and Lotte van de Pol (Basingstoke, Hampshire: 1989), p. 87, conclude that the "common folk" were most intolerant of deviance from accepted sexual norms.

when most historians think of "camp followers," sex is the first thought that comes to mind. But beyond the smirks, it is necessary to recognize that the presence of numerous young and sexually active women in the campaign community was important to the very existence of aggregate contract armies.

Professional mercenary troops, who made up so much of these forces, were often hired as bands under their own captains and enjoyed a leverage not possessed by the individual recruits of the state commission army. With little or no connection to the cause or the king they fought for, mercenaries were concerned with the working conditions they would encounter on campaign. How willing would such troops be to serve without the availability of women, for the quick gratification from a prostitute or the companionship, comfort, and consolation of "whore" or wife? To the extent that this argument hits home, the presence of women was a necessary corollary of reliance upon soldiers who would not be separated from what few joys a hard life provided. Men could insist on having women with them, even if they could not insist upon getting paid.[8]

Moreover, recruits who chose to pursue military service because their civilian existence offered them few acceptable prospects were probably attracted by the lure of the libertine lifestyle reputed to rule the camps. Such an image held out the hope of escape from a dreary reality. This is not to say that camp women were enticed by or relished the freer sex of camp life but simply that their presence drew men into service.

Women help explain why men joined the campaign community. It is common to say of foreign mercenaries, as did Voltaire, "Pas d'argent, pas de Suisse," but it may be equally true to say "Keine Frauen, keine Deutschen."[9] Should commanders have excluded women, they would have had a harder time raising and retaining troops. If this logic carries weight, then the tempting prostitute contributed to the army's creation and staying power, rivaling in value the stalwart laundress and the devoted wife.

WOMEN AND THE EVOLUTION OF ARMIES AND THE STATE AFTER 1650

If we accept that women were key to the pillage-driven military economy and that the decline of this economy resulted in the diminished presence

---

[8] Schiller claims that in 1568, Alva used rewarded the "sensuality" of his troops to control them by allowing them women. Freidrich Schiller, *The Works of Friedrich Schiller: The Revolt of the Netherlands and the Thirty Years' War*, trans. E.B. Estwick and A.J.W. Morrison, ed. Nathan Haskell Dole (Boston: 1901), p. 277.

[9] "No money, no Swiss" and "No women, no Germans."

of women, we are still left with important questions. Did the actions of camp women before 1650 help to cause the military and governmental changes that led to their expulsion, or did the fate of women within the campaign community simply reflect greater shifts in warfare and government after 1650?

There are no simple answers, because the different influences and outcomes were so intertwined. The pillage-based economy spawned abuses that led to its rejection as an acceptable way to compensate and sustain troops. Because women were integral to that economy, they contributed to the excesses and inefficiencies that led to its demise and, thus, brought about their own diminished presence. At the same time, the abandonment of the pillage-based economy was wrapped up with greater issues of power and perception concerning armies, warfare, and government. Pillage undermined discipline, control, and command within field forces, as illustrated by Monro's comments mentioned earlier. Effective authority over troops and their officers was a critical attribute of the absolutist state, and reliance upon plunder-based supply caused troops to rampage and also gave local army chiefs logistical independence from the rulers they were supposed to serve. A desire to ensure the reliability and loyalty of troops also hastened the demise of mercenary bands and their captains. Greater discipline and the end of the leverage enjoyed by earlier mercenaries curtailed the libertine lifestyle of the camps. The modernization of armies through the regularization and regulation of military units required that the absolutist state be capable of marshalling the necessary resources and exerting its authority. This also made possible the surprising expansion of the army to a size typical of state commission armies, an expansion that enhanced the power and legitimacy of the state itself. New perceptions and expectations that military forces should conduct war in a less rapacious manner, made possible by improved supply, stricter discipline, and obedient command, encouraged what is often termed "limited war," a form of eighteenth-century combat with which large-scale unregulated pillage would have been inconsistent.

The point has already been made that during the sixteenth century and through the Thirty Years' War, pillage by the campaign community was highly destructive and viciously brutal. Not only ruinous to the inhabitants of town and countryside, pillaging also imposed material and symbolic costs on a prince, particularly when his troops victimized his own subjects. In such cases, pillaging undermined the prince's wealth by eroding his tax base, but plundering also contradicted sacred claims that a ruler was the protector of his people. Louis XIV was explicitly concerned about just this kind of abuse. "Any prince," he wrote, "who cherishes his reputation ... will not doubt that it is founded as much upon defending the goods of his subjects from pillage by his own troops as upon defending against pillage by his enemies."[10] Louis's concern for his reputation, his "gloire," cannot be disregarded. Moreover, his role as war leader and protector was key to the sanctification of his person and the justification of his power.[11]

Troops who were compensated by plunder rather than through direct state support could also be a threat to the authority of a government, because logistic independence gave commanders the freedom to pursue their own agendas. Bear in mind that Albrecht von Wallenstein (1583–1634), who maintained his army by extorting money from civil communities in the war zone, became such a threat to his master, the emperor, that this ruler ordered Wallenstein's assassination. A notable French example of such dangerous independence involved fortress commanders, known as "governors," who maintained their troops by making demands on the localities around their fortresses.[12] In fact, this was a practice with a long history in France.[13] Louis XIV complained, "There is not a single governor who has not attributed to himself unlawful rights."[14] Once the war with Spain ended in 1659, Louis determined to eliminate this challenge to his power. "I began to moderate the excessive authority that the governors of frontier cities had

---

[10] Louis XIV, *Oeuvres de Louis XIV*, Grimoard and Grouvelle, eds. (Paris: 1806), vol. 2, p. 92. On the pillage of French subjects by French troops, see John A. Lynn, "How War Fed War: The Tax of Violence and Contributions during the *Grand Siècle*," *Journal of Modern History* 65, no. 2 (June 1993), pp. 286–310, and *Giant of the Grand Siècle: The French Army, 1610–1715* (Cambridge: 1997, paperback edition 2006), chap. 6.

[11] See Joël Cornette, *Le roi de guerre: Essai sur la souveraineté dans la France du Grand Siècle* (Paris: 1993).

[12] Examples of French local commanders who exerted their own authority include the case of François de Bonne, duc de Lesdiguières (1543–1626), who in 1616 responded to a Spanish attack on Piedmont by marching his troops off to the aid of the Piedmontese as he saw fit, without royal order. Contamine, *Histoire militaire*, 1:339. Plessis-Bellière went so far as to refuse to lead troops in Catalonia during 1652 unless he was named a marshal. André, *LeTellier*, 128.

[13] Local villages in France paid "composition" to French garrisons in the sixteenth century to avoid raids. David Potter, *War and Government in the French Provinces: Picardy 1470–1560* (Cambridge: 1993), pp. 225–30. The payment of "appatis," an earlier form of contribution to a captain to spare a particular population, dated from the middle of the fourteenth century and thrived in the fifteenth. Contamine, *Histoire militaire*, 1:191.

[14] Louis XIV, *Mémoires de Louis XIV pour l'instruction du dauphin.* Charles Dreyss, ed., vol. 2 (Paris: 1860), p. 405.

possessed for a long time; they had so lost the respect that they owed to royal authority that they had imposed the same exactions on my subjects as upon my enemies."[15] And thus he "resolved ... day by day to have troops that *depended only on me* enter all the important towns," thus replacing the governors' soldiers and reasserting "the royal authority."[16]

Restricting pillage of local or foreign populations was also tied to another central issue: establishing discipline within the ranks. By providing pay, food, and other services to his troops, the prince not only forestalled those officers who might use their soldiers for their own advantage, he also ensured the obedience of those troops themselves. A "Discours sur le règlement des trouppes," composed in 1637, spoke of disorder within the French army, concluding that, "The essential cause of all these inconveniences is the lack of pay, the soldiers ... believe with reason to be excused from the rigor of discipline and obedience."[17] As long as troops were not adequately supported by the state, they felt justified in disregarding regulations and marauding town and countryside; authorities could not really bring them to heel. The Dutch military commentator, Everhard van Reyd, put it succinctly: "One could not hang those one did not pay."[18] Louis XIV prided himself on establishing discipline, and higher levels of obedience became a hallmark of the state commission army. The records make clear that agents of the crown exerted themselves in investigating and prosecuting violence and theft by soldiers or officers. Provincial and central archives contain many records of inquiries and directives to punish the guilty and to compensate their victims. As the provincial administrator Turgot declared, "I love discipline enough to spare nothing that can be done to maintain it."[19]

When discussing discipline, military authorities viewed camp women as posing problems beyond their roles in pillage. Commanders and commentators complained that camp women undermined good order and impeded efficient operations. In the face of such criticism, women still remained with aggregate contract armies because they provided valuable

---

[15] Louis XIV, *Mémoires*, pp. 401–02.
[16] Louis XIV, *Mémoires*, p. 402. Italics are my own.
[17] David Parrott, "The Administration of the French Army during the Ministry of Cardinal Richelieu," Ph.D. diss., Oxford University, 1985, p. 114. See Le Tellier's comments on pay as well. Le Tellier to Molé, 13 April 1649, in Louis André, *Michel Le Tellier et l'organisation de l'armée monarchique* (Paris: 1906), p. 274n.
[18] Everhard van Reyd in Tallett, *War and Society*, 123.
[19] SHAT, AG, A12265, #234, letter of 3 March 1710.

services to the men, particularly in pillage, and because soldiers simply wanted them there. Mercenaries possessed considerable leverage, and so authorities could not suppress the libertine lifestyle of military camps without alienating these poorly paid and supplied troops. Therefore, the aura of sexual opportunity provided by the presence of camp women remained. When states came to rely more on individual recruits in native regiments after 1650, and as hired foreign regiments replicated the form and nature of these units, military authorities could assert more control over common soldiers. The leverage enjoyed by mercenaries in the past disappeared, and with it the libertine lifestyle to which women were so integral.

These developments were elements of a transformation commonly referred to as the Military Revolution, and change in the participation of women accompanying armies becomes an essential fact and barometer of this development. Much has been written about the Military Revolution of early modern Europe. Different authors supply varied lists of what was achieved and chart conflicting timetables of change. Michael Roberts first posited his Military Revolution thesis as largely tactical in impetus and running from 1560 to 1660. The more ambitious Geoffrey Parker sees it driven by technological innovation and spanning three centuries—1500–1800. Jeremy Black criticizes both historians and will only grant the existence of a revolution, if there was one at all, after 1660. Although I have tried to substitute an evolutionary model for that of a single great revolution or a series of revolutionary bursts, I certainly agree that a particularly notable change occurred in the mid-seventeenth century.[20]

Ultimately the theory of a Military Revolution is an approach to the issue of modernization. I will evade the semantic and scholarly debates over terminology by offering a modest definition of "modernization" as a convenient way to say that things in the past became more like things in the present. It does not have to imply a particular definition of "modern," explicit intent on the part of those who brought it, or any

---

[20] Michael Roberts, *The Military Revolution, 1560–1660* (Belfast: 1956); Geoffrey Parker, "The 'Military Revolution' 1560–1660—A Myth?" *Journal of Modern History* 48 (June 1976): 195–214; Geoffrey Parker, *The Military Revolution: Military Innovation and the Rise of the West, 1500–1800*, 2nd ed. (Cambridge: 1996); Jeremy Black, *A Military Revolution? Military Change and European Society, 1550–1800* (Atlantic Highlands, NJ: 1991); and John A. Lynn, "The Evolution of Army Style in the Modern West, 800–2000," *International History Review* 18, no. 3 (August 1996): 505–45. The Robert's piece, Parker's 1976 article, and pieces by Black, Lynn, and others can be found in Cliff Rogers, ed., *The Military Revolution Debate: Readings on the Military Transformation of Early Modern Europe* (Boulder, CO: 1995).

sense of inevitability or superiority of the modern. European armies abandoned past structures and practices in a way that made these forces more like modern armies; thus, they modernized. The process included making forces more efficient and effective by supplying them in a more regular and dependable manner that soon allowed commanders to strip down the baggage train and reduce impediments. I have described this as the evolution from the aggregate contract army to the state commission army, but however you label it, the prominence of women in the former and the diminished roles and numbers of women in the latter indicate a critical watershed in the history of warfare.

Modernization of military forces could not have been accomplished without the development of a more effective civil administration accompanied by greater authority, or leverage, in the hands of rulers. This evolution was needed to mobilize necessary resources, disperse essential funds, and regularize and control military institutions. Traditionally this development of administration and government has been called absolutism, as manifested by absolute monarchs such Louis XIV. The terms "absolutism" and "absolute monarch" have fallen out of favor, because historians now recognize that princes accomplished much of what they did through conciliating and accommodating existing elites rather than compelling them to submit and obey.[21] Yet by whatever process, it rates as an enormous institutional accomplishment for monarchs to have curtailed unbridled pillage and created military forces of unprecedented size, as did Louis.

There is another aspect of military/administrative reform that accords with ideas of absolutism: the enforcement of the royal will upon the officer corps. As mentioned, Louis brought his fortress commanders to heel. He also imposed the principle of seniority upon his contentious generals through the *ordre de tableau*. Nobles who were accustomed to independence in command, often based on their social prestige, were regulated in a firm hierarchy of military rank. What began with the highest commanders was imposed throughout the officer corps. Rulers not only imposed discipline and obedience on the rank and file, but on their leaders as well. This went well beyond the conciliation used by monarchs in civil society.[22] Monarchical authority reigned over the state

---

[21] See the extremely useful survey of the literature bearing on Absolutism, William Beik, "The Absolutism of Louis XIV as Social Collaboration," *Past and Present*, no. 188 (August 2005): 195–224. See particularly his discussion of armies, pp. 212–18.

[22] New expectations and controls over officers, which eventually became self-enforcing, should constitute an aspect of the "civilizing process" as propounded by Norbert Elias.

commission army, which was, in a sense the ultimate, the archetypal, theatre of absolutism.[23]

The growth of state commission armies attests to the greater power and efficiency of early modern states. Certainly the size of the French army mushroomed from 1661 to 1693 at a rate it would never again equal, although armies would certain become much larger in the future. The increase in troop levels is most extraordinary in the case of peace-time forces. This remarkable multiplication of troop strength is the most undeniable and important evidence for the theory of a Military Revolution and for the existence of absolutism. Such expansion was, to some extent, an unintended consequence of the radical decline in the number of camp women. Had the proportion of women in the campaign community remained high, it is incomprehensible that European armies would have become so large; the unpaid "woman load" would have made them impossibly cumbrous. Yet states did not cut the number of women in order that they could commit more troops to campaigns; instead, the decline in the number of camp women allowed larger armies to take the field effectively.

From the late seventeenth century through the onset of the French Revolution, princes and governments tried to limit the excesses of war. This is not to say they did not fight wars or that they did not mobilize great armies to do so, only that they tried to control and diminish brutality outside the context of battle itself. This related to an entire complex of social and military values, including the ideal of war as a rational science.[24] Such intentions could only be achieved by the greater discipline, efficiency, and regularity of the state commission army. And the pillage typical of the aggregate contract army and its plunder-driven economy in which women played such a large role, came to be regarded as horrific anomalies to be shunned. By turning away from their rapacious excesses, accepting discipline, and redefining themselves as defenders of the people, armies in this age also contributed to the legitimacy of the state and its rulers.

The sharp fall in the number of women is, along with the decline in pillage and the increase in army size, one of the clearest markers of the rapid transition from the aggregate contract to the state commission

---

[23] As marvelously useful as Beik's survey is, I do not believe he gives adequate attention to this aspect of the monarch's authority.

[24] On eighteenth-century military culture and the quest for scientific warfare see John A. Lynn, *Battle: A History of Combat and Culture* (Boulder, CO: 2004), chap. 4.

228 Women, Armies, and Warfare in Early Modern Europe

army, signifying the heart of the Military Revolution. This transformation has been examined in other and equally valid ways. However, the metamorphosis of the campaign community is particularly convincing evidence of change, and it supports the contention that greatest institutional innovations came after 1650, not in the century before. On the other hand, the relative stability of the role and number of women with the creation of the popular conscript army is surprising and revealing. The French Revolution altered crucial parameters of warfare, but attempts by some to create a new role for the women warrior failed. With regard to women, the revolutionary army exhibited continuity rather than contrast with the army of the *ancien régime*.

WOMEN'S INDEPENDENCE, POWER, AND STATUS

If the decline in women's presence in the campaign community was an important aspect of European army evolution, was it also an important or illustrative development within the context of women's history *per se*? How did the expulsion of so many women from the campaign community impact the civil community and women's opportunities within it?

Reformation and Counter-Reformation ideas on sexual morality and marriage affected the campaign community. Some women fell victim to the zeal of those who sought to ameliorate the libertine atmosphere of the army by banishing prostitutes and debauched women from camps and garrisons. Military and civil authorities outlawed irregular partnerships or free unions, and insisted on marriage. In some armies, notably the Prussian, garrison communities formed, which included many wives and children, although the numbers of women who could accompany troops into the field was limited. Other armies, notably the French, sharply restricted soldier marriage, even among troops in garrison. Garrison communities may have served themselves, but they also had to relate with and obey the regulations of civil society.[25] Thus, they did not enjoy such a marked independence as did the campaign community.

Restricting the numbers of women on campaign probably scaled down the economic alternatives open to women, who seem to have enjoyed more leeway in the economy of makeshifts that powered the campaign community than they exercised in the more regulated civilian

---

[25] On eighteenth-century garrison culture, see Beate Engelen, *Soldatenfrauen in Preußen. Eine Strukturanalyse der Garnisonsgesellschaft im späten 17. und 18. Jahrhundert* (Münster: 2004).

economy. Thus, exclusion from the campaign community may be considered a loss.

Camp women may also have enjoyed greater agency than did their sisters in the civilian world, although the campaign community was a regime of male military authority. Yet despite their agency within the campaign community, women were powerless in the process that excluded the great majority of them after 1650. Military reformers were men who wished to create a more efficient and effective army by stripping it of unnecessary operational impediments, including noncombatants who populated the baggage train. There is no evidence that women negotiated to resist their growing exclusion. Military evolution was state directed, and women were as much pawns in the creation of the state commission army as were the common soldiers whose lives they shared.

Many women lost a life they had known, but it is also fair to remember that the life lost was usually one of poverty, suffering, and danger. So if military reform and the development of the state closed doors that had once been open, what was behind those doors may have best been left behind. Loss of prominence within the campaign community may cause historians to grieve—one less interesting sphere of women's activities—but it is another thing to say that women at the time had cause to mourn. In fact, the status of women who remained in the campaign community rose after 1650. They become wives of good reputation, not the despised prostitutes or "whores" of the past. Even the images of soldiers' women soften and become more respectable, as seen in plates 8 and 13.

Judging the impact of military reform on women involves tracing the lives of essentially anonymous women in and out of the campaign community and making difficult comparisons between their lives with and away from the armies. For this reason, exploring the relationship between women's ebbing presence in the campaign community and the fate of women in civilian society raises more questions than it answers. Conditions were bad in the campaign community, but did plebian women still have more power and opportunity there than in civilian society? What were the incomes of plebian women within the campaign community compared with their earning power in the civilian world? Where did women go when they were excluded from the campaign community? Did the challenges and opportunities they experienced in the campaign community lead these women to alter the institutions and practices of their civilian worlds? Were civilian women's gender definitions affected by the example of so many women who came from an environment in which they were expected to exhibit masculine traits? Did the overlap of masculinity upon femininity increase in the civilian world?

Theses queries point to a far more basic question: What was the impact of the campaign community upon civilian, particularly, urban communities? Military forces on campaign could have horrendous effects on the districts and towns they plundered; that is obvious. However, were there more subtle ways in which, either by imitation or aversion, civil communities changed because of the existence of campaign communities? After all, armies and their entourages constituted marching cities, but with fundamentally different rules and practices.

* * *

I conceded at the start that my study is unavoidably preliminary; it combines sound assertions and convincing theses with more speculative suggestions and admitted conjectures, depending on the level of evidence. The goal has been to collect what we know and to suggest possible lines of future inquiry. Women clearly were present and played valuable roles in the campaign community throughout the early modern era. There is no doubt and really no surprise in this. It also seems self-evident that the large-scale presence of women with aggregate contract armies increased the need for pillage; more mouths required more food. That women contributed to the army's very existence by drawing men to the libertine lifestyle is less documented, but still convincing.

I am on more speculative ground in arguing that women were key pillage managers. Evidence garnered from contemporary literature and military commentary points to this conclusion, as do insights from women's history and from common sense. That women might have played a managerial role in the commerce of pillage will surely come as less of a jolt to women's historians than to military historians. Other issues, such as surmise concerning gender tensions and violence within the campaign community, are founded only upon suggestive evidence in an environment in which conclusive data may never emerge. Inference may be as good as we will ever get. Dealing with camp women's attitudes toward rape during pillage is little more than educated guesswork at this point. And I have only questions concerning the impact of camp women's experience on the civil communities to which they returned.

Yet what is certain or reasonably solid is more than enough to justify this volume. The presence of women with early modern armies was not trivial, but fundamental to the character of military institutions and conduct of war, particularly before 1650. And the participation and fate of women in the campaign community illuminate our knowledge of the evolution in military institutions and practices. Hopefully this study will encourage historians of women and gender to take on this subject as a rewarding focus for research that will add richer and deeper gendered interpretations of the redoubtable women who marched across Europe in the train of armies great and small.

Writing toward the close of the period studied in this volume, Bennet Cuthbertson offered advice to military officers. In his *A System for the Compleat Interior Management and Oeconomy of a Battalion of Infantry*, he displayed many opinions common to his day, including a patriarchal view of officers and suspicion of soldier marriage. He cautioned that no common soldier be allowed to marry without approval of the captain commanding his company, who "should not grant on any account, until he has first had a strict enquiry made, into the morals of the Woman, for whom the Soldier proposes, and whether she is sufficiently known to be industrious, and able to earn her bread." But should the woman in question live up to such scrutiny, he concluded, "it will be right to give him leave" to marry, because "honest, laborious Women are rather useful in a Company."[26] Certainly they were, but we now know that to simply describe camp women as "useful" diminishes the full range of their contributions.

Future discussions of early modern armies must address their impact on the conduct of war or be incomplete. *Women, Armies, and Warfare* has surveyed the state of our knowledge, added to that store, and issued a challenge to advance the story farther. Such formidable women demand our attention; they earned it.

---

[26] Bennet Cuthbertson, *A System for the Compleat Interior Management and Oeconomy of a Battalion of Infantry* (Dublin: 1768), pp. 192–93.

Index

CPSIA information can be obtained
at www.ICGtesting.com
Printed in the USA
LVHW081950130722
723431LV00005B/379

9 780521 722377